To Know the Soul of a People

To Know the Soul of a People

Religion, Race, and the Making of Southern Folk

JAMIL W. DRAKE

OXFORD

UNIVERSITY PRESS

OXFORD
UNIVERSITY PRESS

Oxford University Press is a department of the University of Oxford. It furthers
the University's objective of excellence in research, scholarship, and education
by publishing worldwide. Oxford is a registered trade mark of Oxford University
Press in the UK and certain other countries.

Published in the United States of America by Oxford University Press
198 Madison Avenue, New York, NY 10016, United States of America.

Library of Congress Cataloging-in-Publication Data
Names: Drake, Jamil W., author.
Title: To know the soul of a people : religion, race, and the making of
Southern folk / Jamil W. Drake.
Description: New York, NY : Oxford University Press, [2022] |
Includes bibliographical references and index.
Identifiers: LCCN 2021027749 (print) | LCCN 2021027750 (ebook) |
ISBN 9780190082680 (hardback) | ISBN 9780190082697 (paperback) |
ISBN 9780190082710 (epub) | ISBN 9780190082727 | ISBN 9780190082703
Subjects: LCSH: African Americans—Study and teaching. |
African Americans—Religious life—Southern States. |
African Americans—Folklore. | Poor African Americans—Southern
States—Social conditions—20th century. | Rural African Americans—Southern
States—Social conditions—20th century. | Folk religion—Southern States. |
Ethnology—United States—History—20th century. |
Sociology—United States—History—20th century. |
Southern States—Religious life and customs. |
Southern States—Race relations—History—20th century.
Classification: LCC E184.7 .D73 2022 (print) | LCC E184.7 (ebook) |
DDC 305.896/073075—dc23
LC record available at https://lccn.loc.gov/2021027749
LC ebook record available at https://lccn.loc.gov/2021027750

DOI: 10.1093/oso/9780190082680.001.0001

1 3 5 7 9 8 6 4 2

Paperback printed by LSC Communications, United States of America
Hardback printed by Bridgeport National Bindery, Inc., United States of America

For my four "Little Women"

Contents

I have decided to use Black to refer to the communities under study. I am capitalizing the B to acknowledge the humanity of a people under the persistent history of white supremacy. But I am not capitalizing black folklore or folk and other constructs because I am interrogating and critiquing the category as used in the social sciences and liberal reform. Additionally, I have decided to lowercase white to decenter its normativity and supremacy.

Preface

The Legacy of Hampton: Folk, Religion, and Classifying the Cabin People

> To know the soul of a people and to find the source from
> which flows the expression of folk-thought is to compre-
> hend in larger measure the capabilities of that people.
>
> —Howard Odum (1909)

In the 1893 December periodical, *Southern Workman*, Alice
M. Bacon circulated a letter about a "new line of work" in "folk-
lore and ethnology" at Hampton Normal and Industrial Institute
in Elizabeth County, Virginia.[1] The youngest daughter of the famed
Congregationalist pastor Leonard Bacon, of the First Church of New
Haven, Alice Bacon was a long-standing teacher, missionary, and
administrator at the Institute since 1883.[2] She was also a regular editor and contributor to the *Southern Workman* in the areas of culture and health.[3] In the December issue, Bacon informed alums and
broader community about the recent founding of the Hampton Folk-
Lore Society that had received early endorsements from Thomas
Wentworth Higginson, Booker T. Washington, George Cable, and
Alexander Crummell, to name a few. In addition to Bacon, the local
professional society was composed of teachers and residential staff,
who had recently graduated from the Institute. Cadet disciplinarian
Robert Moton, treasurers Frank Davis and Frederick Douglass Barrett,
and nurse-trainee Susie J. Rix were all residential staff who comprised
the leaders and members of the Hampton Folk-Lore Society.[4]

This professional society held monthly meetings at which a member read a paper aloud and members exchanged stories on the selected topic in black folklore. The discussions from the monthly meetings were printed in the "Folk-Lore and Ethnology" section in Hampton's monthly periodical, *Southern Workman*. In addition, Bacon and members traveled to the annual meetings of the American Folk-Lore Society (AFLS).[5] At the Ninth Annual Conference of the AFLS at Johns Hopkins University in December 1897, Bacon presented on the "Work and Methods of Hampton Folk-Lore Society," while Robert Morton presented on "real" Black music (i.e., spirituals) over and against the "imitations by white nigger minstrelsy" to an esteemed professional audience of anthropologists and folklorists.[6] The Hampton Society organized its own conferences, where Anna J. Cooper, president of the D.C. Folk-Lore Society, AFLS founder William Newell, and Wilberforce University's classicist William Scarborough gave keynote lectures. The Hampton Folk-Lore Society was one of the first nationally recognized black folklore societies in American history.[7]

Alice Bacon also solicited distant alums to submit folklore materials. Her letter targeted alums whose professions put them in "close contact with the simple and old-ways of their people" in county districts of the rural South.[8] Bacon welcomed the "simple and old-time ways" that included animal tales and myths; birth, marriage, death customs; African words and sayings; ceremonies and superstitions; proverbs and riddles; and music.[9] These cultural practices were lumped under "folklore" because they were considered traditional relics that reflected a distant past in human evolution. The society continued the antiquarian trajectory of folklore that considered "folklore" as "observances and customs of the olden times."[10] This trajectory understood modern industrialization as a historical and social force responsible for relegating certain observances and customs to the ever-growing distant and fading past. More specific to the postbellum period, Bacon encouraged alums and members to preserve these vanishing relics due to the rapid raise of the "American Negro" from the "conditions of ignorance and poverty to a position among the cultivated and civilized people on earth."[11] By her lights, Protestantism, scientific, and industrial advancement contributed to the making of modern civilization and the obliteration of the so-called traditional, simple, and old-time cultures.

No other materials in folklore generated more interest than "superstition." In Hampton's lexicon, superstition referred to erroneous thought processes and immoral beliefs outside Protestant and scientific norms.[12] According to Bacon, these superstitions included a range of beliefs in "nature, supernatural beings, animals, and medicinal and magical properties."[13] The first monthly meeting took place on December 8, 1893, and was dedicated to "Popular Signs and Superstitions," such as both "good and bad luck-signs." The following month's meeting, on January 8, was on "Dream-signs and Hag stories." The "hag" referenced "witches" that African bondspeople and their American descendants carved out of West African cosmologies, coupled with their borrowing and adapting aspects of Native American and Western European cultures in the diasporic world.[14] The hag captured the importance of female-embodied spiritual power.[15] To Bacon, the hag was the personification of evil in black folklore and ethnology. The hag "oozed through the keyhole, pervades their [victim's] room with her malicious but invisible preference, rides them in their sleep."[16] "Riding" denoted the act of persecution that could result in the death of the victim after a year or two from the nightly visitation.[17] Members also exchanged oral stories about the ways to identify a hag through the human senses: sights of the "twitching dog," and "lifeless skin" of the hag on the doorstep, or hearing gurgling sounds. They also discussed different strategies said to conquer a hag, such as blocking keyholes and/or spreading wheat or grits on the floor.[18]

On April 8, 1894, the professional meeting was dedicated to conjuration, or "medicine magic," another popular study of black folklore. Hampton's librarian Leone Herron collected and complied papers and letters on conjuration from former students who had attended the Institute in 1878. The different conjure-practices were thought to be a mixture of "relics of African days" and European lore. Conjure was couched as part of the wider "fetishism, divination, quackery, incantation, and demonology" of the relics of African days. Members heard about the extraordinary powers of the conjure-doctors who had the ability to heal and harm people. Bacon shared exact formulas used by the conjure-doctors to diagnose and cure patients. For instance, she shared an incident where a man told a conjurer about his stomach pains. The conjurer explained that the man had been conjured with snakes in his stomach. The society collected conjuration as one of many folklore practices used to chart the "spiritual agencies" said to be at work in the daily lives of Black southerners.

Collecting folk superstitions was just as much about generating knowledge about the present social conditions of Black southerners as about understanding the "vanishing past" of the race. The romantic and historical importance of folklore was actually secondary to "applied sociology" at Hampton.[19] Not only did collecting folk superstitions prove an invaluable resource for the "future historian of the race," but it was also considered a resource for social thinkers and reformers invested in knowing the social conditions of Blacks after Emancipation. Bacon wanted to establish a repository of folklore data to inform knowledge about the social problems of the Black communities in the postbellum South and the broader nation.[20] Following social scientists, Bacon attributed social problems to mental and cultural factors.[21] She surmised that knowledge about the mental development of southern Blacks could provide the necessary knowledge about their social and economic conditions. Moreover, Bacon and other members highlighted the sociological importance of folk superstition and broader folklore.

The Hampton Folk-Lore Society had a specific population in mind in their study of folklore. The "folk" in folklore was a designation for a specific population. The sociological importance of folklore research revolved around studying the social conditions of a specific subpopulation. The Hampton Folk-Lore Society engaged in folklore, and superstitions in particular, to generate knowledge about a population known as the "cabin people." Thus, Bacon considered the collecting of folk superstitions and other spiritual expressions to be a sociological database of the "mind of the cabin people." She asserted that the aim of the Hampton Folk-Lore Society was to "gather together and mass into shape the ideas and beliefs that form the mental background of the cabin people of the South."[22] Cabin people denoted a subpopulation who inhabited the old slave cabins in what was called the "suburbs" or outskirts of Elizabeth County and other counties in the rural South. "Folk" was a class designation that referenced their impoverished material conditions. But more importantly, it functioned as a euphemism that classified them by their underdeveloped or primitive minds and cultures. Thus, "cabin people" was not only a reference that identified their material conditions in the rural county districts. Rather, the reference captured a population considered untouched by the "civilizing processes" of Protestantism, scientific and industrial development, unlike their counterparts at Hampton Institute. Not only were the folk religions of the cabin people couched as a reflection of the bygone past; they also supposedly illustrated a lower stage of human development in "modern civilization." Bacon and other members of the society tried to amass superstitions in order to acquire knowledge about the mental and cultural behaviors of the cabin people that was perceived as the main cause of their social and economic predicament. The preoccupation of folk religion of the cabin people underscored how class designations were refracted through certain religious, moral, and cultural frameworks. In the history of ethnology and anthropology, "folk" was also a category that produced and managed racial differences. For instance, much of the use of "folk" in American ethnology (e.g., the Bureau of Ethnology) was dedicated to the study of Native Americans and contributed to governmental reservation policies during white colonial expansion.[23]

Folk was a modern concept used to classify the southern Black poor by their perceived mental, cultural, and moral differences and deficits. To focus on the sociological aspects, folk was mainly associated with specific demographics whose cultures were considered outside the flows of modern progress. Early twentieth-century Black philologist Georgiana Simpson asserted that "folk" initially denoted a "common people," a "multitude," a "family," a "tribe," or an "army" within Old English and Old High Germanic languages.[24] But by the nineteenth century, "folk" had gradually turned into a cultural concept that identified an underdeveloped, primitive, and lower population(s), such as the "uneducated, lower and vulgar classes," "European peasants," and/or backward races (e.g., "natives of Australia," "American Indian tribes," and "Southern Negro").[25] Philosophers, philologists, antiquarians, folklorists, anthropologists, and psychologists described the cultures of these "folk" populations as native, old, rustic, and/or backward within the contours of evolutionary history. Bacon was a product of the evolutionary thought in the "science of culture" (i.e., anthropology) that sought to chronicle the long and extended history of modern civilization by gathering and studying a population who supposedly occupied an early and lower stage of cultural development. Moreover, the history of the folk category discloses how ideas about race and class are entangled.

The collection of folk superstition in the society was aligned with the broader Hampton missionary and reformist agenda. Bacon's preoccupation with the sociological application of collecting folk superstitions underscored how she incorporated the society into the Institute's efforts to civilize Blacks a generation removed from enslavement. Collecting the beliefs and practices of the southern folk was integral to the Institute's modern project. Established by the American Missionary Association in 1868, Hampton Institute trained freed people and indigenous populations in Christian and industrial education. The Institute's founder and principal, Samuel Armstrong, had already started the process of creating a repository of folk superstitions in order to know and eradicate them from the student population. He strongly felt that the eradication of folk religion was crucial to the modern reformist project of human development. Religious historian Yvonne Chireau rightly asserts that Armstrong firmly believed that introducing new "standards of character would free the freedperson's sons and daughters from their own superstitious roots and be forced to break away from the slave background."[26] Armstrong was a nineteenth-century "racial liberal" who rejected the notion that postbellum Black populations had fixed and natural racial traits that prevented them from acculturating into modern civilization.[27] He adamantly believed that a proper Christian and industrious environment, like Hampton Institute, could significantly obliterate their so-called folk and bad habits and customs to ensure their modern development. Bacon continued the liberal missionary and reformist impulse of the founder in her vision of folklore and ethnology at Hampton Institute. At the Ninth Annual Conference of American Folk-Lore Society at Johns Hopkins University in December 1897, Bacon asserted,

Our [Hampton Folk-Lore Society] interest in folk-lore is used, not so much to help us in interpreting the past as it is to aid us in understanding present conditions, and to make it easier for us to push forward the philanthropic work that Hampton is doing.[28]

By Bacon's lights, folklore studies stage an opportunity to know the mind of the cabin people for reform and uplift. It presented the opportunity for educated Black members of the society to gain access to the private homes of the cabin people. This access would establish trusting relationship between the "civilized" Hampton affiliates and "uncivilized" cabin people, and allow the former to have an intimate knowledge of the folk customs of the latter. This encounter would be the basis of reform. Bacon asserted that folklore collecting "bridged the great gulf fixed between the minds of the educated and uneducated and civilized and uncivilized of the race."[29] Folklore extended the "civilizing process" of the Protestant and industrial Institution to the outskirts where the cabin people lived.

This liberal reformist agenda in collecting the folk "superstitions" of the cabin people was most exhibited in the modern project of health and medicine. Bacon's preoccupation with the mind of the cabin people emerged out of her concerns about their poor health conditions. Before she founded the Hampton Folk-Lore Society, Bacon was instrumental in the founding of Dixie Hospital and subsequently its nursing training program at Hampton in 1891 and 1892.[30] More importantly, her concerns about the health of the cabin people—the poorest population—was demonstrated in her role in establishing the "charity case program" in the curriculum at the nursing school.[31] Bacon wrote that "[o]ne of the most interesting features of the work of the Dixie Hospital [was] the charity work among the cabins of the poor."[32] The charity cases sent nurse-trainees to provide and extend medical services for communities who could not afford it. Dixie Hospital physician Harriet Lewis noted that "[t]he possibility of moral influence on the part of a high-minded woman employed in this way among the ignorant and unfortunate is incalculable."[33]

One of the charity cases for the cabin poor was the mission wagons. Beginning in July 1892, the school secured the funds to purchase a light box wagon pulled by a horse for the purpose of sending nurses to the "cabins of the poor" in the countryside of the county. The light box wagon also had a small bed to transport patients to Dixie Hospital. The mission wagon was aimed at the "poorest classes of the people of color" who inhabited "the rudest and direst cabins."[34] One student entered one of the rude and dirty cabins and found a six-year-old girl who was extremely ill and on the brink of death due to her unsanitary cabin and lack of resources. The student recalled that the girl was laying on a dirt and vermin-infested floor, without hot water or fresh air, and coarse food.[35] Nurse-students traveled to the rural "suburbs" and extended modern medicine to the poorest of Blacks who had the most "densest ignorance and prejudice against the new-fangled notions of bathing, careful feeding, and use of disinfectants."[36]

Bacon attributed the poor health and unsanitary conditions of the cabin people partly to their reliance on ill-informed superstitions. Her interests in conjuration correlated to her preoccupation with extending modern medicine and health to the cabin populations. Folk religion was removed from modern advancement in health and sanitation in American civilization. Her allegiance to Protestantism and medicine animated how she defined folk superstitions (or, a case of bad religion) that hindered the moral and social development of the race in modern society. The mission wagons placed nurse-trainees in the homes of the cabin poor to understanding their most intimate folk superstitions. The wagons helped the knowledge production of the religions of the cabin people and the discovery of the best strategies to eradicate them. It was no wonder that Susie J. Rix was both a nurse-trainee and member of the Folk-Lore Society. Collecting superstitions was most connected to health reform.

The Hampton Folk-Lore Society was short-lived. In 1899, the folklore society ended with the 41-year-old Bacon's resignation from her position at Hampton. She headed to Japan to modernize its women.[37] Yet Bacon left a category that became a familiar way to classify the Black poor in the rural hinterlands by social sciences and liberal reform in the early twentieth-century South. Bourgeoning sociological and social anthropological researchers and reformers after Bacon deployed folk religion in their work that amassed data on the socioeconomic conditions of the Black southern poor. "Folk" disclosed the modern logic about the religion of the Black rural poor that animated liberal social scientists' efforts in research and reform. The concept was deployed by these social scientists to further explain the moral and cultural differences and deficits of the Black poor. Folk religion was a way to point to an "underdeveloped" subpopulation who remained isolated from standard moral and cultural stages of modern American society. Early twentieth-century liberal social scientists never quite abandoned the evolutionary logic that projected the view of history in a linear, teleological, and progressive scheme. This logic undergirded how they deployed folk to classify the premodern religious cultures of the Black poor in accordance with "advanced" thought-processes, behaviors, values, and manners that supposedly constituted modern (or "mainstream") society. Thus, they still adhered to a developmental model of culture that animated their use of folk in their studies of an underdeveloped population who lagged behind the rest of modern society. The religion of the southern folk was a product of the secular discourse of modern progress in the bourgeoning social sciences and liberal reform in the first half of the twentieth century. Like Hampton, their earnest analyses of race and poverty remained beholden to certain moral and cultural interpretations that animated their classifications of the Black poor. Thus, folk religion was not simply a romantic mode to preserve or collect vanishing traditions to understand a primitive past. The sociologists and social anthropologists also used folk religion to study and reform poor Black populations in accordance with what they considered moral and cultural norms, imperatives, and expectations that characterized modern society.[38] The liberal study of religion understood modernity or modernization as a regulatory idea of culture and morality. Bacon also left the legacy of folk religion within liberal reform. Her use of folk religion was tied to Hampton Institute's reformist project that championed the idea that the formerly enslaved and their descendants were malleable and fully capable of being a "civilized" people with outside Christian, scientific, and industrial programming and uplift. Managing their religion was also a central part of the Hampton idea that latter liberal-minded social scientists adopted and replicated. Like the founder, Armstrong, Bacon rejected fixed race traits while denigrating the religious and cultural practices of the "uncivilized" Blacks. Thus, the folk category in the study of religion captured the importance that early twentieth-century social scientists and liberal reformers gave to moral and cultural behaviors in their classi-fication of the Black lower class in the rural South. With the Hampton Institute, folk religion was an important concept that shaped ideas and perceptions about the Black lower class in the early twentieth century. In the end, folk religion brings into view the history that identifies race and class by cultural and behavioral markers in American social thought.

Acknowledgments

Our individual accomplishments are never simply the result of our heroic acts. Rather, our individual accomplishments are made possible by the doings and sufferings of the community. My book is a testament to a collective of people in my life. I know that my acknowledgments cannot do justice to the many people who have profoundly contributed to the book.

I first want to pay tribute to my mother, Regina Drake, my first intellectual inspiration. Working many late nights, participating in my many activities, sharing insight and wise counsel, first exposing me to an African American intellectual and artistic tradition, and even traveling to secure archival information, you have laid the foundation that has made this book possible. I hope to model the love, strength, courage, sacrifices, intelligence, wisdom, and care to my daughters the same way you have for me. To my grandfather, William "Big Daddy" Harris; you had to suspend your dreams in higher education to care for your family when your father died. Working in the meat industry in Chicago, you poured your energies and resources to help me pursue your dreams in higher education. To my grandmother, Jean Shaw; your unwavering love, tear-jerking humor, and honesty gave me perspective to weather the difficult times.

Special thanks to Michael and Mark Gumm for their love and support. To my in-laws, Matthew Johnson and Arnetta "Ya-Ya" Johnson and family, for your love and support. Matthew Johnson, I definitely benefited from our critical conversations and your extensive library (lol). Thanks to Chrystal and Gabrion; Andre and Pamela; Keith Lewis; Derrick Barnes; Floyd Woods; Reginald Figures, the Favors, Turner, and Williams families for your compassion, support, and belly-aching humor.

To my past and new religious communities for reminding me that everything I do should connect to a larger purpose. On this note,

I want to thank Pastors Kenneth Samuel, Mark Lomax, and R. B. Holmes. I am forever indebted to Victory Church in Stone Mountain, Georgia; First African Presbyterian Church in Lithonia, Georgia; and Bethel Missionary Baptist Church in Tallahassee, Florida.

This book has benefited from my personal experiences at universities and colleges. This project was an extension of my dissertation in the Graduate Division of Religion at Emory University. Special thanks to my former advisor and friend, Gary Laderman, and dissertation committee, Barbara "Bobbi" Patterson, Earl Lewis, and Alan Tullos for seeing the potential of this project. You made the arduous journey enjoyable, stimulating, and humane. I also want to acknowledge Dianne Stewart, Lawrence Jackson, Carol Anderson, and the late Rudolph Byrd for contributing to my intellectual formation during my graduate experience. Emory University's Office of Community Partnerships provided me with firsthand knowledge and experience in the power of community organizing to combat socioeconomic inequalities in Atlanta.

I am thankful to Aline Kalbian and my wonderful colleagues in the Religion Department at Florida State University. Your encouragement, patience, and wisdom have aided my research and overall professional maturation. Thanks to John Corrigan, Amanda Porterfield, Michael McVicar, Matthew Day, David Kirkpatrick, and Charles McCrary, and Daniel Wells for reading chapter drafts, offering feedback, and taking notes. Thank you to the graduate students in the American Religious History Department for your comments during colloquiums. To the Religious Studies Department at Bates College for giving me an opportunity to serve as a Visiting Professor; you provided the space for me to think about the transition from a dissertation to a book manuscript. My family and I will never forget the rich and transformative experiences that we were afforded at the college and in Maine.

I have continued to benefit from the mentorship, scholarship, and the community in the fields of Religious Studies. Several mentors have set aside time in their extremely busy schedules to read my manuscript at different stages in the process. I want to thank Marcus Bruce, Judith Weisenfeld, Sylvester Johnson, and Sally Promey. Thank you for exemplifying the generosity, dedication, and intellectual rigor that I hope to model in my own teaching, research, and advisement. I have been

blessed to be part of many academic communities that have contributed to the book's maturation. Thank you to Philp Goff, Joseph
Blankholm, Melissa Borja, Chris Cantwell, Matthew J. Cressler, Sarah
Dees, Katharine Gerbner, Samira Mehta, Shari Rabin, Alexis Wells-
Oghoghomeh, and Lauren Schmidt in the Young Scholars of Religion
program for your invaluable feedback on chapter drafts, encouragement, and laughter. I continue to benefit from wonderful conversations
with many faculty members, fellows, and graduate students that have
enhanced the book project. I am excited to be a participant in rich and
generative conversations in Black religion with extremely engaging
and amazing colleagues in Princeton University's Crossroads Project
and AAR's African-American Religious History Unit. I also want to
thank faculty, fellows, and graduate students at Princeton University's
American Religious History Seminar, Yale University's Center for the
Study of Material and Visual Cultures of Religion, and Dartmouth
College's Society of Fellows for taking time out of your busy schedules
to read or listen to chapters and offer your perspectives.

Special thanks to the several archivists in special collections at
various universities and colleges, and foundations who provided
documents that had a significant impact on the direction of the book.
You provided information that allowed me to blaze new pathways in
the study of Black religion in the social sciences and liberal reform.
I want to thank Matthew Turi of the Southern Historical Collection
at the University of North Carolina; Delisa Harris of the Special
Collections at the John Hope and Aurelia E. Franklin Library at Fisk
University; Kerry Bowden of the Archives and Special Colleges at
Oxford College Library; Jonna Rios in the Rare Book and Manuscript
Library of Columbia University; Fordyce Williams of the Archives
and Special Collections at the Robert H. Goddard Library at Clark
University; Tom Rosenbaum of the Rockefeller Archive Center (de-
ceased); and Lauren Rogers of the Archives and Special Collections
at the University of Mississippi. I also want to thank Rhondalyn Pairs
for sharing your erudite knowledge on the local history of Oxford and
Lafayette County in North Mississippi.

I want to extend a special appreciation to Lawrence Morehouse,
Phyllis Reddick, and the Florida Education Fund for the McKnight
Fellowship which provided the resources to complete my entire

manuscript. I would be remiss if I did not acknowledge Ulrike Gutherie and Kali Handerman for reading and editing drafts of the manuscript at various stages.

I have been blessed to have many friends in the academy. I have the privilege to have friends who inspired me to finish the book. Special thanks to Laura McTighe, Alexis Wells-Ogohomeh, Joseph Winters, Alison Greene, Vaughn Booker, Melvin Rodgers, Matthew Pettway, Theri Pickens, Ameenah Shakir, and Timothy Rainey for your friendship, thought-provoking conversations, and humor.

To my big brother, Jonathan Walton, for your love and counsel for nearly 30 years. You have been an inspiration to me from the day you picked me up and took me to Morehouse when you were an undergraduate student. You never let me forget my potential and the larger meaning of why I do what I do. You also never stopped reminding me about the value of this book project. (I must extend my heartfelt appreciation to Cecily Walton for all you have done for me and my family.) To Lerone Martin, for all your encouragement, support, and tremendous historical sense. In addition to scholarly feedback, you have been a constant wise and calming presence throughout the highs and lows of the book. My acknowledgments cannot capture all you have done for me. I also must thank Josef Sorett for your scholarly and personal advice, particularly telling me to value my unique journey and to "breathe."

I wish to express my gratitude to Oxford University Press and my editor, Theo Calderara. Theo, thank you for seeing the importance of the project from the first time I submitted it to you. Your guidance, patience, generosity, and responsiveness helped to bring this book into fruition. Thank you to Zara Cannon-Mohammed for preparing the book for production. I also want to thank Alison Greene and another reviewer for the close and laser-like readings and critiques. I benefited immensely from your extensive comments.

Last but not least, I owe everything to my wife, best friend, confidante, and editor, Muriel Drake. You are the reason why I am able to do what I do. Despite your exhausting work schedule, you never failed to read, listen, challenge, and edit endless drafts of the entire manuscript late nights and early mornings. Your faith, strength, and honesty have grounded and sustained me throughout this whole process. I hope to fully support your aspirations as you have mine. Also, I hope to forever reside in the shadows of your smile. I dedicated the book to our four "little women," Mariah, Nya, Autumn, and Lorraine. You never cease to amaze me! You are precious gifts that have made and continue to make me a better human being. You are the reason why I do what I do. It is truly an honor to be your father.

Introduction

Before the Black Underclass Concept

The southern Negro is our principal folk.
—Robert Redfield, *Tepoztlan, A Mexican Village* (1930)

Poor people are real. However, ideas about poor populations are invented. *To Know the Soul of a People* chronicles how the idea of "folk" in the social scientific study of religion contributed to perceptions about the Black southern and rural poor in the early twentieth century. This book discusses a cadre of second-generation social scientists who used the idea of "folk" to classify distinct beliefs and practices in their field studies of Black laborers in the rural regions of the lower South. Their use of folk religion was designed to illuminate the effects of poverty on the cultural behaviors of Black southern laborers. Moreover, these social scientists were responsible for folklorizing Black southern conjurers, Spiritualists, Baptists, Methodists, and Pentecostals that associated them with lower-class religious cultures. *To Know the Soul of a People* argues that the uses of folk religion in the South contributed to the ideas of the Black poor in American thought. I argue that the use of folk religion in the social sciences has helped to classify the Black southern poor as lagging behind or outside "modern" standard culture. This classification was designed to regulate religion in service of reforming the Black poor and the broader agricultural economy in the Jim Crow South.

This book contributes to the literature on poverty in American history. Historians have written extensively on the idea of the *black underclass* that fueled liberal welfare policies and subsequently neoconservative crime laws in the latter half of the twentieth century.[1] The

To Know the Soul of a People. Jamil W. Drake, Oxford University Press. © Oxford University Press 2022.
DOI: 10.1093/oso/9780190082680.003.0001

idea of a *black underclass* captured the cultural and moral frameworks of poverty. Postwar social scientists (e.g., Kenneth Clark, Nathan Glazer, and Patrick Moynihan) extended ideas of the *black underclass* to highlight a Black urban population with a different (and consequently, "pathological") culture that was considered separate from "middle-class" or "mainstream" America. In her rich history, *Poverty Knowledge: Social Science, Social Policy, and the Poor in Twentieth-Century U.S. History*, Alice O'Connor argues that the idea of the underclass underscores how "poverty-knowledge" in the sciences has been refracted through explanations about "individual deprivations."[2] These so-called individual deprivations helped to facilitate the racialization of poverty in American social and political thought and policy. Additionally, historians have explained that the idea of the underclass in the Moynihan Report revealed the contradictions of postwar liberalism that acknowledged racism while remaining wedded to a racially tinged meritocratic culture.[3] The underclass concept was informed by Oscar Lewis's terminology, the "culture of poverty," which concluded that the Black poor in the urban ghettos were totally marginal from mainstream values and posed a threat to the American modern state.[4]

To Know the Soul of a People contributes to the literature by extending the ideas about the Black poor to social scientific studies of a subpopulation, otherwise known as "America's folk."[5] Early twentieth-century male social scientists—Howard Odum, Charles S. Johnson, T. J. Woofter, Guy B. Johnson, Allison Davis, Gunnar Myrdal, and Lewis Jones—generated ideas about folk "peasants" and their subcultures in the American South.[6] This book demonstrates how these ideas about culturally distinct Black lower-class populations have southern and rural "roots" in the social scientific studies after World War I.[7] Moreover, the antecedents of the black underclass concept rest in the idea of the "folk Negro" with their "folk cultures." The "folk Negro" was imagined in the social sciences as a subpopulation isolated from modern and advanced culture.

The main contribution of the book is its concentration on the importance of religion in producing ideas about the Black poor in the social sciences. "Religion" is not normally considered a factor in the ideas about Black poor in the social sciences and policy. *To Know the Soul of a People* underscores that religion was a central mechanism in the social sciences to delineate cultures and behaviors of human groups along racial, class, and regional differences. Like religion, folk is not a native category. Rather, it is a second-order category that has been primarily imposed on a group from the outside within specific arrangements of power and domination.[8] It has played a significant role in shaping knowledge that has raced, classed, and gendered populations. Thus, folk religion was one of the examples used by social scientists to identify the behavioral and cultural deficits of Black lower-class workers, which supposedly resulted from regional rural poverty and racial segregation. Moreover, their use of folk religion grounded their liberal or secular narrative of modernization that sought to identify the Black southern poor as occupying an earlier and lower stage of human and social development. Folk religion supposedly revealed that the Black southern poor were isolated from more advanced stages of human and social development. It was also used to bolster their liberal reformist agenda to modernize the Black poor in accordance with "advanced" culture. Ideas about modernization (or, what some refer to as the secularization thesis) in social scientific research and liberal reform did not just entail an acknowledgment of the historical and social processes of industrial, urban, technological, and commercial change. But social scientists and liberal reformers framed modernity (secular society) within a developmental model of culture that privileged certain epistemological, religious, and moral behaviors over and against the premodern, lagging, stagnant, bad, residual counterpart. Their project of modernization was designed to classify and manage the religion of the southern folk by subsuming it under (e.g., Black southern poor) advanced liberal cultural and moral standards of self-control, labor efficiency, scientific rationality, cleanliness, nuclear family, and independence.[9] These social scientists and reformers thought that modern social and economic change would automatically cause the Black poor to free themselves from their so-called bad and lower folk religion. "Folk" was a category integral to their liberal modern project of human development.

To be sure, the folk concept has generated rich discussion about the spirituals, blues, gospel blues, chanted sermons, and other musical and cultural expressions of Black lower- and working-class communities from the American South. In fact, the scholars in this book aided the conversations about the rich "folk expressions" in Black southern religion and cultures. For instance, sociologist Charles S. Johnson was considered the "Entrepreneur of the New Negro Renaissance" and helped to market and popularize rich black folk musical expressions (e.g., "arranged" folk spirituals) in commercial culture during his tenure with the National Urban League in the 1920s. Contemporary scholars have revived the idea of folk to valorize the specific religious worlds of Black southerners and migrants.[10] "Folk" is often used in Black religious and broader American religious scholarship to accentuate the local or specific religious lives of communities over and against conventional or "official" forms of religion. In this sense, it is no accident that folk religion has been associated with "popular," "vernacular," and "lived religion."[11] To be sure, this book is not meant to police the folk term. But I do diverge from its "romantic" underpinnings that attempt to shed light on the religious cultural agency of Black southerners and migrants. Instead, this book wants to show how the modern idea of folk entailed certain assumptions about the cultures and behaviors of lower-class populations. It also operated as a way to classify a population that was supposedly isolated from American modern (mainstream or, later, middle-class) values and morals.[12] Following contemporary historian Robin Kelley, the folk idea used to classify the religious worlds of the Black poor "[has] something to do with reproduction of race, class, and gender hierarchies in order to police the boundaries of modernity."[13] *To Know the Soul of a People* shows how this part of the idea of folk was found among these racial liberals in their attempt to reform the Black lower-class and the broader segregated rural South after World War I. Using folk in their study of religion, these social scientists had a hand in shaping the knowledge and perceptions of the poor in American social and political thought.

Social Science, Liberal Reform, and the Poor South

This intellectual history of folk religion is situated in the lower South in the early twentieth century. To be sure, the book extends back to the Progressive period at the turn of the century to trace the use of "folk" in race sciences. But the historical setting mainly focuses on the different southern regions after the Great War. After World War I, the agricultural South (former Confederate states in particular) was ensconced in regional poverty. It paled in comparison to national averages in per capita income and property value. By the late 1930s, Franklin D. Roosevelt declared that the "South" was the "Nation's Number 1 economic problem." This book on the religion of southern folk is about the social scientists who worked to highlight the reasons that accounted for the regional poverty while attending to racial segregation. They knew the roots of southern poverty were intimately tied to the legacy of slavery.

These social scientists thought of their research in service to racial and regional reform. They were joined by a plethora of civic organizations, trade unions, philanthropies, and industrial schools, as well as the federal government, that were all seeking to transform the Dixie South, particularly in the Depression. These scientists undertook their field studies while the Communist Party USA, Southern Tenant Farmers Union, Southern Conference for Human Welfare, National Association for the Advancement of Colored People, and others challenged southern Democrats, absentee landowners, industrialists, and merchants. More specifically, the social scientists in this book represented a petit-bourgeois intellectual class who worked at research universities (University of North Carolina, Fisk University, Harvard University, to name a few) and partnered with the Commission of Interracial Cooperation, Rosenwald Fund, Carnegie Corporation of New York, and New Deal agencies to extend education, health, social services, employment, and landowning opportunities to Black laborers in the "one but many souths."[14] They were also deeply invested in reform. These university-affiliated scientists championed reform from the standpoint of "scientific engineering" and "social planning." They were responsible for spearheading rural and agricultural social sciences, and alerting philanthropic and governmental organizations about the long agricultural depression in the southeastern regions of the South.

These university social scientists were born a generation after emancipation. Many of them were raised in the Jim Crow South, then trained in areas of psychology, sociology, and social anthropology in graduate programs at northern universities in the early twentieth century. For instance, Howard Odum struck out from his family's farm in Piedmont Georgia in 1908, to attend Clark University and then Columbia University in 1909 and 1910. Guy B. Johnson grew up in a rural town in northern Texas and later enrolled in a master's program to study sociology with Robert Park at the University of Chicago in 1922. Amid the Great Migration, these scientists returned to the South to apply their scientific expertise and training to modernize what they took to be poor and lagging regions. Additionally, they represented a mixture of liberal Protestants and agnostics. Although Charles S. Johnson grew up in a Baptist household in Virginia, he would later join and serve as a deacon at Fisk's University Congregationalist Church in Nashville. Guy B. Johnson renounced his southern Baptist upbringing when J. Frank Norris and other conservative ministers forced his mentor and former professor, G. S. Dow, to resign from his position for teaching Darwin evolution at his alma mater, Baylor University. He later became a member of a Methodist church at the University of North Carolina in Chapel Hill, due to its emphasis on "perfectionism," that suited his sociological research and reformist impulse. Allison Davis grew up in an Episcopal church among the Black middle class in Washington, D.C., only to become an agnostic in his adult life. Despite their different affiliations, they all were committed, to some extent, to a liberal modern narrative of religion. Thus, they believed that religion of the so-called southern folk should be governed by liberal modern standards of scientific rationality and instrumentalist and civic morality. Their earnest efforts to work toward racial social progress and/ or equality correlated with freeing Black rural communities from their folk religious traditions in industrial America.

This class of social scientists comprised a diverse cast of liberals in the vast sea of various political networks and organizations in the rural South. On one level, these scientists believed that specialized social scientific research ("social facts") could guide state government, philanthropic organizations, and civic societies in modernizing the rural South on par with the rest of the industrial nation. They championed scientific expertise and governmental intervention in addressing social problems. But my use of "liberal" underscores their approach to race. On one level, they worked across the *color line* and promoted interracial harmony and cooperation. As part of their interracial cooperation platform, these social scientists supported the idea that Black communities had the capacity to fully acculturate into modern (or mainstream and "middle-class") market society with scientific and bureaucratic assistance.[15] Thus, this book focuses mainly on their liberal ideas about race in their field studies of Black farmers and unskilled laborers in the Carolina Sea Islands, Carolina Piedmont, Mississippi Delta, and Alabama Blackbelt. Unlike their progressive predecessors, these second-generation scientists jettisoned biological theories of race that framed the "Negro problem" into a separate problem. Instead, they framed the race problem within a broader regional economic problem. In this sense, they used folk religion to challenge the staple-crop and tenant-farming system that kept Black farmers and migrant workers suspended in debt to landowners and merchants. The agricultural system was part of the larger low-wage, unskilled, labor-intensive, low commodity value culture that characterized the South's regional economy and its depression before the 1929 stock market crash and the subsequent New Deal administration.[16] These scientists accredited the Great Depression with helping whites rethink race within the broader social and economic problems of the South. In fact, they sought to use the Depression to fit Black communities into the broader petitions for regional and agricultural reform. They sought to move the discussion about race to class and culture within a specific socioeconomic environment in rural America.

In his 1938 essay, "Rise of Liberalism in the South," Charles S. Johnson celebrated the emerging liberal social scientific institutions that couched the "Negro problem as a phase of the south's broader economic and cultural problems."[17] While he confirmed the "class consciousness" of the Southern Tenant Farmers Union, he accredited emerging university scientists with extending the liberal view that the race problem was essentially an "economic problem and would be solved as such."[18] Their use of folk religion was part of this effort to accentuate the role of the racially segregated and antiquated labor economy in Black life. They also extended their analysis to poor white farmers and mill hands. Contemporary scholars have discussed the importance of class consciousness across the racial divide in the 1930s, particularly in the agricultural economy. These scholars point to the interracial grassroots organizations and religious cultures in the Depression to highlight class over and against racial consciousness.[19] However, this book on folk in the study of religion highlights the entanglement of race and class after the World War. It shows that the approach to race and class by these professional scientists was just as much a part of their strategy of reform to navigate the contours of entrenched racial segregation and violence. For instance, Charles S. Johnson told administrations in the Rosenwald Fund that white powerbrokers would extend health services to their Black workers if they understood that it maximizes labor productivity. An advocate of Black equality, Johnson considered his appeal to be a practical and temporary strategy to aid Black southerners in the face of entrenched racial segregation and violence. Guy B. Johnson and others often made appeals to white powerbrokers by pointing to the negative impact of urban migration on labor and the economy. In fact, Johnson and other UNC white southern liberals were gradualists who emphasized Black rights (meaning access to quality education, housing, health and medicine, work, landownership, and welfare) while ignoring political justice in their research and reformist efforts. They considered calls for racial equality and justice to be a bad political strategy that only intensified racial conflict and violence. They placated to Jim Crow segregation on the grounds that southern white segregationists were not ready for racial integration and equality at that moment in the early twentieth century. Within the political climate, these social scientists used folk religion to draw attention to the larger economic problems that plagued the Black working poor by calling attention to their economic benefits to the region. These social scientists felt that white powerbrokers would extend certain rights to Black communities if framed in the broader regional and economic progress of the poor South. Race and class informed one another in the Jim Crow South.

Not only did they document the shotgun houses, unsanitary privies and water; illiteracy; scaly hands, bent legs, and enlarged stomachs, in order to reveal the Black and Brown faces of regional poverty. But they also documented the spiritual possessions, chanted sermons and ecstatic singing, conjure, dreams and visions, to support their conclusions about the impact of the regional socioeconomic conditions on the Black working poor. These social scientists, in their seemingly earnest denunciation of the agricultural economy, actually contributed to the knowledge production of a folk or lower-class religion. They did not necessarily interpret that these practices and customs arose out of racial or class consciousness. Rather, they supposedly arose out of individual and collective deprivation due to their socioeconomic lack. Moreover, the knowledge and erasure of the folk religion undergirded the logics of racial liberal reform. They assumed that a greater acculturation into the advances of modern society—education, medicine and health, employment and land opportunities, and commercialism—would spur the "vanishing" of the folk spiritual relics. *To Know the Soul of a People* shows that moral engineering was an important aspect of racial liberal reform, just as much as changing social and economic conditions.

They did not reproduce the idea of the "undeserving poor." Such scientists were earnest in their efforts to petition white state powerbrokers to extend social services and opportunities to the Black working poor in the Jim Crow South. Additionally, they were right to concentrate on the racial division of the labor economy in agriculture and extractive industries. Yet, this book shows that their use of folk religion actually undermined their research and reformist agenda. Their circulation of folk religion recycled the moral and cultural frameworks of poverty that white powerbrokers used to maintain the racial division in the labor economy. Although they substituted biological traits for cultural behaviors in their racial thinking, they nevertheless still did not escape the modern logics of race and class that rendered Black workers and their religious cultures as irrational, sexually deviant, superstitious, pathological, lazy, dependent, and undemocratic. They remained steadfast in articulating a developmental model of culture and behavior that played a significant role in subjugating Black southerners. The folk concept was meant to show a religious culture that had developed in isolation from modern society. Moreover, these social scientists collectively used folk religion to show a lower stage of mental, moral, and cultural development that needed moral and cultural, just as much as social and economic, reform.

The Structure of the Book

This book on folk religion is organized around five separate researchers and their case studies in various regions in the American South. In their collaborative field studies in the lower regional South, they all used "folk" to denote the religious practices of Black yeoman farmers, sharecroppers and tenant farmers, domestics, mill and migratory workers. The first chapter sets the tone of the book by exploring how the folk concept emerged out of the "Negro Problem" after Reconstruction. The concept was used to identify a population based on moral and social deficits. The chapter will discuss the early progressive roots of folk religion through the graduate work of Howard Odum, who wrote his two dissertations on black religious folksongs and oral practices in small southern towns. Moreover, we will see how the folk category was related to behavioral deficiencies that marked Black southerners as an industrial problem of the South. I will show how the folk category was designed to regulate the interior life of Black southerners in order to make them into moral working subjects. The subsequent liberal social scientists after World War I replicated the modern (or civilizational) logics of their predecessors as they abandoned sociobiological racial theories. They perpetuated the hierarchy of culture and behaviors in their study of Black religion in agricultural lower South.

The next three chapters examine folk religion in case studies in the lower South. It will explore individuals who understood themselves as liberals in their field studies. As self-described "liberals," these social reformers placed more emphasis on economic conditions over and against racial biological traits in their analysis of southern Blacks in agrarian America. By emphasizing economic conditions, they shared a belief that Blacks were more than capable of modern progress into mainstream society. They also sought to strategically situate Black southerners within the broader industrial and economic development of the impoverished and backward South. They understood that the welfare of Blacks was instrumental to the welfare of the South. Yet, Guy B. Johnson, Charles S. Johnson, and Allison Davis examined black folk religion—Protestants and conjure—to bolster their claims to bureaucrats and policymakers that a racially tinged impoverished economy had drastic effects on Black southerners. These racial liberals erased distinctly black folk religion for a biracial folk religion to demonstrate that Blacks, like poor whites, needed modern social and economic resources for their welfare, and the entire welfare of the South. They understood folk religion to be the result of the feudal conditions of southern agriculture. However, their emphasis of class in their examination of folk religion was a strategy to navigate the Jim Crow South.

Chapter 5 anticipates challenges to this book regarding other ways in which intellectual practitioners have used the folk concept. I could have written more chapters about the folk in the works of Zora Hurston, Ralph Ellison, Katherine Dunham, Albert Murray, William Levi Dawson, Paul Robeson, Ruth Landes, Pete Seeger, the American Folklore Society, the Popular Front, or the Columbia School of Anthropology. One book cannot capture the category in all its complexity in the long twentieth century. In this book, I am explicit that I am exploring the folk category through the works of liberal social scientists who sought to reform Black communities and the broader regional southeast in rural America. However, I argue that the more romantic vision of the category recycles the secular-modern discourse of liberal science and reform. In this vision, the folk category simplifies the complexities of Black rural southerners by defining them as isolated and removed from modern society. The more romantic modes that seek to authenticate and validate the unique religious cultures of the Black rural poor still reproduced the binary knowledge that the liberal reformers and researchers used to standardize conduct in their logic of modernization. The romantic preservationists tried to show the authentic, uncontaminated, natural, and counter-folk religious songs of Black rural workers even as they facilitated its "modern" commodification, which was not lost on the informants. Many American romantics recycled the "noble savage" in their quest to present authentic folk cultures of pastoral America.

To make my argument clearer, I will turn to the tensions and controversies between Fisk sociologists and folklorist Alan Lomax in their field study of Coahoma County in Mississippi in 1941–1942. In Clarksdale, Fisk University faculty and graduate students focused on the industrial changes that had altered the religious cultures of Black southerners. Fisk University's sociologists Lewis Jones and Samuel A. Armstrong argued that the modernization processes were contributing to a vanishing folk culture. As a representative of the Library of Congress, Alan Lomax was not happy with the Fisk sociologists' observations or the embrace of the modern changes that altered the religious and secular music in the juke joint or the Baptist Convention.

Lomax took his federally funded technological equipment to local plantations, where he was able to record the "real" and "authentic" folk musical sounds that he felt Fisk University Black faculty members and graduate students, whom he criticized as too bourgeoisie, did not appreciate. Lomax approached the religious expressions of the folk in a different manner than the Fisk sociologists and the broader liberal social research community. As part of governmental cultural programs, such as the Library of Congress, that flourished in the New Deal era, Lomax wanted to archive the sounds of the people of the "Negro farthest down." This chapter will briefly chart his trajectory that caused him to later fetishize "old-time religion" in Coahoma, Mississippi, while he overlooked how his recording sessions were just as "artificial" and constructed as the gospel blues that he criticized. He failed to bring to light how his own informants performed specific songs in a particular way in order to fulfill a specific want and need, such as a reduced jail sentence or money. Although Lomax represented the other side of the category of folk, his knee-jerk anger because the church choirs had moved to sheet music or that couples in local juke joints preferred to dance to Duke Ellington's "In the Mood" represented a different side of the same coin that linked him to the Fisk community that he claimed to oppose. While my book shows how the category set the stage of the later deprivation theories, I also underscore how it reduced the complexities of a people who were at the center of "modern" America with their various religious, social, and cultural aspirations and goals. At the heart of the perceptions and policies is the logic that reproduces the Black lower class as marginal to so-called American modern values and moralities. This book seeks to shed light on that history, which underscored how a category can and does ultimately simplify the complexity and aspirations of a people and their religious and cultural practices.

The conclusion lifts up famed journalist Nicholas Lemann and his two-part article on the "Origins of the Underclass" in the *Atlantic Monthly*. Lemann's argument highlights the book's central claim about the southern and rural roots of the culture of poverty in urban America in the last two decades of the twentieth century. Examining public housing in urban Chicago, Lemann countered both liberal and conservative claims about the underclass by highlighting its southern antecedent in rural Mississippi. Thus, Lemann reproduced the long liberal and scientific viewpoint that looked to the "Folk Negro" and their religious cultures to capture the behavioral deficits that needed moral and social reform. These social scientific reformers laid the seeds of the moral and cultural frameworks of poverty that shaped welfare and crime policies in the latter twentieth century . This book will trace the southern and rural roots of the culture of poverty in liberal social scientific study of the "Folk Negro" and their religious cultures in the first half of the twentieth century.

1

Moralizing the Folk

The Negro Problem, Racial Heredity, and Religion in the Progressive Era

> . . . the Folk—to people who have shared [least] in the general advance.
> —Lee J. Vance, "The Study of Folklore" (1896)

In the summer of 1908, Howard Odum left his parents' small dairy and trucking farm in north-central Georgia and headed for northern Massachusetts to attend graduate school at Clark University. He would become a part of the stampede of white southern males who struck out from the countryside and small towns to devote themselves to the "new sciences" at universities in northern cities at the turn of the century.[1] What was interesting about his trip to the Northeast was what he decided to bring to graduate school. The 24-year-old white Georgia native toted his collection of transcribed Black songs that he would later refer to as "treasures of folk-gems."[2] Beginning two years earlier, in 1906, Odum began collecting folk spirituals and "secular songs" (i.e., blues) during his field study of local Black communities first in Oxford, Mississippi, and then later in Covington, Georgia. With total populations of less than 2,500, both Oxford and Covington were county seats with railroads and remained dependent on farm produce in the surrounding countryside.[3]

Before he arrived at Clark University, Odum had made an agreement with university president and advisor G. Stanley Hall that his research on Black southern populations would be grounded in his folk songs and expressions.[4] More specifically, he said that the folk songs in his collection were from the "average Negroes" who were "less in

To Know the Soul of a People. Jamil W. Drake, Oxford University Press. © Oxford University Press 2022. DOI: 10.1093/oso/9780190082680.003.0002

the refinement and culture of the white man."[5] These "treasures of folk-gems" would be the basis of his 1909 dissertation, *Folk-Songs and Character-Traits of the Southern Negro*.[6] A year later, in 1910, he re-transported his black folk collections with him to another northeastern graduate program in sociology at Columbia University. His collection proved invaluable to his second dissertation, *The Social and Mental Traits of the Negro*, which continued to examine Black southerners in small and rural towns. Years later, after World War I, Odum handed his graduate student Guy B. Johnson the suitcase full of transcribed folk songs and other expressions, which were repurposed in their collaborative book, *The Negro and His Songs*, at the University of North Carolina in Chapel Hill in 1925 (see Chapter 2).

Howard Odum brought his folk collection to Clark University with the intention of confronting the social problems that plagued his beloved South after the Civil War and Reconstruction.[7] Born in 1884 in Bethlehem, Georgia, Odum grew up on a modest dairy farm. His father spearheaded Newton County's dairy industry by breeding the New Jersey–Avon cattle.[8] But like most farmers in the New South, the Odum family faced economic hardships in a growing interdependent commercial market that upended their Jeffersonian dream of independence and self-sufficiency. Amid industrial boosterism in nearby Atlanta, he witnessed populist farming movements and subsequently local Farmers Unions' strikes and protests against interdependent markets due to fluctuating crop (especially cotton) prices.[9] Odum came to graduate school with the sense that his unique experiences provided him with a bird's-eye view on knowledge about southern culture and its problems. His graduate work on the folk songs would be his first attempt at a southern-based social scientific study that would define his entire professional career until his death in 1954.

Odum brought his collection of folk songs to graduate school to confront the "Negro Problem." Like budding American folklorists, he acknowledged the literary and poetic value of black folk songs. But he felt that his collection provided so much more than insights into the "vanishing" relics from a bygone era.[10] Instead, he presumed that the folk songs contributed to "efforts toward racial adjustment and [discovery of] new aids in the solution of race problems."[11] He was shaped by the broader progressive impulse of social and racial reform. He approached black folk songs amid the wide array of diverse issue-focused organizations that had entered the public sphere to address the separate yet interrelated social problems associated with urban industrialism. Moreover, he intensely studied the black folk songs while various professional, civic, and philanthropic organizations, such as the Negro Business League, National Association for the Advancement of Colored People, Jeanes Fund, and University Commission on Southern Race Questions were addressing the Negro Problem in the Jim Crow South. But Odum represented another trend in the Progressive period: the emergence of professional experts who championed that the objective sciences could address the Negro problem in particular, and facilitate social and racial progress. University-trained experts imagined the new social sciences—sociology, psychology, economics, and anthropology—as instrumental to racial reform. Moreover, Odum brought his collection to Clark University to advance the notion that the social sciences, particularly psychology and sociology, could help to solve the Negro Problem in the South. With a view that the different reformist organizations and groups did not really know the southern "Negro," he intended that his collection of folk songs would fill the void.

This chapter shows how Odum used his collection of folk songs to examine Black religion, particularly Baptists and Methodists in the two southern towns. Howard Odum came to the study of the religion of the southern folk with a family background in southern Methodism. His family's farm in Covington was within walking distance from his alma mater, Emory College, in Oxford, the hub of Methodism (Figure 1.1).[12] But he came to the study of black folk songs and religion while Clark University was developing its psychology of religion, particularly in child studies. At the time he arrived on campus at Clark University, G. Stanley Hall and other faculty members in the psychology department spearheaded the discipline in America by establishing professional journals, graduate seminars, and collaborative experiments. The department wanted to move the study of religion from theology to "new" or "experimental" psychology to advance knowledge about human behavior. New psychology described the complexity of human behavior by empirically studying what is called the "reflex arc" in the neuromuscular system.[13] Moreover, Hall and the psychology department couched its study of religion within developmental psychology

Figure 1.1 Howard Odum's graduation photo from Emory College in 1904. He received an A.B. in classics. This image was drawn from the Early Emory Class Photograph Project.

Courtesy of Oxford College, Archives and Special Collections.

that studied human behavior by exploring the history of the human mind, especially in its primitive and elementary stages. Known as the "Darwinist of the mind," Hall's developmental psychology influenced Odum's use of folk to classify and explain the religious behaviors of Black southerners within a mental evolutionary framework. Moreover, Odum privileged folk religious songs as scientific data that disclosed the primitive mind (i.e., "nervous system," or "soul") of Black southerners. In fact, Odum used "folk" also as an adjective to described their inherited and elementary mind. And he privileged religious folk expressive practices as providing a window into the inherited and inferior physiological traits (e.g., instincts and impulses) that accounted for the collective behaviors of Black southerners. Odum understood that folk religious songs and oral expressions generated knowledge about the mental traits that he considered key to knowing Black southerners and solving the Negro Problem.

But the folk category in the social scientific study of Black religion supported what contemporary anthropologist Keane Webb called the "moral narrative of modernity." This narrative established a modern hierarchy of culture (or civilization) that was used to identify the moral deficiencies of the southern folk and to inform progressive racial reform. Odum folklorized Black religion to show an underdeveloped and deficient population without higher, progressive, civilized mental and moral traits, such as rational self-control, labor efficiency, and disciple. He deployed folk to explain "bad" and black religion as anathema to modern civilization.[14] Moreover, these scientists were just as invested in religion to legitimate certain moral norms deemed commiserate with human and social progress. A product of the late Victorian evolutionary sciences, Odum used folk religion to show how the southern black masses were isolated from the highest forms of moral and cultural development of "modern civilization." Therefore, he used folk religion to equally identify a racial mass population supposedly devoid of "civilized" moral and cultural habits. Not only did folk religion identify a population outside moral and cultural traits of modern civilization; it also bolstered moral imperatives to guide progressive racial reform in the South. What I will show is that his appeal to modern civilization legitimated a religious and moral culture of labor that contributed to racial violence and inequality in the southern economy.

Howard Odum's use of folk religion in his dissertations before World War I sets the tone of the following chapters. He was not a folklorist. Odum came to folk spirituals and other oral expressions (sermons and prayers) as a racial liberal who was preoccupied with reforming the black southern masses according to the moral and cultural standards of modern civilization. To be sure, like other progressive scientists, his aim to reform Black southerners existed alongside his perspective that they were naturally inferior. But, as a theme of the book, he deployed "folk religion" in his social scientific research and racial reform. And more importantly, he used folk religion to classify a mass subpopulation on the basis of their different moral and cultural habits. His view of the folk religion of "unrefined" black southern masses planted the seed that later liberal-minded social scientists would use to identify the Black poor in the Cotton regions of the lower South after World War I. Although the postwar liberal-minded social scientists did not adhere to Odum's evolutionary view of race heredity, they nevertheless still espoused the same developmental view of human culture to differentiate a folk religion of Black rural southerners. In the end, Odum brings us to the progressive roots of the folk religion concept in the social sciences and liberal reform.

The nature of this chapter is threefold. First, I will discuss the progressive sciences in the Negro Problem. Many progressive scientists defined the Negro Problem as a black mass population who struggled to adjust to the social and cultural norms in modern civilization. He adopted a view of the Negro Problem that spurred his turn to what he called "folk-gems." Thus, his folk-gems were connected to his view that the Negro Problem was a behavioral "problem" that reflected certain inherited mental deficiencies of Black southerners in the two small towns. Secondly, I will demonstrate how his training in the Psychology Department at Clark University enriched his study of black folk religion. The department used folk religion of the "primitive races" to understand the evolutionary history of the human mind in their efforts to reform child education. This chapter will offer a window into why he used the folk category to understand the religious songs of Black southerners. In the end, folk religion was used to identify the underdeveloped mental and moral traits of a primitive population in need of moral and civilized reform.

Scientific Expertise and the Negro Problem

Howard Odum was a byproduct of the changes in American education beginning in the late nineteenth century.[15] These changes in American colleges and universities contributed to the professionalization of the social sciences after the Civil War. Such changes signaled the transition from religious, moral, and classical to an empirical scientific research-based curriculum to accommodate industrial capitalism. Bourgeoning American scientists had traveled abroad to study in graduate programs in Europe while consuming Charles Darwin, Auguste Comte, Herbert Spencer, and Wilhelm Wundt, to name a few. They also began to professionalize their disciplines in the social sciences through graduate education, research journals, and conferences. Additionally, early American social scientists began working and researching for emerging state bureaus, like the Department of Labor and Bureau of Ethnology.[16]

By the 1890s, the new sciences, like their counterparts in the natural sciences, were increasingly gaining authority over knowledge production about human nature and society. Within professional and institutional arrangements, bourgeoning social scientists asserted their authority on grounds of their so-called objective knowledge of the natural laws governing human and societal development. Moreover, they extended this authority to the realm of social problems directly associated with Gilded Age corporatism and urban industrialization, such as wealth, poverty, labor, immigration, and health. In the period between the 1880s and the 1920s, known as the Progressive period, the new sciences played an important role in social amelioration in the emerging bureaucratic state.

Prior to Odum's travels to Clark University, scientific experts were already busy trying to extend their specialized knowledge and authority to the Negro Problem. The Negro Problem revolved around the discussion about the social status and capacities of the formerly enslaved persons and their descendants in the republic. Professional scientists were petitioning policymakers, reformers, and the broader public that the Negro Problem should be guided by the objective new sciences. Much of their petitioning arose from their interpretations that the Negro Problem had been distorted and corrupted by what they took to be the subjective and biased nature of politics. Not only were they referencing the corrupt machine politics of their day, but their petitions were driven by what they considered to be the failure of American Reconstruction. One of the scientists who called for more scientific investigation against politics in the Negro Problem debates was Nathanel S. Shaler. A Harvard University geologist, Shaler took a temporary break from his study of minerals to write about the Negro Problem in a series of articles for the *Atlantic Monthly* and other American periodicals. In his "Science and the African Problem," he encouraged his fellow scientists to sacrifice and dedicate themselves to addressing the race problem like their white ancestors had in the Civil War. The Kentucky native's scientism with regard to the Negro Problem was animated by what he took to be Reconstruction's "rude machinery of legislation."[17] Rejecting slavery, he still asserted that Congress contributed to the "fatal disunion and destroyed the sympathy and understanding of the races."[18] Shaler's petition for scientists to collaborate together, especially in the southern states, to study the Negro Problem in its various facets inspired Christian missionary Alice Bacon to organized the Hampton Folk-Lore Society at the Hampton Normal and Industrial Institution.[19]

Others also joined the professional campaign to place the Negro Problem in the social sciences. For instance, Odum's later academic advisor, G. Stanley Hall, explained to the Massachusetts Historical Society in 1905 that the Negro Problem should be transferred from the "hands of politicians, sentimentalists, or theorists" to "economists, anthropologists, and sociologists."[20] He further noted that emancipation and legislation contributed to the "destruction of the intimate knowledge of blacks by whites in the south."[21] Later, as president of the Congo Reform Society, Hall was inspired to make good on his petition by founding the *Journal of Race Development* that sought to leverage race sciences to inform religious missionaries and international politics.[22] There was a chorus of natural and social scientists who felt that the fate of Black people and the nation rested in its scientific community and their specialized knowledge of human nature in society. As I will show, years later, Howard Odum sang the same tune, calling for policymakers, educators, and philanthropists to consult the social sciences in their efforts to remedy the race problem.

The Negro Problem was a national debate in the postbellum period. Progressive social scientists had deviated from their predecessors' view of racial difference. In the antebellum period, American ethnologists—Louis Agassiz, Josiah Nott, and Samuel Morton—located racial difference (and inferiority) in cranial size, face structure, lungs, and other physical structures.[23] Progressive scientists deviated from their predecessors by locating racial difference in behaviors. As progressives, they tended to evaluate these behavioral differences with an eye to advanced or modern American civilization. Not only did civilization denote the scientific, technological, and industrial advancement in America, but it also represented higher forms of manners, morals, aesthetics, and knowledge-skills. Moreover, the Negro Problem was reduced to the problem of social and behavioral adjustment of a lesser population to modern life.

In his 1890 "Negro Problem" essay in the *Atlantic Monthly*, Nathaniel Shaler defined the problem as "blending a folk, bred first in savagery . . . , and then in slavery" into a "self-governing society."[24] But this behavioral model of the Negro Problem cuts across the vast spectrum of the progressive sciences in the late nineteenth and early twentieth centuries. Black sociologist W. E. B. Du Bois even replicated the evolutionary behavioral model in his study of the Negro Problem and consequently embraced "civilization." Unlike Shaler, Hall, and later Odum, Du Bois attributed uncivilized behaviors of Black people to the social and political history of white supremacy (e.g., slavery and segregation) that impacted a generation removed slavery. Nevertheless, Du Bois still cast the problem as a failure of group adaptability to advanced society. In 1897, the Atlanta University professor defined the Negro Problem within the textbook definition of a "social problem" in the social sciences: the "failure of an organized social group . . . to adapt a certain desired line of action to a given condition of life."[25] He further explained that the problem constituted a "large percentage of the black [southern] population" who displayed a "peculiar weak[ness] in the nice adaptation . . . to the life of the national group which is the essence of civilization."[26] The failure of the southern "masses" was exhibited by their "grosser forms of sexual immorality, disease and crime. . . ." This view of the Negro Problem was most exhibited in his discussion of the Black southern migrants who became the "submerged tenth" in Philadelphia in the late nineteenth century. He would later discard his progressive scientism and appeals to modern "civilization."

Sociologist Robert Park replicated a similar frame to shed light on the Negro Problem. Taking his que from Booker T. Washington, he defined the Negro problem as the "race facing for the first time all the complexities of a technological civilization; all the difficulties of that race making its way in the modern world."[27] Preoccupied with collective behaviors in natural and social evolutionism, Park was focused on the "process by which the Negro was making and has made his slow yet steady advance."[28] Similarly, Howard Odum would later articulate that the Negro problem revolved around the problem of adjustment of black southern folk to modern—and for many social scientists, white—civilization.[29] But, more importantly, the social scientific definition of the Negro Problem accounts for why Odum turned to new psychology and religion, and considered his folk collection gems and treasures.

It is not clear in his biography how he understood the Negro Problem during his early years in Georgia. The *Atlanta Journal Constitution* circulated articles about black crimes and vagrancy in Newton County. His alma mater, Emory College, had white Methodist clergy, such as paternalists Atticus Haygood and later Andrew Sledd, who supported black education and criticized white mob violence. But Odum developed an interest in the Negro Problem around 1906. After graduating from Emory College in Oxford, Georgia in 1904, Odum moved to the hills of north Mississippi to pursue a master's degree in classics at the University of Mississippi. He came to the state the same year the ultra-white supremacist and populist candidate James Vaardman was finally elected governor of the state that reportedly had the most lynchings in the United States.[30] While completing his master's thesis on the "Religion of Sophocles," Odum's interest in the social scientific study of race was the result of his enrollment in Thomas Bailey's course, "Psychology of the Negro Problem."[31] Odum later remarked that Bailey "got him heeped up over sociology and studying the South and the Negro."[32] Born in 1867 in Georgetown, South Carolina, Bailey obtained his first doctoral degree at the University of South Carolina in 1894 before receiving a second one in the Psychology Department at Clark University in 1897. Bailey was part of the bourgeoning southern white progressivism, which he called, "southern humanitarianism." True to his Episcopalian faith, Bailey's southern humanitarianism professed a paternalistic responsibility that college-educated and professional white communities should extend sympathy and lend a hand in the development of an inferior race. But he was equally a proponent of the professional currents that championed the sciences in guiding politicians, statesmen, philanthropists, and especially educators in the Negro Problem. He noted that the "star-eyed, truth-loving, spiritually intellectual sciences" should direct and solve the Negro Problem.[33] He further noted that the "race problem should be studied, and by competent, trained minds, and with all methods known to the biological, psychological, anthropological, and social sciences."[34] He believed that the Protestant ethical and truth-loving sciences would determine the proper education policy to ensure the development of a so-called naturally inferior racial group in the South. In his estimation, one cannot know the best course of reform without knowing the nature of Black southerners.

Bailey reduced the Negro Problem to uncivilized and primitive behavioral traits of Black southerners. Thomas also focused his study of the Negro problem around "whether [Blacks] were assimilable as a man and as a citizen."[35] A Lamarkian-evolutionary psychologist, Bailey recycled the behavioral paradigm of the Negro Problem that focused on the inheritance of acquired race traits in the physiology of Black southerners.[36] Trained in new or experimental psychology, Bailey interpreted the Negro Problem through perceived natural and unique instincts that explained the behaviors of Black people in specific southern environments.[37] Therefore, Odum picked up on his mentor's views that the "unassimilable" black southern masses were bound by certain physiological inheritances of instincts and impulses that needed more exploration to identify their behavioral problems and natural capacities. He accepted Bailey's approach to the Negro Problem that placed him in an already established professional company of progressive scientists who were applying their evolutionary theories of the mind to elucidate the behavioral differences of the black southern masses. The science of the Negro Problem was simply a way to generate knowledge about an undeveloped and inferior population with deficient behavioral traits and tendencies.

This psychological approach to the Negro Problem further explains why Howard Odum considered his collection of folk songs and expressions "scientific-treasures." Odum began collecting folk songs and expressions while working with Bailey at the University of Mississippi, from 1905 to 1907.[38] To be sure, it is not clear what exactly propelled his interest in black folklore. It is plausible that he already had an interest in black folklore before he arrived in Oxford. Growing up near Atlanta, he and his family could have enjoyed Joel Chandler Harris's *Uncle Remus* tales in the *Atlanta Journal Constitution* in the 1880s. Black "folklore" was a familiar genre in the "Lost Cause" and southern romantic literature popular in the United States after the Civil War and Reconstruction. Or, given his background in literature and classics, he could have been exposed to literary folklore research popular in English Departments at American universities and colleges. For example, in 1888, Francis Child's research on English and Scottish ballads inspired his students, like George Kittridge, who carried his legacy of studying ballads and tales into various English departments in the twentieth century.

But the study of "folk" cultural expressions contributed to the developing social sciences in the United States. Bailey strongly encouraged his student to collect folk culture near campus. Folklore studies was a popular mode of study, first in ethnology and anthropology and subsequently in psychology and sociology in the nineteenth and twentieth centuries. By the time he began frequenting Black communities in Freeman's Town in Oxford, cosmopolitan intellectuals, like G. Stanley Hall, W. I. Thomas, and other social psychologists, were busy studying German folk psychology (à la Wilhelm Wundt), cultural anthropology, and biological evolutionism in order to address the Negro and other social problems.[39] These social psychologists were using folk songs and other expressions (language, myths, and customs) of the so-called primitive and underdeveloped races to know "aspects of the human mind and behavior that emerged from cultural life."[40] Folk myths, songs, and customs of primitive and underdeveloped races helped social and cultural psychologists understand the evolutionary laws of the human mind and behaviors. Clark University further supported his interests in the study of folk religion—spirituals, sermons, and prayers—to advance scientific knowledge about the mentally and morally underdeveloped black southern masses for the sake of racial and moral reform and management. Its psychology department was already deploying and incorporating folk religion of the so-called primitive races to reform public education by aligning it with child development. Odum's notion of folk religion was further influenced by the department's child psychology, otherwise known as genetic or development psychology. Folk religion was a classification for a "child-race."

"Folk Religion," Child-Primitive Mind, and Developmental Psychology

Clark University was one of the institutions that helped to pioneer graduate education and new psychology in America.[41] The university's reputation in psychology was accredited to Hall, the first doctorate in psychology in the United States, who had joined his advisor William James and others in spearheading new or experimental psychology in American higher education. But more importantly, folklore and folk religion were already a part the curriculum in the psychology department before Odum arrived to start his courses in the fall of 1908. Folk religion was attributed to Hall and the broader department's investment in anthropological or cultural psychology. German Jewish anthropologist Franz Boas's former graduate student Alexander Chamberlain took over his advisor's seminar, Anthropological Psychology, that Odum most likely took in the fall. Chamberlain's seminar examined "myths, customs, and beliefs; comparative religion and psychology of religion, primitive art, and the study of the life of savages and children, adolescence, and senescence."[42] American folklore chronicler Lee J. Vance had Hall and Clark University in mind when he noted that psychologists delved into "[a]nthropological psychology [to] largely [study] the lore of rude and primitive folk."[43]

The study of the religious lore of rude and primitive folk was directly related to the department's interests in child psychology and progressive education. Folk religion was part of Hall's and the department's interests in understanding the natural mental development of the child and adolescent. Moreover, folk religion was used to support their commitments to the recapitulation theory popularized by German evolutionist Ernest Haeckel. Haeckel argued that ontogeny (individuals) recapitulated phylogeny (the human race). Hall, Chamberlain, and other students and faculty in the department considered folk "natural" religion (which they called superstition or myths) to provide information about the "ancestral records of the human mind" that children repeated in their daily behaviors. Hall ultimately argued that the child *should* repeat the psychic experiences of their primitive ancestors.[44] Rehashing the antiquarian roots of the category, Hall felt that the folk religions of primitive races provided a gateway to see the history of the human mind that should ground school curriculum and activities for children and adolescents. Hall and later Clark University "f[ound] abundant material for studying the problems of mind-history of simple-minded folk."[45] Psychology faculty and graduate students argued that schools should structure curriculum on the knowledge of the natural mental development of the child and broader human race. It was no accident that Howard Odum used "child-like" to frame the folk religion of southern Blacks. Odum followed Hall's perspective that the savage or primitive races had the underdeveloped mind of a white child.

The department understood religion to be a natural and universal instinct in individual and human development. Folklore provided the ancestral record of religion (i.e., "natural religion") that children and adolescents re-enacted in their daily lives. Hall and other psychologists deemed religion to be a natural instinct that educators and administrators had to understand in order to properly implement curricula that would facilitate the natural development of the child. Hall noted, "If religion can be taught or revealed, it must already be performed in us by nature. . . ." Therefore, he further explained, "[t]he teacher, then, must ever regard and inculcate religion as in a sense a growth or development, and in such a way that this natural predisposition be neither neglected, repressed, nor distorted."[46] For instance, Hall and his colleague J. E. W. Wallin performed one of their many experiments that sought to prove how children and adolescents "recapitulated" the folk religion of their primitive ancestors. The two psychologists sent out a questionnaire for students to answer questions about their emotional responses to certain clouds.[47] One of their conclusions was that children often said that dark clouds generated feelings of fear. Both Hall and Wallin concluded that the children "recapitulated" the folk-myths of the Sioux tribe, who prayed to the thunder god out of fear. The thunder god was said to inflict great harm. In his 1900 work, *The Child: An Evolution of Man*, anthropologist Alexander Chamberlain espoused the biogenetic law of parallelism when he claimed that children repeated the folk cosmologies and superstitions of the lower races. The biogenetic law of parallelism in folk religion had implications for non-white races and Black southerners in particular. The Psychology Department espoused the view that understanding the mental development of the child would help educators, administrators, and parents better facilitate their moral progress for the sake of cultivating adult citizens.

No doubt, Odum was shaped by the racial implications of the department's recapitulation or biogenetic parallelism in developmental psychology. He would turn to folk religion to explore the souls of Black southerners to further know their mental development. Hall's student would look to the folk religious songs of southern Blacks to explain their underdeveloped or child-like mind. More importantly, he would use his study of the folk religious songs to extend his advisor's racial biologism. Odum extended Hall's claim that Black people had "far deeper differences than color of skin and crookedness of hair that included cranial and thoracic capacity, proportions of body, nervous system, glands and secretions, *vita sexualis*, food, temperament, disposition, character, longevity, instincts, customs, emotional traits, and disease."[48] Odum was certain that the racial difference of the black folk was located in their behavioral deficits. He felt that folk religious songs added to objective knowledge about their inherited mental traits and social behaviors. He believed that gaining knowledge of their inner lives—just as for children—would better position philanthropists and reformers to implement policies and programs to ensure mental and moral development of the southern folk.

Black Folk Religious Songs and the Primitive Mind

Odum's use of the "folk" category was shaped by the Clark University department's psychological study of the mind of primitive and child populations. The folk prefix was part of the broader mind-history problem that preoccupied Hall and the department. Black southerners were objects of inquiry that complemented the departments' study of the "savage and primitive races, children and adolescents, defects, and animals."[49] Odum eclectically borrowed from the theories in developmental psychology, folk psychology, and comparative sciences (religion, folklore, and anthropology) to bring into view the inherited mental character of the Black population. Also, folk music, along with religion and nursey tales, was another useful source of knowledge in understanding the genetic and behavioral history of a certain population as well as the broader human race. He was encouraged to utilize the folk religious songs that he had previously collected in the Lower South to ground his dissertation on the natural and undeveloped mind of a population to clarify the meaning of the "problem" in the Negro Problem.

Odum embarked on the study of the folk spirituals with knowledge of the literature on black folk music during and after the Civil War. He framed his contribution to the study of black folk songs in juxtaposition to the previous white northerners who introduced the "weird" yet emotionally beautiful plantation spirituals (e.g., "Roll Jordan, Roll," "Hail Mary," and "Bound to God") to the American white public.[50] These northern abolitionists framed the songs within their American racial romanticism that championed the spirit-feeling over and against crass materialism of the industrial age.[51] Colonel of the Ninth Regiment of South Carolina, Thomas Wentworth Higginson, took to the *Atlantic Monthly* to boast of the "unwritten songs, [that were] simple and indigenous as the Border minstrelsy, more uniformly plaintive, almost always quaint, and often as essentially poetic." The abolitionist further opined that the "quaint religious songs were more than a source of relaxation; they were a stimulus to courage and tie to heaven."[52] Higginson's romanticism led to his claim that the formerly enslaved were natural transcendentalists.[53] Odum, too, called attention to the "beauty and weirdness of negro singing."[54] In addition to romantic racialists, he also lifted up his approach to the folk songs in contrast to the interpretations of "race men." He recalled how Booker T. Washington's and W. E. B. Du Bois's interpretations of the folk religious songs were bound by the history of enslavement. In other words, he highlighted how the emotional quality of the songs captured the enslaved people's message of "death and suffering and unvoiced longing toward a truer world. . . ."[55] Odum quoted Booker T. Washington in his dissertation: "the negro folk-songs fostered race pride and in the days of slavery it furnished an outlet for the anguish of smitten hearts."[56]

Odum acknowledged the historical religious context of the songs that emerged during the camp-meetings, revivals, and other religious exercises in the antebellum period. He followed the course of American social scientists who preferred to model their analyses of the society on the natural over and against historical processes.[57] He felt that the early abolition romantics (à la Higginson) and later "race men" (à la Washington) oversold how "bondage and oppression" shaped the religious songs. He further remarked that "[s]lavery has passed, four decades of liberty for slave people have signalized the better civilization, and there still remains among the negroes the same emotional nature, the same sad, plaintive, beautiful, rhythmic sorrow feeling in their songs."[58] He listed one of these songs: "Sometimes I hangs my head an' cry / But Jesus goin to wipe my weepin eyes." But the racial romantics and subsequent "race men's" recognition of the pathos and sorrows in the songs ignored the underlying the power of the inherited nervous system. Despite the previous literature, he concluded that the Black folk songs had never really been scientifically studied within the scope of the Negro Problem. His call for more science in the study of the songs privileged the mental processes of Black southerners over the historical and social experiences in the "nadir" of Black life after Reconstruction.

Odum's central argument was that the religious folk songs were an invaluable scientific source of knowledge that displayed a true portrait of the psychic life of Black southerners. In the early parts of the dissertation, he quipped that the scientific community "remained ignorant of the treasures of folk-gems that lay hidden and wasting about." Since these folk-gems had largely been ignored by the professional community, the "hearts and souls of the real people [were] unknown and deprived science of a needed contribution, and the world was consequently hindered in its effort to discover the full significance of the psychological, religious, social, and political history of [human] kind."[59] Following Hall, Bailey, and Clark's Psychology Department, the folk religious songs were considered ancestral records of the primitive mind that was considered the source of their racial character traits and tendencies. Cast within developmental psychology, these folk cultural artifacts alert the community and the society to the natural laws of the human mind.[60] Odum, like Hall and others, considered that the folk songs were scientific data that disclosed the persistence of racial polygenetic thought in early twentieth century American social thought.[61] Odum highlighted the distinct mind to support his claim that Black southerners were different in kind.

Odum noted that the folk songs he collected were mostly the "present-day spirituals." While he said that Black southerners still performed the old antebellum spirituals, he said that the present-day spirituals were representative of the consciousness of the race. The difference between the present-day and the old spirituals was a matter of style and form. He attributed the present-day folk spirituals to "broken and unbroken melodies, rapid minor cadences, improvised arrangements, meaningless and disjointed phrases and refrains."[62] He attributed the meaningless words and disjointed phrases to the present-day Black southerners' preoccupation with "sound impression" and rhythm. He noted that the "Southern negroes of today" sacrificed coherent meaning and words for rhyme and sound. He struggled in his characterization of the different music in Black southern Protestantism. I will show in the next chapter how his trusted graduate student Guy Johnson admitted that Odum did not know or care very much about the actual music. For instance, in, Odum's dissertation he noted that how Black southerners sang the old, present-day, church, and denominational hymns the same way. He noted that the "negroes sing their regular denominational hymns with the same feeling, often, as they do the spirituals, and while mention must be made of their church hymns as such, they often reach a climax similar to their most fervent outbursts, and freely mingled them with the old songs."[63] The grouping of different and complex musical songs and styles under the category of folk was more about the so-called mind-character than about the actual songs. He opined, "[t]he preaching, praying, singing, and with it shouting and unity of negro worship—perfection of rhythmic sing-song, these with the throbbing instinct of the people make the negro music what it is."[64]

The songs were more about the psychological forces in the inherited mental character traits that Odum deemed responsible for their style, dialect, thought-content, and emotional character. The feelings and attitudes that characterized the folk religious songs were attributed to mental processes, and not historical, social, or personal experiences. Like G. Stanley Hall, he magnified the racial instincts and impulses that generated the "plaintiveness," "simple-longing," "child-like" thoughts, pathos, rhyme, incoherent words in the old and present-day spirituals, hymns, and denominational songs and the other oral practices. Moreover, the religious folk songs were rooted in the actions of the underdeveloped and primitive mind. Odum underscored that these religious folk songs represented the ancestral mental record wherein the instincts and impulses dominated the behavioral thoughts and actions of Black southerners.[65] Odum's ideas were inchoate. Like most of his writing, he often confused attributes for explanations and arguments. For instance, he often relied on vague terms like "feeling-attitudes," "child-like and psychological cravings," "throbbing instincts," and "pleasure-giving qualities" to explain the folk soul of Black southerners. He provided incomplete and vague anecdotes and examples to validate the connection between ecstatic worship and the folk-mind. He noted, ". . . the negro loves to mourn and if his songs were full of sadness and pathos, he also loves to shout and vigorously defend the right to shout as he pleases."[66] The songs boiled down to psychological explanations that accounted for overly emotional conduct or the "frenzy." In the end, the folk captured a mind that was under the spell of the lower registers (instincts and impulses). It was an overstimulated and reactive mind. The songs revealed the lack of the higher mental registers (e.g., rational control or restraint) that reportedly ensured good conduct and habits.

Odum's dissertation was not reduced to explaining the styles and forms of the folk songs. He also noted that the primitive mind also gave way to the peculiar thoughts and imaginations that formed the content of the folk songs. Even Christian concepts, such as sin, the devil, Jesus, Heaven, and hell, were attributed to the underdeveloped folk mind. A unique characteristic that constituted the folk songs was what he called the vivid imaginations and portrayals of these religious symbols. He equated the vivid pictures of heaven in the songs to mere fancies of the black mind that did not exceed children's fairy tales, like Mother Goose.[67] He mentioned how their ideas of heaven displayed vivid and imaginative portraits, such as golden paved streets, crowds, and white robes. He listed one of the songs:

In the morning—um-u'
In the morning—um-u'
In the morning—um-u'
I goin put on my golden
Shoes.

In the midnight—um-u
In the midnight—um-u
In the midnight—um-u
I goin' put on my long
White robe.

Talk about it—um-u
Talk about it—um-u
Talk about it—um-u
I goin' waer that starry
Crowd.

The devil played an important part in the folk songs. "He" was depicted as a trickster and personified a "concrete man who constantly inflicted terror often real or imaginative."[68] He would later trace their preoccupation with the devil to the hereditary "fear-impulse." The so-called fear impulse once again neglected to situate Black people in a specific historical and social context. The devil was placed alongside other objects of fear, like black cats, police officers, gamblers, debt collectors, thunder, and lightning.[69] Odum further noted that the naturally inherited "fear-impulse" overwhelms their religious orientation. He later linked the hereditary "fear-impulse" to the superstitious nature of Black southerners he studied in southern towns. He further noted that "when in excitement from fear the Negro is without control, he sees all sorts of images and hears all sorts of sounds."[70] Again, Odum left his reader guessing as to how the poetic symbols in the songs relate to the folk mind. He was content with just providing the words to the songs and restating the characterization of the symbols without clear explanation of the distinct racial nervous system. In his second dissertation at Columbia University, he further explained why the folk songs and Black Protestantism displayed the moral deficiencies of a population. We will, in this chapter, see how his treatment of the folk songs revealed why he considered Black religion a social and economic threat.

Folk Expression, the Protestant Church, and Moral Deficits

Howard Odum used his second dissertation to extend his research on folk religious songs to the entire nature and function of Black southern Protestantism. He was more explicit in what he meant by the peculiar or "folk" mind of the "average black population" inhabiting these southern towns. He extended his previous argument about the primitive and folk mind by arguing that Blacks were a "mass of physiological reactions and reflexes" to natural and external stimuli without inhibitive control. He asserted that their "whole being [was] volatile, without continuous or stable form, easily disturbed, as easily quieted."[71] But, unlike the first dissertation, here we see how these traits purportedly underlying Black folk religion posed a social threat to southern industry.

After Clark University, Odum focused on sociology in the Department of Political Science, Philosophy, and Pure Science at Columbia University in the 1909–1910 academic year. He specialized in sociology under the advisement of the first-generation sociologist Franklin H. Giddings. Also, he enrolled in William Dunnings's courses on American history, with special reference to the Civil War and Reconstruction.[72] Dunnings's discussions of Reconstruction and "forced legislation" confirmed what he heard in his household growing up, where his mother resented the federal government after the Civil War for her family's economic and social lot.[73] The Confederate organizations—Confederate Veteran's Association and Daughters of the Confederacy—coupled with racial progressive paternalists in Covington, Georgia, prepared him to consume Dunnings's ideology about Reconstruction at Columbia.[74] But nothing changed his views on race and religion in the span of a couple of months since he had completed his previous dissertation. He still framed the Negro Problem in the same neo-Lamarckian terms, "inheritance of acquired mental traits" to which Giddings remained beholden. Giddings was a chief proponent of the biosocial evolutionary concept "consciousness of kind." Consciousness of kind was used to explain that social and group associations formed on the basis of their shared genetic mental traits and tendencies. Odum also enrolled in Giddings's and Alvana Tenney's sociology course on Principles in (Historical) Sociology.[75] Under Giddings's advisement, he simply expanded his early dissertation on folk songs to a study of Black institutions and associations in southern towns. In this sense, Odum's community studies focused on the genetic traits and tendencies that contributed to the formation of Black social institutions and associations—schools, lodges, churches, and homes. He stated that one could get a "bird's-eye view" of the true racial character of a people in their group associations and natural environment. His claim about group associations and natural environment was based on the fact that Black people supposedly did not reveal their natural character while interacting with whites. This very premise undermined his ethnological study as well as entire argument about the so-called natural traits and tendencies of black southerners.

Odum noted in his second dissertation that he collected oral data—songs, sermons, prayers, and testimonies—in predominantly Baptist, Methodist Episcopal, African Methodist Episcopal, and Colored Methodist Episcopal churches in the South. He collected the folk oral practices in Sunday services, class meetings, and prayer-meetings. He noted that the average number of congregants in the churches was approximately 190. Despite the local and communal nature of the study, the Georgia native did not reveal any specific details about the communities and completely glossed over the specificity of the churches in the southern towns. One can only assume that he visited at least one of two predominantly Black churches in Freemen Town in Oxford, Mississippi: Methodist Episcopal Church and Colored Baptist Church of Oxford. Around the time he did his field study, the Trustees of the Colored Baptist Church had just purchased a new plot of land from Hattie Anderson for $650,000 after the first structure was damaged in a fire. The Methodist Episcopal Church, like the Colored Baptist Church, was established in the aftermath of the Civil War when the formerly enslaved left the white churches to form their own by buying land. For instance, he did not mention actual congregants, like storeowners and landowners or account for how the churches served as schoolhouses for children and adults after the war. In Freeman's Town, the Methodist Episcopal Oxford Church formed a relationship with the Freedman's Bureau where the minister served as a teacher.[76]

Odum remained stuck on his use of the category of folk religion. His folk category was an abstraction that ignored pertinent details about the actual congregations and broader communities that he visited and studied. The folk category was used to collapse the specific churches into the "Negro Church" that complemented his generalization of the songs and oral practices. In fact, he used the folk category to understand the songs and other expressions to bolster his claim about inherited racial traits and tendencies (e.g., consciousness of kind) that led to the formation of the "Negro Church." Interpreted through consciousness of kind, the Negro Church was not an institution forged out of historical and social experiences in American life. Rather, the Negro Church was forged out of a unified mind where congregants were bound by the same hereditary traits that they passed to their offspring. From the study of folk songs, he noted that the nature and function of the church was to "give expression and satisfaction to the social and religious emotions. . . ."[77] It was the same argument where he noted that Black southern religion showed that "Negroes were more excitable in nature and yield more readily to excitement than does the white man." To bolster this claim about the character traits, he casually stated examples without providing any context. He noted that "church satisfie[d] as much as anything else his social wants, and relieve[d] his psycho-physical cravings. His worship [was] music to his soul, whether it be in the word-music of prayers and sermon, or in the natural music of his song, or in the rhythm of all combined."[78] He called their religious programs "satisfying services." Again, it was the overly excitable nature that made them prone to these religious and social behaviors. Their folk religious orientation did not provide psychological mechanisms of self-control and restraint.

Odum was not alone in his physiological framing of the Negro church and Black southern religion in particular. He joined a chorus of social scientists who focused on the pathological emotionalism that characterized their folk Protestantism. Religious historian Curtis Evans rightly noted that "the social sciences, and the psychology of religion in particular, were the key cultural authorities in pathologizing the religious experiences of blacks in the South."[79] Another one of Giddings's students, Frederick Morgan Davenport used his research to focus on pathological emotionalism in Black southern religion. A political science professor at Hamilton College, Davenport's research recycled the view that Black southern religion was an outgrowth of the African primitive animistic religions that were furthered developed in the "tropical" West Indian sugar plantations and antebellum South cotton fields. These primitive rites continued in the "charm and magic" used among Black populations in the "lower Mississippi Valley." But he also highlighted how the "primitive phenomena" was most displayed in the emotional character of Black southern religion. The emotional character was attributed to the ancestral and inherited mental traits that were woven into the nervous motor system of Black southerners. He noted that the "group of motor manifestations, the rhythm, the shout, the falling out," [were] exceedingly characteristic."[80] Davenport, a progressive Republican politician, lifted up examples of the "sheep-calling," "Hard Shell," and "Primitive Orthodox Zion Baptists" to emphasize their abnormal, high, and violent emotions, muscle contractions, foaming at the mouth, "falling out," and dancing. He attempted to show the "herd or crowd mentality" in Black religion (and overall primitive religion) that underscored a "sympathetic like-mindness" of a people under the spells of hypnotic suggestibility, imagination, and emotionalism. He furthered noted that the "[h]igh feeling, discharing itself in muscular action, and discharging itself rhythmi-cally, [was] everywhere a spontaneous manifestation of children and of child races."[81] Davenport, like Odum, highlighted the "underdevel-oped and rudimentary mind" to identify the bad religious behaviors of Black southerners. Both were indebted to Giddings's "consciousness of kind" that W. E. B. Du Bois criticized as speculative.[82]

Most importantly, folk religion was defined in contrast to morality. Rehashing the scientifically informed religion and character via Bailey, Hall, and broader religious liberals, Odum classified the religious culture of black southern "folk" because it was supposedly devoid of morality. He wrote that the "Negro [was] not censured, therefore, because the moral and ethical in his religion does not exert so strong an influence as it should."[83] He asserted that the folk religious expressivism at the heart of Black southern Protestantism had no direct bearing on moral conduct. What drove Odum, like other social scientists, to the study of religion, and Black southern religion in particular, was their underlying investment in normalizing moral behaviors and conduct. In fact, the study of religion was a means to legitimate moral values and norms to regulate industrial democracy in the early twentieth century. Odum felt that their folk religion did not prevent their overly natural susceptibility to criminal instinct. The folk and "bad" religion fed into the criminalization of black southerners. Both the religious and criminal instincts pointed to the overpowering of the lower registers of the human person. In his estimation, their religion offered no real salvation.[84] This point was not lost on Davenport either. Davenport noted that some Black communities in parts of the South had been in possession of "Anglo-Saxon consciousness" with a "high capacity for high thought and heroic deed."[85] Here, he was referencing the Hampton and Tuskegee Institutions and their civilizing mission. But he reiterated the point that the black masses in the sections of the Black Belt South had a "small sense of morality." He also noted that the masses exhibited clear marks of their savage inheritance in their "primitive simplicity." Davenport pointed to the disconnect between religion and morality when he told of "a colored house-girl seeking religion . . . who extracted a pound of butter from the day's churning of her employer, and carried it as a compensation to her mother. . . ."[86] Unlike Odum, Davenport attributed the bad conduct of Black southern masses not to their inherited immorality, but their "unmorality."[87] Yet, many progressive researchers still deployed folk religion (or primitive, in Davenport's case) to identify a supposedly morally deficient population that lacked "inhibitive control."

Black Folk Religion and Moral Standards of American Industry

What did Odum mean by morality in his study of character and behaviors? Morality was not a descriptive or universal term. It is a

value-laden historical product that takes form within specific social and political contexts. To be sure, there were multiple and competing moralities across different communities. But the social sciences
worked to standardize morality that was compatible with modern
industrial and human progress. American civic morality took on the
spirit of the scientific, technological, and industrial age. Odum's embrace of the age illuminates why he used complex civilization to evaluate the character of Black southerners. Interestingly, Odum and
others organized their moral discourse around self-control as it related to work efficiency.[88] To be sure, self-control related to adjudi-
cating good conduct from deviant sexual and criminal practices. But
work efficiency is often left out of the equation in discussions about
self-control and morality in the early twentieth century. Therefore, folk
religion was considered bad religion because it did not foster modern
subjects who were efficient and productive in the labor industry in the
South. In other words, folk religion was defined by its inability to influence the moral work habits and dispositions of Blacks in small towns
and the surrounding countryside. Efficiency was considered a public
good within the emergence of scientific management and bureaucratic
organizations. With Frederic Taylor's early essays that culminated in
the *Principles of Scientific Management* in 1911, managers sought to
apply different techniques and strategies designed to maximize productivity from their laborers. Odum's focus on efficiency lacked the
specific techniques and strategies that later scientific engineers and
managers sought to apply to factory and manufacturing industries. He
elevated efficiency to provide an ethic of work in the southern labor
market. Odum's focus on efficiency alerts us to his preoccupation with
the standard moral conduct of the worker. Efficiency, according to
Odum, demanded inhibitive control of the lower registers of the mind
that redirected psychic and physical energy to productive, efficient,
and responsible work. Folk religion directed energy to other activities
that were outside work production. Folk religion's uncontrollable passionate energies supposedly caused Black southerners to work less, to
loaf, wander, or waste time. Odum asked, "Is it surprising that he does
not want to leave until a late hour (in their religious events), when he
has little to attract him to his home, where he must begin again to think
of work which is disagreeable to him?"[89] In his eyes, modern subjects

possessed the psychic control that reserved their mental and bodily energy for work productivity. The modern subjects were moral in their attitudes and orientations toward work.[90] Efficiency was lauded as a religious, moral and civic good in the professional sciences in industrial democracy.

For Odum, folk religion was too expressive and uninhibited, and generated bad character and social actions, such as restless migrations, unemployment, idleness, and vagrancy. The folk concept was designed to identify a religious disposition that was isolated from moral standards of labor habits. Later he romanticized his father and the white folk due to their strenuous, honest, Protestant orientation to labor in the farming fields.[91] He was able to reconcile his small-town Protestant southern values to the emerging scientific and industrial value of work efficiency. It appeared that he was simply referencing general character outcomes of consistent, committed, ambitious, and hard work.

Odum blamed the poverty of Black southerners on their elementary inferior mental traits. Additionally, and most important to him, was scapegoating southern Black people for the poor economic state of Oxford and Covington. He argued that the financial situation of these two southern towns was the result of the Black population's unwillingness to work in their designated jobs. He said that postbellum Blacks contributed less to southern industry and wealth. This accounts for why he supported the racist vagrancy laws that were designed to politically, economically, and personally manage and contain Black strivings in the New South.

Howard Odum was part of a broader scientific and progressive contingent who linked morality to work. Work was considered a moral good. These progressive scientists collectively despised loaferism and vagrancy. Both Booker T. Washington and Robert Park perceived idleness as both a religious and civic wrong. The valorization of work informed notions of civilized citizenship. In 1912, Park had hosted the Second International Conference on the Negro at Tuskegee Institute that brought educators, scientists, and colonial representations from all over the world. In his address on "Education by Cultural Groups," he celebrated how the Tuskegee Institute (i.e., its open door policy where poor girls and boys could work and earn an education) instilled discipline that brought out the best in students.[92] He noted that Tuskegee was "at the base of the moral discipline of the school, since it requires that the students choose a vocation and make personal sacrifices in order to prepare themselves for it. It dignifie[d] labor because it makes the student feel . . . the value of common and ordinary labor when it is performed with a high purpose."[93] Park did not critique the racially tinged labor suppression or structures that conditioned Black and white relations. Similarly, Odum used attitudes to address what he took to be the labor and economic problems of the South. In this sense, moral character served as a panacea to solve the Negro Problem and overall racial tensions. Both black adjustment and racial peace went hand and hand in the study of the Negro Problem. To be sure, his turning of race and labor problems into a moral character problem of a population overlooked white supremacy that reinforced the servitude, poverty and debt, and subjugation of Black workers. The stress on morality and hard work in the evaluation of religion ignored the plight of Black workers in the Jim Crow South. In many instances, hard work and ambition were also perceived as a threat to white supremacy.[94] The New South economy was predicated on racial inequality and the lack of legal representation. Black workers knew that hard and committed work was not a guarantee for economic advancement or citizenship. One Black worker in Covington, Georgia, sang:

> Ain't it hard, ain't it hard,
> Ain't it hard, to be a nigger, nigger, nigger?
> Ain't it hard, ain't it hard?
> For you can't git yo money when its due.[95]

Odum criticized the "general laborers" and failed to highlight the labor exploitation and suppression that stunted their social strivings. A large number of the Black laborers were predominantly general laborers, tenant farmers and sharecroppers, and domestic servants in the two towns. The New South's perpetuation of Black dependency and submission to semi-skilled and unskilled labor industry, lack of landownership, and debt was not a factor in his study of black folk religion in the Negro Problem.

Odum felt that the best way for Black people to adjust to modern life was only through subjugated labor and the unequal economic domain.[96] On this note, he rejected the quest for social and political equality for hard work and efficiency within modern civilization. Good character was relegated to the work ethic that should guide Black southerners in general labor, agricultural, and domestic industries. Similar to some extent to Washington's "gospel of work," Odum asserted that Blacks must adopt a "policy of faithful, consistent, and industrious application of [their] work." Progressives also equated good conduct with thrift. Therefore, they believed hard and consistent work should correlate to the "reasonable amount of judgement and economy in the expenditure of [their] money."[97] Good religion must abide by the moral policies by cultivating the Protestant work ethic that German sociologist Max Weber saw during his visit to Tuskegee Institute and the broader South in 1904.[98] Like many progressive reformers, Odum equated good religion and character with the dignity of work.

Howard Odum's policy was premised on the importance of scientific knowledge about the natural character of Black people. Scientific knowledge revolved around the natural "fact" that Black southerners were a mass of physiological reflex and stimuli without rational mechanism of control. This knowledge contributed to developing effective policies to manipulate the good natural traits to morally manage a population. His mentors and other scientific progressives simply privileged industrial education as an ideal model of racial governance. G. Stanley Hall, Thomas Bailey, and Fredrick Davenport all celebrated Booker T. Washington's Christian and industrial programs. Odum also confirmed that an adequate adjustment policy should revolve around moral and industrial training. Not having much faith in Black churches, he gave an example of the positive effects of white intervention in Black religion. He briefly noted that the most effective organized church work revolved around white Presbyterian "Sunday-schools" for Black southerners. While he extolled Black race leaders to help in the endeavors of morally developing the race, he called on whites to assist in guaranteeing the "exalted idea of labor" that simultaneously would obliterate folk religion. Right and good moral Protestantism would channel the psychic energy of Black southerners to more productive outlets in general, domestic, and farm work. To be sure, economic and industrial development required religious and moral precepts.

Folk religion arose out of the study of the Negro Problem. Folk religion supposedly exhibited an underdeveloped natural mind that resulted in behavioral problems. The "problem" in the Negro Problem was a character problem. Odum juxtaposed folk religion with a moral and practical religion that was deemed compatible with human and industrial progress. He thought that black folk religion did not cultivate the standard physiological comportment to productive work. Howard Odum was a product of the social sciences and progressive reformers that privileged work productivity as an American civic good. Thus, good religion complemented industrious productivity in American civilization.

This modern or civilization logic of religion and work would have appeared strange to Black laborers in Oxford, Covington, and the broader lower South. It was especially so for the disproportionate Black population who worked in domestic, mill, road, service, railroad, and agricultural areas in both counties, as well as the few skilled laborers, such as painters, shoemakers, blacksmiths, brick masons, plasterers, [mechanics], and wheelwrights.[99] In an ethnographical study of Covington, Georgia, W. E. B. Du Bois concluded that the "[m]ass of the Negroes [were] hard-working people with small wages." He further asserted, that many of them manage to buy homes with their savings.[100] If modern civilization was equivalent to hard and committed work, then these workers would have considered themselves the ideal modern exemplars of the Protestant work ethic that Odum and other progressives promoted. In minds of Black laborers, there was no way they were outside modern American conduct. For instance, in Odum's backyard in Newton County at the Union Grove Church, he ignored how a large group of local Black farmers attended the agricultural convention to "improve their conditions." This convention was organized for Black farmers by the Agricultural Department at Atlanta University.[101] But to focus on the hard work of Black laborers in the lower South reified the racialist logics used to exploit and subjugate Black workers and communities. In short, Odum's folk religion was an abstraction that perpetuated the modern ideals designed to confine Black southerners to a life of subjugated semi-skilled and unskilled labor, enterprise, landlessness, violence, and poverty. Odum's category of folk in his study of religion was an abstraction that bolstered Jim Crow governance. Additionally, his attention to morality distracted attention from the problems of the labor market in southern towns and surrounding counties.

Howard Odum was a progressive reformer. He noted that "strength of moral character and mental stability with economic prosperity never yet came to a people by leaps and bounds." He further noted, "[s]uch growth can only be effected through the coming generations, by means of training which will give a permanent character basis upon which to build and a capacity to retain. . . ."[102] He recommended state, local, and private (e.g., church) policies and programs that could effectively develop the race through industry and good homes. As a neo-Lamarkian progressive, these policies and programs of moral and labor training could alter the inherited mental traits (like the frontal lobe of the brain) of Black southerners for the sake of their welfare. He also thought the alteration would benefit southern race relations and industry. Like G. Stanley, he noted that Black people possessed some good traits (e.g., plasticity) that scientists and bureaucrats could manipulate with their psychological and moral engineering. But again, their natural inferiority limited them to a lower station in social life. Odum represented the progressive roots of the Black folk religion concept that highlighted character deficiencies and privileged moral training in their reformist agendas. In fact, he was ambiguous about class position of the concept. He noted that the average or common uneducated Black workers in the southern towns were representatives of the religious folk songs (although he noted that educated and successful Blacks sang them too). His ambivalence was tied to his commitments to a biological view of race and religion. Liberal social scientists jettison his view of race and religion. After Swedish economist Gunnar Myrdal met with Howard Odum in North Carolina in 1939, he concluded that the latter was an old, kind fool who struggled to modernize his ideas. Odum's successors were explicit about the class position of the communities who practiced "folk religion." They noted that Black lower-class workers were representatives of folk religion in the American South. But they continued using the concept's moral and cultural presuppositions to normalize and standardize conduct for the sake of producing modern subjects. Like Odum and their progressive predecessors, the following postwar liberal social scientists used their study of Black folk religion to (1) highlight the character deficiencies of the Black poor and (2) standardize their conduct in accordance with American modern culture.

2

Assimilating the Folk

White Southern Liberals, Revival Religion, and Regional Isolation

In 1928, white sociologist Guy B. Johnson, along with his wife and social historian Guion Johnson, sociologists Frank Ross and T. J. Woofter, and educator Grace House, attended a program on communion Sunday at Scottsville Baptist Church.[1] Scottsville Baptist Church was one of the six predominantly Black Protestant churches on St. Helena Island off the coast of South Carolina. Before the program, Johnson took note of the rural church's "above average interior" with what he described as wooden floors and "smooth white plastered walls" with a few cracks and water stains, presumably from the Island's subtropical climate. Seated with the aforementioned "several white people" in the second row of wooden-carved pews, Johnson fixed his attention on the oral practices of the Black congregants. He intentionally watched the service's song leader, Paris Capers, who sang a spiritual, *No Harm*, in a loud and rhythmic voice while swinging his body and patting his hands. Johnson noticed Capers's son, who sat with the choir in the gallery and appeared as if he were trying to outdo his father with his own loud singing. After the singing, the University of North Carolina (UNC) sociologist then heard what he described as the "typical rhythmic sing-song Negro prayer" from an individual who had "plenty of help from the Amen corner." After the greetings from Scottsville's pastor, Issac Brisbane, Johnson then described how Capers "lin[ed] a hymn" that he said was "atrociously slow."[2]

Then, Guy Johnson noted a "Deacon Barnswell" who gave an atypical "quiet and reserved prayer" before the sermon.[3] Johnson opined that his prayer disappointed some of the congregants. The program's sermon was preached by D. C. Washington of Ebenezer Baptist Church. Ebenezer was reportedly the largest church on the Island that

To Know the Soul of a People. Jamil W. Drake, Oxford University Press. © Oxford University Press 2022.
DOI: 10.1093/oso/9780190082680.003.0003

split from the Brick Church. According to Johnson, Washington, at times, "grew fervent, and almost lapsed into the old style of preaching." During this moment, Johnson recorded a male congregant shout, "step on the gas, push man, push!" Yet, Washington reportedly executed his "sound and homely advice" on moral citizenship with a particular emphasis on prohibition. At one point in the sermon, he asked the congregants: "Are you a good citizen?" After his message, one of the white visitors, Grace House, vice principal of the local Penn School, stood in front of the congregation and addressed them for 25 minutes on prohibition.[4] Established in 1862, the Penn School was the result of the "Port Royal Experiment" during the Civil War before it later evolved into an agricultural and industrial school at the turn of the century. At the time of the service, House and the principal, Rossa Cooley, also white, were on a crusade to rid St. Helena in Beaufort County of local bootleggers.[5]

But Johnson said that the most "interesting" part of the program took place during collections. Capers performed another spiritual, *Death So Hard on Me*, and then started to "wave his arms and shuffle" in a lively manner. Other congregants came forward to place their offerings on the table at the front of the sanctuary before they also began to shuffle. Johnson noticed two women shuffling "as if they were about to break out into a shout." During announcements, an individual reported to the congregation that $21.00 had been collected from the evening program. Johnson and the white visitors left the church around 3:30 p.m. before the communion segment of the program began.

Johnson's visit to the evening's religious program at Scottsville Baptist Church was part of his field study of what he called black "folk cultures" in St. Helena and other nearby islands off the Atlantic coast of South Carolina. For six months, Johnson attended funerals, class meetings, and Sunday services at predominantly Baptist and Methodist churches and praise houses on St. Helena, Edisto, and Ladies Islands to document and analyze the oral practices of rural Black communities. He came to the study of St. Helena religious cultures as a liberal Methodist, after leaving the southern Baptist tradition in graduate school. In February 1928, Johnson attended a nightly service at a praise house on Frogmore plantation in St. Helena Island.[6] According to a

Black landowning farmer, Maria Chaplin, each separate church on the islands had either one or two praise houses located in one of the plantation neighborhoods where members would usually meet on Tuesday, Thursday, or Sunday nights.[7] With a total of 31 congregants (including 7 white visitors) in the meeting, Johnson listened intently to the hymns, spirituals, prayers, and the short sermon.[8] He documented old Watts hymns, a "quite fervid, rhythmic and chant-like prayer" and syncopated spirituals. He jotted down on a notecard that, toward the end of the meeting, the "class leader" had a young boy finish lining a hymn that sent the congregants into a "frenzy."

In addition to songs, he collected conversion narratives and good and bad luck customs in his broader study of black folk religion. Informants, like Mollie Robinson, told Johnson about her visions in the woods during her conversion experience. Another informant, "Mrs. Whaley," retold a story to the sociologist where praise house members visited the home of a "nearly dead" old woman to pray and sing all night. Johnson recorded Mrs. Whaley's testimony that the members stayed there until she "got well" the next morning. He also recorded daily good or bad luck beliefs from residents. Informant Samuel De Veaux told him that wearing a dime around the ankle generated good luck.[9]

Guy Johnson's field study of the folk culture patterns was part of a collaborative social scientific study of the predominantly Black small landowning communities in St. Helena right before the stock market crash of 1929. Peter Capers, Maria Chaplin, D. C. Washington, Mollie Robinson, "Mrs. Whaley," and other Black residents in churches, praise houses, and schools toiled their small plots of land on former plantations.[10] The study was sponsored by the UNC's Institute for Research in the Social Sciences (IRSS) and the Social Science Research Council (SSRC). Johnson was joined by other social scientists (e.g., sociologists, psychologists, economists, historians, and anthropologists) who also traveled to St. Helena and other neighboring islands to explore a particular aspect of the Black yeoman families on former large-scale plantations. In addition to folk studies, these social scientists examined labor, wages, and taxes; urban migration and education; health, sanitation, and home; and social history. The SSRC provided $1,600 to the St. Helena community study and praised it as one of the first comprehensive surveys where all the separate social sciences merged together to examine a specific population in a concentrated area.

There was something more at stake in the study of St. Helena than just advancing the social sciences in America. With the IRSS, the St. Helena study was created out of a real concern about the poor and agrarian South after World War I. Before the market crash of 1929, St. Helena, like other southern regions, were already in an "agricultural depression" due to the staple-crop arrangements and market depreciation of cotton; low and fair wages; lack of mechanization and industries; and harsh environmental factors. Johnson's UNC colleague, rural sociologist T. J. Woofter, explained that the farming families in the Sea Islands were still coming to terms with the collapse of the phosphate industry in the late nineteenth century, and more importantly, that of the cotton industry from the boll weevil and the hurricane of 1927. The annual per capita income of a St. Helena yeoman, like the greater southeastern region, was $420, in comparison to the national average income of $3,347.[11] Most of the yeoman farming families on the Island lived in substandard conditions. From the standpoint of the IRSS, the St. Helena study was part of their broader research program to explain the socioeconomic problems arising out of "state and regional conditions." The St. Helena study was tied to the IRSS's aim to "lead the way to a new state and new south through scientific research and social planning."[12] Under the tutelage of Howard Odum, the IRSS's southern and regional scientists joined other scientists and bureaucrats to support governmental intervention for the sake of southern and regional modernization.

Guy Johnson's collection of St. Helena folk religion must be situated within the IRSS's intent to expose the factors that reflected and contributed to the stagnant and poor southern regional economy.[13] His role in the St. Helena study contributed to the "Negro and Folk Background Studies" subunit of the IRSS. This subunit operated from the premise that culture arose out of southern and regional conditions. Therefore, his deployment of black folk religion was part of his colleagues' concentration on St. Helena's isolation from the economic and commercial processes of mainstream America. It was no wonder that he referred to the St. Helena Black yeoman farmers as "cultural isolates" from his assessment of their so-called obsolete folk spirituals and other religious customs. Unlike Howard Odum, he did not understand folk religion as a cultural product of inherited race traits. Rather, it was a byproduct of the poor and isolated southern regional conditions. Therefore, Johnson understood folk religion as a cultural concept that accentuated class and regional isolation from industrial and commercial society. Thus, he used the term "folk" to point to the "obsolete" religious cultures of Black farmers who remained wedded to an old revival religion of the antebellum period while living in the second half of the twentieth century. For Johnson, their folk religion highlighted how they remained stagnant and frozen in a rural past, isolated from modern progress.

But I will demonstrate that Johnson's move away from inherited race traits to regional environment in his study of the southern folk was aligned with white southern liberalism of the "Chapel Hill group." While he thought about his field study within anthropological and ethnomusicological studies, his use of "folk" was also designed to navigate Jim Crow society with regard to racial liberal reform. In the first half of the early twentieth century, UNC's IRSS was known as the "hub of southern liberalism" in professional circles that comprised universities, philanthropies, and governments. Their reputation was based on the IRSS's belief in scientific and governmental planning to modernize the regional South on par with the rest of the country. Yet, the reputation of the Chapel Hill group was also due to their scientific and reformist work toward interracial harmony and cooperation and racial progress within the Jim Crow South.[14] For instance, Johnson and his UNC colleagues spearheaded the North Carolina division of the Committee on Interracial Cooperation (CIC). Thus, Johnson's use of "folk" in his study of Black farmers was part of the IRSS's racial reformism that also sought to alter white people's perceptions, especially the powerbrokers, of Black southerners. More specifically, "folk" sought to alter the attitudes and perceptions about Black people by accenting the significance of the regional economic environment over and against perceived inferior racial traits. Johnson understood that the religion of the St. Helena "folk" reflected southern and rural lower-class culture. In fact, he deployed "folk" to situate the St. Helena farmers within a larger interracial southern and rural lower-class Protestantism. Moreover, Johnson's folk category correlated to the logics in Chapel Hill liberal reform that integrated the racial problem into the broader social and economic problem of the regional South.

But folk was proscriptive. Johnson's deployment of folk was grounded in his commitment to liberal modern ideas that espoused a developmental model of culture. Thus, Johnson deployed folk to classify a population on the basis of their so-called obsolete, residual, and premodern religious culture of a bygone past. He deemed the St. Helena farming communities to be behind or marginal to the standard, advanced, and modern culture of mainstream America. This chapter will demonstrate how his use of the folk category provided the impetus for his fellow UNC liberal colleague T. J. Woofter to associate the Black rural poor in St. Helena with certain moral and cultural deficits that were isolated from moral norms and standards of a modern wage-economy, especially with regard to work and sex. Although Johnson and other white southern liberals transitioned from race traits to class and culture in their research and reformist agenda, they still nevertheless replicated the old racial logic of the folk category that substantiated black inferiority due to their isolation from an advanced "American" modern monoculture. Not challenging Jim Crow or petitioning for racial equality directly, white southern liberals focused on interracial cooperation and the capacity of Black southerners to assimilate into modern monoculture and consequently contribute to the southern economy. Thus, white southern liberals petitioned for state policies and programs for the social and cultural development of Black people that would be in the best interest of the regional southern economy. They felt that interracial cooperation and racial progress were beneficial for the modern development of the region. Johnson and his colleagues in the St. Helena study paid close attention to D. C. Washington and a few other landowning families who were affiliated with the Penn School to show the value of interracial cooperation and consequently the capacity of Black rural communities to be law-abiding and morally responsible landowners and consequently assimilate into modern culture with "white paternalistic reform."[15] D. C. Washington's "modern religion" was exemplary of the capacity of Black southerners to assimilate into advanced civilization with outside and white Protestant, industrial, and agricultural scientific programming. White southern liberals, especially the Methodists, like

Woofter and Johnson, championed a modern or ethical religion that was exhibited in Washington's sermon on moral citizenship and pro- hibition. Regulating religion was integral to the liberal social scientific study and reform.

The nature of this chapter is threefold. First, I will discuss Johnson's early research on what he called "folk music" before the St. Helena Study. He entered graduate school at UNC with the perspective that the biological theories of race were anachronistic and ill-informed. Under the advisement of Howard Odum, his studies of black folk songs replaced biological racialism for the socioeconomic environ- ment in the formation of Black religious culture. Second, his early studies in the Negro and Folk Background Studies unit of the IRSS anticipated his argument about the folk spirituals and broader lower- class Protestant cultures of the St. Helena yeoman farming community. In the St. Helena study, he identified what he saw as the white origins of the Black folk spirituals and broader Protestantism. Lastly, I will dis- cuss the implications of his use of "folk" in white southern liberal re- form in the regional South. His classification of the so-called folk and obsolete religious cultures of the St. Helena yeoman farmers correlated to Woofter's description of their bad habits that resulted from their iso- lation from the higher modern industrial and wage economy. Woofter openly associated modern American culture (or "civilization") with white cultural (or civilized) traits. I also show how Johnson's view of race in the folk category highlighted white southern liberals' project of altering ideas about race in the South by highlighting that Blacks had the capacity to assimilate into white and American modern culture. They looked to the Penn School to support their claims.

Guy Johnson's Study of Black Folk Music before St. Helena

Guy Johnson's work in black folk religion in St. Helena was shaped by his previous work on folk songs. His conclusions in the St. Helena study were an extension of his previous study of black folk songs in grad- uate school. Born 1901 in Caddo Mills, Texas, Johnson had developed into a decent piano player in his hometown, Caddo Mills, Texas.[16] In addition to working on the home farm and his store, Johnson's father was the choir director at their local Baptist Church that his family had helped to build and establish during the Civil War. Johnson's father's love of religious and other music rubbed off on his middle son, Guy.[17] With training from his older cousin, Johnson had cultivated his skill for the piano by playing at church, school events, and community recitals. He continued playing the piano at Baylor University in nearby Waco, and traveled as the pianist for the glee club. Yet his playing came to a temporary halt once he decided to pursue sociology, first at Baylor University, and later in the master's program at the University of Chicago.[18] He later renewed his earlier interest in the piano and composition after he retired from teaching at UNC in 1969.

His experience with music came in handy the moment he arrived in Chapel Hill for graduate studies at UNC in the spring of 1924. As stated in Chapter 1, Johnson was immediately assigned by his then advisor, Howard Odum, to look through his old collection of black folk spirituals and blues, and to edit his first dissertation. Odum wanted to quickly publish *The Negro and His Songs* (1925) to put the IRSS on the professional map at the height of the New Negro Renaissance. Although his advisor made Johnson the coauthor, he actually did not really contribute anything substantive to the book. Yet, his previous musical experiences, coupled with his studies at the University of Chicago, certainly shaped the structure and content of the coauthored second book in the Negro and Folk Background Studies unit, *Negro Workaday Songs*. Published in 1926, this book was a culmination of the field study of black folk songs that they collected while observing chain gangs, railroad and domestic laborers, and students in various parts of Georgia, Virginia, Alabama, and North Carolina. They also collected a lot of their data from Black construction workers (many migrant laborers) who constructed new buildings and renovated old buildings at the all-white public university in Chapel Hill.[19] Johnson recalled that he heard the "plaintive calls and hollers" of the workers from their living camps near his house, close to Pittsboro highway. Johnson explained that "most any day you could go out there on campus . . . and just hear these gangs singing away while they were digging and shoveling . . . and you'd just sit there by the hour and pick these things up and put them in your notebook."[20] Odum reportedly exchanged liquor with one of the construction workers, John "Leftwing" Gordon Wesley, a one-armed migrant worker, in return for folk songs and stories.[21]

With Johnson's influence, *Negro Workaday Songs* included more songs—250 ballads, work songs, blues, spirituals, and love songs. Johnson remarked that Odum did not have any knowledge of or use for the actual folk music he wrote about. More importantly, the coauthored second folk song book was different in its approach to race and culture than the first one. The first book showed how his advisor could not quite relinquish his sociobiological and evolutionary ideas of inherited and primitive race traits that animated what he meant by black folk religion and culture. These ideas were not as popular in the social sciences after World War I. *Negro Workaday Songs* featured an environmentalist approach to race and culture. Prior to his tenure at UNC, Johnson was a part of the postwar social scientific culture that privileged environment in their assessment of cultural expressions and practices. Due to his previous training at the University of Chicago, Johnson, like other second-generation sociologists, had abandoned the theory of fixed biological race traits in shaping black culture.[22] The second book was explicit that the folk songs were products of the social and economic environment of the workers. Moreover, it was more explicit that the folk category in the folk songs represented the uneducated and "unsophisticated" lower working class. With Johnson's influence, these songs were products of their external social experiences that the workers negotiated on a daily basis. The book discussed the folk songs within the testimonies and experiences of Black workers. The authors noted, "[i]dealism in song and dreams, in workaday songs as well as spirituals, alongside sordidness in living conditions and physical surroundings, appear logical and direct developments from the type of habitation which the Negro common man has ever known."[23] This explains Johnson's section on the John Henry ballad among Black railroad workers on the Big Bend Tunnel.[24] Protestant themes of death and heaven, sin and hell, and exodus were briefly mentioned in light of the daily toil of the "songster." The workaday songs shed light on the Black workers' daily interaction with exploitative white bosses, landowners, and prison guards in the eddies of the Jim Crow South. After World War I, Johnson contributed to the definition of "folk cultures" as a category reserved for Black lower-class and working-class communities in the South.[25] Like other second-generation social scientists, he noted that many Black people had surpassed "folk culture" and had entered another phase of human and cultural development on par with the rest of modern populations.

Yet Johnson's dissertation project further challenged the previous claims about the role of race traits in black folk songs.[26] In centering his dissertation around the religious spirituals that he classified under folk songs, his argument in his dissertation played a significant role in his study of the folk spirituals among Black farming communities in St. Helena.

His dissertation project emerged out of the inquiry he formed in the last chapter in *Negro Workaday Songs:* "Is the vibrato more frequent among the Negroes than whites?" "Is the Negro's capacity for harmony greater than the white man's?"[27] His dissertation applied psychologist Carl Seashore's musical test to quantify musical aptitude, such as pitch, intensity, time, rhythm, and memory. Seashore was a psychologist at the University of Iowa and began working on musical aptitude tests after World War I. Johnson used a portable phono-photographic camera in his fieldwork to record over 3,000 Black and white elementary, secondary, and college students in Carolina and Virginia. The phono-photograph visually detected the soundwaves and vibrations to determine the pitch, intensity, time, and rhythm of the folk spirituals. Johnson was joined by Seashore's former student, Milton Mettessel, in the fieldwork for his dissertation research in the Carolinas and Virginia. What Johnson apparently discovered from applying the Seashore test in his fieldwork was that both Black and white students had virtually the same musical aptitude. Johnson opined that Black singers were neither superior nor inferior to whites in music. His dissertation research showed that race was not a variable in musical and cultural differences. This argument set the tone for his later argument about class over and against racial difference in religious music and culture in St. Helena Island in Beaufort County. He would come to question the existence of a distinct Black religion and culture.

The St. Helena Study

Guy Johnson submitted his dissertation to complete the requirements for his doctorate degree in 1927. He was encouraged to join the faculty in the Sociology Department and the IRSS at UNC–Chapel Hill. He was one of the new white and younger hires to join the faculty and to help Howard Odum shoulder the research load.[28] Johnson and the new hires were all assigned to participate in the St. Helena study the same year they were hired. One of the new faculty, sociologist T. J. Woofter, was responsible for proposing the idea to study Black farming communities in St. Helena. Raised in a prominent Methodist family in Athens, Georgia, Woofter matriculated in the undergraduate program at the University of Georgia (UGA) before he eventually completed his doctorate degree in sociology at Columbia University.[29] After graduating from UGA in 1912, Woofter received a fellowship from the Phelps-Stokes Fund that had jump-started his long-held research interests and reformist work on Black southerners. Before he came to UNC, he already had a reputation in white southern liberal and Protestant circles due to his work with fellow socially minded Methodist colleagues at the Phelps-Stokes Fund (e.g., Thomas Jesse Jones) and later at the Commission of Interracial Cooperation (e.g., Will Alexander). His interest in St. Helena was the result of his previous work as a research assistant with the Phelps-Stokes Fund. While assisting Thomas Jesse Jones on his survey of schools for Black people in the American South, he developed an interest in the Penn School while visiting St. Helena.

At the time of the study, UNC social scientists considered St. Helena a wonderful laboratory for scientific study due to its unique racial demographic and geographical composition. Woofter was amazed that Blacks made up approximately 90% of the Island's population. The 1920 census reported that St. Helena Township had a total population of 5,157 with approximately 5,100 Black residents. In 1930, the census reported that out of a population of 4,626 people in St. Helena township, 4,458 were Black. Woofter thought of the racial demography in St. Helena in comparison to other regions in the lower South. He noted that the composition provided an opportunity to examine "a truly homogenous community, and not a bi-racial community." Woofter and others were equally excited by the barrier islands that supposedly isolated St. Helena from the mainland. Woofter understood that the physical barriers provided an opportunity to study "one of the most primitive and isolated groups of Negroes in the United States."[30] Johnson interpreted the barrier islands as isolating the predominantly Black population from the broader world of modern commerce. Thus, there was a sense of urgency to complete the study because the townspeople had voted for a city bridge that would connect the barrier islands to the Charleston "mainland." The bridge was touted by the white city elites for its ability to bring business and commerce to the islands through hotels, industry, and tourist reservations. This bridge was intended to be the gateway to modernizing the Island through industrial and commercial capitalism. Yet, Johnson, Woofter, and the UNC social scientists viewed the highway bridge as contributing to the obliteration of the folk cultures of Black rural farming communities.[31] The bridge generated a sense of urgency to study a unique population in a peculiar region. Yet, the perceptions of the rural geography of the islands factored into his definition of "folk" in his study of religious practices.

Guy Johnson's St. Helena Folk Cultures

Johnson arrived in South Carolina and took the trolley across the Beaufort River to St. Helena Island in January 1928. His acquaintance with both Rossa Cooley and Grace House of the Penn School gave him access to the intimate worlds of the Black farming families on the islands, including Edisto and Ladies Islands. While attending praise house meetings, funerals and communion services, school classes, and visiting churches and plantation neighborhoods, he was able to record and transcribe approximately 200 spirituals, along with conversion narratives and "superstitions." With his UNC colleague, social psychologist Ernest Grooves, Johnson observed the materially decorated gravesites of the community.[32]

His study of the spirituals underscored the meaning he ascribed to folk religion of the Black rural farming community. Johnson noted that "isolation made [St. Helena an] excellent laboratory for the study of the spirituals." The common trope of isolation informed the meaning he ascribed to "folk religion." He listened to the Islanders sing old Watts and Wesley hymns, and "new choir songs" in their class meetings and church services.[33] But Johnson noted that the spirituals stood out as the "characteristic mode of religious expression of these people." He further explained that they provided Blacks with a freedom to express themselves without formal restrictions.[34]

Johnson had come to St. Helena with knowledge of the previous studies of Black folk spirituals in folklore, musicology, and anthropology. Four years before his fieldwork, Sierra Leone musicologist N. G. J. Ballanta visited St. Helena while on a southern tour to observe Black musical culture. Visiting the Penn School, Ballanta called attention to the African patterns in the spirituals. Yet, unlike Ballanta and previous fieldworkers, Johnson did not attribute the distinct patterns to West African musical styles. Instead, he noticed similarities between his transcription of the St. Helena spirituals he gathered from the farmers and nineteenth-century white revival songbooks. Johnson explained that "some of the best or most characteristic spirituals can be traced back in whole or in part to white revival songs." Johnson's reference to revival songs was a nod to the popular printed songbook in the camp-meeting revivals and prayer meetings during and after the Second Great Awakening.[35] These songbooks were accredited with being America's first book of popular music that reportedly "broke free of the constraints of formal church music or cleric authority."[36] He compared the St. Helena spirituals to *Christian Lyre, Southern Harmony, Milleniall Harp, Musical Companion, Zion Songster,* and other hymnbooks popular during the antebellum period. Johnson claimed that there were striking "parallels" between the St. Helena folk spirituals and the white spirituals in popular songbooks in content, form, tunes, and rhythm.

Johnson asserted that these popular songbooks contained the same repetitive refrain, solo-chorus structure, syncopation, and pentatonic scale that he heard, recorded, and transcribed among Blacks on St. Helena Island. He found the typical stanza or repetitive form in the stanza and chorus of the popular Black spiritual, "Swing Low, Sweet Chariot," was also exhibited in the white revival songs: "Together let us sweetly live,/I am bound for the land of Cannan/Together let us sweetly die,/I am bound for the land of Cannan."[37] The repetitive stanza and chorus signaled the standard solo and chorus structure that he discovered in the white revival songs, like the St. Helena Black spirituals. His comparison to white revival songs was an extension of his previous arguments that denied race traits, and in this case, African ancestry, in the development of black folk songs on St. Helena Island and in the broader South (e.g., Virginia and North Carolina in particular).

His comparison of the St. Helena spirituals to white revival songs encapsulated the meaning he ascribed to folk religion. Like Woofter, Johnson also considered that the so-called regional isolation had a tremendous impact on the religious development of the Black yeoman farming communities. For him, the tidal waters separated the farmers from the outside world of commerce, transportation, and technology. To Johnson, his deployment of folk spirituals and religion was aimed to explain that the St. Helena yeomanry were suspended in an American religious and cultural past. His concept of folk bolstered his perception of them as "cultural isolates." Later, at a 1939 SSRC conference on cultural island groups, he further opined about the Sea Island Black community: "isolation figured as a factor which made for the preservation of obsolete cultural forms."[38] In his estimation, folk was evidence of old cultural relics from an agrarian past that the majority of American populations had abandoned due to their daily interaction with modern life. His comparison of the folk spirituals to old revival songs confirmed his view that their Protestant cultures were relics from the nineteenth century.

Johnson's "folklorization" of the spirituals had nothing to do with race traits or West African cultures. His comparison between the St. Helena and old revival spirituals had implications for his thinking about the contours of race and class. But Johnson did not just highlight the musical similarities between old white and St. Helena Black spirituals.[39] Instead, similar to Duke University's English professor Newman White, Johnson argued that the St. Helena spirituals were actually derived from white spirituals set in the revivals and camp-meetings in the American South during the antebellum period.[40] Along with White and later George Jackson Pullen, Johnson was part of the "white derivative camp" in the study of black folk spirituals in American thought.[41] Johnson took his derivative argument to contest what he saw as the pervasive "sentimentalizing" of the black spirituals, presumably in "New Negro" aesthetics, that he felt obscured how they were largely borrowed from "white folk music" during slavery.[42] He was gradually more assertive in his argument after the study. Three years after the 1930 *Folk Culture on St. Helena Island*, he asserted that some of the best or most characteristic [Black] spirituals can be traced back in whole or in part to the white revival songs."[43]

Johnson situated the "white roots" of black folk spirituals in broader white and American Protestant history. He looked to the Scots-Irish population from Ulster, Ireland.[44] He argued that the St. Helena spirituals were derived from the Scots-Irish folk ballads in the Carolinas (most notably, Charleston) and other parts of the lower antebellum South in the late eighteenth and nineteenth centuries. The Scots-Irish settlers came to the Sea Islands by way of the Upper South (e.g., Virginia and Kentucky) after leaving southern Pennsylvania and Maryland in search of better land. Johnson noted that the Scots-Irish (and English) population had singlehandedly infused the revival songs with their unique style in the Piedmont and Appalachian regions of the South. He asserted, "The Scots-Irish and English peasantry, with their love of song and their religious zeal, undoubtedly played a conspicuous part in shaping the folk music of the camp meetings." These old Scots-Irish ballads from Midland and northern Europe contained the "flat sevenths, neutral thirds, and other musical traits" that had been noted as a marker of the distinctiveness of the St. Helena and black spirituals in general. This was demonstrated in the pentatonic scale that broke away from conventional music. Johnson argued that the old Scottish ballads had the "gapped or pentatonic scale" that Ballanta and other ethnomusicologists had cited as distinguishing the black spirituals from others. Johnson asserted that the "pentatonic mode [was] very frequently used in these English folk songs and in their American derivatives."[45]

Johnson's white derivative hypothesis was not limited to the spirituals. He also extended his claim to the distinct dialect and speech patterns of the Islanders. He refuted previous claims that St. Helena was a bastion of the Gullah or Angola dialect. Rather, he argued that the perceived Gullah dialect was actually the result of old English speech patterns. By old English speech patterns, he was referencing the seventeenth-century mode of English dialect that Blacks borrowed during their daily contact with English peasant settlers and indentured servants in the colonial periods before the rise of the large plantation economy in the antebellum South. These white settlers and servants were representatives of the "man of small [economic] means." These peasants and settlers spoke an English dialect (in contrast to literary English) that the St. Helena farmers in the late 1920s still mimicked in their speech patterns. He noted, White speech has undergone "some degree of change, moving a little nearer, perhaps, toward a standard American English, but, because of cultural isolation, the Negro lags behind, thus conserving the white man's linguistic past."[46] Visiting the local schools, Johnson noted that the "native teachers" often taught in the Island's vernacular and concluded that "standard English" will probably not make much of an impact on the pupils. He asserted that "fifty years, perhaps even a hundred years, from now, the English of the sea-island Negroes will still be looked upon as something unusual."[47] UNC social historian Guion Johnson also endorsed his claim in her own research in the collaborative study. In her *Social History of the Sea Islands*, Guion Johnson concluded that the "folk-ways, [of the Black communities on the islands] were the outgrowth of slavery; their songs, the ones they sang in bondage; their speech, the English of their ancestors when they were 'tamed.' "[48] The Sea Islander's folk English linked them to whites in the southern Appalachians, Ozarks, and North Carolina banks.[49]

Guy Johnson's claim about St. Helena folk spirituals and cultures was published during the Depression, in 1930. After the initial publication of the book, he never wavered from his argument, which he continued well into the 1980s, though he faced mounting criticism from Black and white social scientists, ethnomusicologists, aestheticians, race leaders, and pundits. For instance, banker and philanthropist George Peabody explained in a personal letter that Johnson did not have sufficient knowledge of African music to make his claim regarding the English and white roots of the spirituals. He then went on to say that he personally knew scholars who visited Africa and that they all confirmed the convictions that "possess Mr. Ballanta."[50] Ethnomusicologist Henry Krehbiel critiqued Johnson on his comparative method. Krehbiel challenged Johnson's sole use of written sources to outline his argument. He furthered noted that Johnson failed to make an important distinction between written sources and actual performance in music. The written could not capture the essential musical differences of specific racial and cultural groups.[51] Others were merely dumbfounded that Johnson would make a claim about the roots of black folk spirituals.

After the St. Helena study, an older W. E. B. Du Bois had found out that the Phelps-Stokes Fund selected Guy Johnson to work with him on the *Encyclopedia of the Negro* in the 1940s. Du Bois responded that he "could not see how a man who seriously argues that Negro folk songs originated and were developed by white people has exactly the mental balance for this work."[52]

Guy Johnson's conclusions about the European and white folk roots of the Black spirituals were meant to be a broader cultural commentary on Protestant culture in the American South. And his commentary was couched in a cultural evolutionary framework. He understood that his use of the folk to show the cultural isolation of the yeoman farmers was deliberately meant to rethink Black religion and its relationship to white American Protestantism. Moreover, Johnson's reference to the revivals and camp-meetings as well as the Scots-Irish songs were part of his broader argument that there was nothing distinctly racial or African in Black Protestantism. His early work in black folk songs and cultures had culminated in the St. Helena study. He thought that the "parallels between Negro and white Protestant institutions and cultures were almost perfect." Johnson noted, "that every denomination known to white people was also found among Negroes . . . and the Negro creeds, rituals, ceremonies, church architecture, etc. [were] patterned after the whites."[53] The "cultural isolates," according to Johnson, were suspended in the web of old revival Protestantism that white isolates had practiced, too. As outlined in his 1927 dissertation, Johnson wanted to conceal the role of race that separated black religious and cultural differences from whites. Instead, he wanted to demonstrate that black Protestantism demonstrated the lower stage of American cultural development for populations inhabiting remote and underdeveloped regions. The designation of "folk" showed that they were still lagging in religious development and suspended in an old web of the antebellum period.

Johnson was not necessarily clear on what he meant by "almost" with regard to the parallels between Black and white religious institutions and cultures in the isolated South. Like his conclusions on animal tales, he probably traced some parts of black folk religious cultures to West Africa.[54] But he seldom discussed them in his work on folk religion and white American acculturation. For instance, he did not provide an explanation on the origins of the folk Protestant conversion narratives, otherwise known as "seeking," that he collected on the islands. "Seeking" was part of the process in which a candidate was required to enter the woods (usually several times in the early morning and/or late night) to pray (i.e., seek) in order to receive confirmation of their conversion. The confirmation usually came in the form of a spiritual vision that was evaluated by an assigned teacher and the congregation. Johnson interviewed Mrs. Mollie Robinson, a resident of Frogmore plantation, about her experience.[55] At the time of the interview, Robinson was actually promoted to a spiritual teacher who had actually validated the spiritual experiences of converts. Robinson explained to Johnson one of her many spiritual visions that confirmed her conversion. She noted that she had a vision about walking out to Eddings Point with a candle and stumbled on a baby in the road. She explained that the baby was wrapped in white sheets. Robinson, then, noted that she cleaned the baby, which signified that she had found her soul. In another report, Johnson noted Robinson's other vision, where she heard a voice: "your sins were forgiven and your soul set free." Where does the Protestant conversion narrative fit in the broader American Protestantism in the South? Although he did not account for the conversion or seeking customs, he titled the top of his notecards with Mrs. Robinson and other converts' stories "superstition." Under the category of superstitions, these experiences were still couched as religious fossils from a stagnant population.

Additionally, he also recorded the daily superstitions—the good and back luck—of the population. For instance, he recorded one of the "signs" provided to him by Samuel de Veaux on a white note paper: "if a dog howls during the night, near someone's house, somebody will die in that family soon." Or, he recorded another sign from an Isabella Coleman, a fourth grader on the Island: "bad luck to plant crop when it's a moonshine night." On March 21, 1928, Johnson recorded what he titled the "superstitions" from an informant who "believ[ed] in ghosts." He did apply his English and/or white derivative claim to the superstitions on the Island. After the study, a film producer, William Laidlaw, sent a letter to the IRSS about his interest in doing a film on Blacks in what he called "remote parts of the Carolinas and the small islands off the coast." Laidlaw wanted to learn more about the "enthusiastic devotees of voodooism." Johnson replied, admonishing the film producer that voodooism was not present, as in New Orleans or Haiti. He further opined that the few superstitious charms and signs were merely "remnants of European superstitions."[56]

Johnson's framing of the obsolete folk spirituals underscored his privileging of class and regional differences over and against racial difference in the formation of American Protestant culture in the South. He essentially used the folk category to highlight the peasant and lower-class roots of Black spirituals and Protestantism that evolved out of the antebellum period. His explanation of the Scots-Irish and English peasants and the white origins of the folk religious lag of the yeoman Black farmers downplayed African differences in order to re-narrate the history of lower-class southern Protestantism in the isolated South. Folk expressions underscored the idea that poor and rural Blacks and whites shared the same antiquated Protestant cultures. His reference to the emotional evangelical camp-meeting revivals and ballads of Scots-Irish and English peasants were not only meant to display the origins of Protestant history in the American South, but rather, to highlight the revivals and the European peasant to show the persistence of lower-class Protestantism in "backward" and remote rural environments. His folk history of the white roots of the spirituals and broader Black Protestantism was done intentionally to show its parallels to poor white communities inhabiting the Piedmont and Appalachia regions in the American South. For Johnson, the folk religious expressions show how the lower-class Protestant culture was cultivated in underdeveloped regions removed from commerce, technology, and industry. His St. Helena fieldwork was the beginning of his adamant claim that social scientific studies of Black "lower-class" religion ignored the history and presence of poor southern whites in southern Protestant culture.[57]

For Johnson, Protestant revivals and camp meetings were the origins of the folk or obsolete forms of religious practices. The shouting, groaning, and bodily exertions, and the same sort of simple, repetitive singing in the nineteenth-century evangelical revivals continued among white and black cultural isolates. He asserted, "they [whites and Blacks] sang songs more adapted to the common people and to the emotional turmoil of the meeting."[58] Johnson was part of a cast of southern racial liberals that elevated the revivals—particularly the Second Great Awakening and its aftermath—to explain the antecedents of the twentieth-century lower-class and southern Protestantism and other "cults" in American life. He joined a cast of second-generation social scientists and historians—Charles Johnson, E. Franklin Frazier, Hortense Powdermaker, Carter Woodson, and John Dollard—who studied religion in order to identify and categorize the economic and regional differentiations within Black life. To refute fixed biological differences, they often pointed to poor whites to make the case about culture and class differentiation in American religion.

Johnson's use of the folk was meant to alter perspectives about race and culture, particularly with regard to Black rural communities. Johnson's conclusion about the European, white, and peasant roots of the obsolete folk patterns of the Black yeoman community was directly linked to his UNC colleagues' attention to the stagnant rural economy. Rural sociologist Woofter extended Johnson's arguments about the so-called cultural isolates. His focus on the folk cultural patterns intersected with their study of the economy recovering from the "agricultural depression." Long gone were the days of the long staple crop of the Sea Island that advanced industrial capital markets in Manchester and Liverpool, England, at the height of the cotton boom in the antebellum period. Additionally, Woofter and others spoke with the male informants on the islands who worked with the Coosaw Mining Company and other companies as wage-earning divers during the phosphate boom in the 1890s. Then, South Carolina governor Ben Tillman's extensive state royalties on corporations, coupled with the creation of the other markets in Florida, contributed to the collapse of the phosphate industry. As Woofter noted that at the time of the study, the Islanders were still in the process of adjusting to the collapse of the staple cotton economy. He noted that only a few of the Black farmers raised a "small bale of short staple cotton" for $10 to $30. Some farmers were experimenting to find the "money crop" to replace cotton. The majority of Black workers acclimated to the new environment by splitting their time between domestic farming and wage-earning labor in truck farming, fishing, oyster canneries, on public roads, and as artisans. As Columbia University graduate student Clyde Kiser recorded, a few Islanders (mainly, younger people) responded to the new agricultural depression by leaving the fields and migrating to southern and northern cities, such as Savannah, New York, and Philadelphia, in the 1920s. Additionally, the yeoman farmer did not have enough acreage to make a sufficient profit from farming while falling prey to "antiquated" agricultural techniques that were familiar during the antebellum time period. For instance, Woofter highlighted that many of the workers were unable to purchase commercial fertilizer and relied on the concoction of old composting techniques.

The sociologist underscored how the Black landowners on the barrier islands were removed from the wage economy. Woofter noted that rural sociologists all understood that the landowning farmers did not necessarily live in accordance with the money economy. This was partly the result of farmers producing their own goods and services. But the IRSS social scientists noted that the landowning residents still faced mounting struggles as a result of the lack of wages and resources. For instance, the community still needed wages to pay for private land and highway taxes, clothing and school tuition, church dues, and food. IRSS economist Clarence Heer described how the county land and highway taxes put an added strain on the small landowning community. Heer noted that out of their meager income they had to support governmental activities that benefited sections of the county far wealthier than their own. This matter was most evident in public school education. Heer was also making a point about the economic struggles of farmers in relationship to their inability to have representation in state and municipal government. Racial segregation was still a factor in their everyday lives. Johnson was personally privy to the financial strain on the Islanders when one of the Black domestic servants, "Callie S.," who tended to his family laundry and cleaned his living quarters, asked for $20.00 to keep from losing her house. Callie S. promised him that she would "work it out and pay it back."[59]

UNC sociologists could not resist highlighting the relationship between the material and cultural deficiencies. Woofter added to Johnson's claim about the folk and obsolete cultures of the rural community by concentrating on their premodern behaviors they cultivated due to their isolation from the mainstream wage society. He acknowledged certain behaviors that underscored how the St. Helena rural community had yet to adapt to American modern standards.

Woofter asserted that the rural community had yet to culturally adapt to American standards of ambition and energy. Woofter explained that the rural residents exuded an "easy-going attitude toward life, held by the great majority,—a contentment with less than would satisfy the average American family."[60] Similar to the folk Protestant cultures, Woofter, as a rural sociologist, noted that the lack of ambition was the result of the deficient habits they purportedly had developed during slavery. His attention to the lack of ambition was a reference to their—most notably the male "breadwinner"—attitudinal complacency toward low to no wages. Although Woofter said that rural economy does not adhere to the wage economy, he argued that the rural families were all right with living and functioning with less than $20. Woofter assumed that the wage economy generated ambitions, desires, and habits of men to accumulate more wages in their daily work. For majority of the St. Helena community, he asserted that "life is an Oriental pursuit of a calm, unhurried destiny, rather than a drive under the spur of ambition."[61] The few that exuded the culturally standard values and comportment were young migrants and the "energetic" successful farmers. He further noted that the difference between the successful and unsuccessful workers led him to note that "there are intangible differences in personality which lead the [successful] men to do the right thing at the right time and not to dilly-dally or delay."[62] As a folk population, they were not exposed to these cultural and moral standards. Yet, he concluded by noting that the St. Helena community's lack of ambition and energy extended their life and not their social status or "luxury."

Woofter also said that the rural community was isolated from American cultural standards in their failure to accumulate extra or surplus money that would have been pivotal to the advancement of family and community. The failure of the cotton economy reduced the desire to accumulate and save extra wages. In Woofter's eyes, the failure produced complacency and fatalism. What is interesting is that Woofter reduced the lack of surplus wages partly to energy and motivation. The community had internalized the farming depression that had destroyed their motivation. His creation of the cultural standards was rooted in certain behavioral norms and attitudes—ambition and energy—commensurate with modernization.

As I will discuss further in the next chapter, another cultural habit that reflected their cultural isolation was in what Woofter described as the community's "loose sexual morals." Rummaging through the census reports, Woofter highlighted the high rates of illegitimacy and broken familial structure on the islands. He attributed these factors to agrarian isolation from modern standards of family and sex. As in his text on urban migration, Woofter maintained a rural and agricultural romanticism that partly objected to the Black northern migration that jeopardized the stability of the nuclear family unit. Woofter standardized the nuclear family as a modern moral norm way before the Moynihan Report of 1965.

In the end, Johnson's attention to the cultural isolation in religious songs and oral culture was inseparable from his colleague's claims about the bad habits that supposedly resulted from their lack of interactions with modern wage culture. Their scientific explanation of cultural and moral isolation was a way in which they identified lower-class rural religion and culture. But the St. Helena study was also an evaluation of the "improvability" of the black folk in light of intellectual and moral paternalism. D. C. Washington and other farmers were portrayed in the study as showing that Blacks could assimilate into the standard culture with white Christian and industrial aid and programming. Johnson's statement about the white origins of black folk Protestant culture connected to the larger white southern liberal reformist project to modernize agricultural economy through scientific and state planning. While Woofter and other colleagues discussed the programs designed for agricultural and domestic science, they also accented the school's religious, cultural, and moral reformism. This accounts for why Johnson accredited Washington's sermon on citizenship, described at the beginning of the chapter, to Grace House and the Penn School.

Liberal Reform and the Penn School

Guy Johnson's deployment of the folk category was inseparable from the UNC southern liberalism (Figure 2.1). Southern liberalism was part of the Chapel Hill group's support of bureaucratic state-regional

From the University of N. C.
Mr and Mrs T J Woofter Jr
Clyde V. Kiser, Miss Jessie Alverson
Mr and Mrs Guy B Johnson,
Ben Johnson

Figure 2.1 From Left to Right: T. J. Woofter, Ethel Woofter, Clyde V. Kiser (graduate student at Columbia), Jessie Alverson (UNC staff), Guy B. Johnson, Guion Johnson, and Benny Johnson (son). Triuna Island, Lake George, near Saratoga, New York, in July or August 1929. They were guests of Penn School's trustee, George Peabody, who lent his estate to the social scientists and staff to finish their St. Helena monographs.

Manuscripts and Archives Division, The New York Public Library. "From University of N. C. Mr. and Mrs. T. J. Woofter, Jr., Clyde V. Kiser, Miss Jessie Alverson, Mr. and Mrs. Guy B. Johnson, Ben Johnson," New York Public Library Digital Collections.

development to modernize the South on par with the rest of the country. This chapter has already established how the use of the folk category was designed to identify and explain the persistence of obsolete cultural practices that characterized low-income working communities in the isolated South. He privileged social and economic factors against racial traits to underscore that black folk songs and religion were essentially white and, consequently, American, and not distinctly

Black. Such a claim answered the question about the acculturative capacities of Black populations and their place within the wider state-regional development of the poor South. His reading of the origins of
the folk culture fit into the study's objective to evaluate the effects of
the Penn Agricultural and Industrial School on its rural Black affiliates.
Culture was a site to examine the potential of adapting to modern
standards of moral behavior and agricultural labor.

Woofter organized the St. Helena study with an interest in assessing
the Penn School and its impact on some of the few Black small landowning families. He understood that the school presented a model
for modernizing agricultural labor in the poor South. To be sure, the
school lacked the money and resources to stem the tide of the economic struggles that impacted predominantly Black landowners on the
Island. Nevertheless, Woofter praised the school for "reshaped agricultural policy" for its students and their families with their curriculum
and programs for the rural community. He highlighted the curriculum and programs of the Penn School that were targeted at small
landowners to show white powerbrokers in other regions an efficient
and beneficial alternative to the pervasive yet defunct staple-crop and
tenant farming system in other regions in the Cotton South. He argued
that "Southern counties could well afford to assume as governmental
functions some of the semi-private activities of the Penn School."[63]
Students and families took courses and became involved in programs
in scientific agriculture to learn crop diversification, soil cultivation,
animal husbandry, and adequate tillage. Additionally, adolescents
and adult males excelled in carpentry, blacksmithing, housing construction, shoemaking, and car mechanics. Female students and families were involved in the school's domestic science department and
programs that taught cooking, sewing, gardening, animal husbandry,
canning, and raising animals (e.g., pure-bred poultry). Adults were involved in the school's Credit Union and Cooperative Associations that
distributed affordable loans for farmers, as well as collaborating to purchase expensive agricultural products, such as fertilizers.[64]

Affiliates of the Penn School also had access to a residential doctor
and nurses to administer "modern medicine." The School also provided midwifery and childcare courses for women on the Island.
Woofter noted that the "public health nursing, farm demonstration,

home demonstration, and teaching of agriculture," of the Penn School should be adopted as "legitimate government activities" for Blacks (and whites) in the rural South.[65]

But Woofter's attention to the Penn School was also to demonstrate that Black rural farmers could assimilate into modern society. Guy Johnson's rejection of fixed and inferior race traits in his study of black folk religion played into the broader white southern liberal reform. But Woofter's white southern liberalism was paternalistic in scope. In his "Preliminary Confidential Report for the Trustees of the Penn School," Woofter noted that the St. Helena study would "thr[ow] light upon the question as to what can be accomplished with a group of pure-blooded, isolated Negroes, when they [were] given the stimulus of intelligent paternalism."[66] He also told Penn School principal Rossa Cooley that the comprehensive study sought to disclose the "improviability [sic]" of Black students and families affiliated with the Penn School. And this is where Ebenezer Baptist Church's pastor D. C. Washington comes into the picture regarding Black people and their capabilities to acculturate into modern culture. Washington was affiliated with the Penn School and consequently worked with its various organizations, like the Credit Union. In the early 1900s, he was one of the beneficiaries of the school's partnership with the United States Department of Agriculture (USDA) for a scientific demonstration on diversified farming. USDA's Seaman Knapp instructed Washington and local yeoman farmers in the science of growing corn.

D. C. Washington also alerts us to the ways in which southern white liberalism prioritized a "moral narrative of modernity" that privileged so-called ethical religion. Thus, modern development in the liberal sciences and reform contained the management and regulation of the religion of the Black rural and lower-class community. This was not lost on Guy Johnson's observation of the service in Scottsville Baptist Church. He presumed that House, vice principal of the Penn School, held the strings to the organization of the service for the white visitors. Johnson noted that House was probably responsible for selecting the evening's preacher, D. C. Washington, over Scottsville Baptist Church's pastor, Issac Brisbane. Washington provided more expository sermons that resembled "middle-class black churches." He even accredited Washington's homily on moral citizenship and prohibition to House and her crusade against bootleg-ging. Penn School affiliates were assigned to sign pledge cards where they vowed to resist booze. They presented good or modern religion as an instrument that could facilitate broader social development in rural life. Washington was the designated pastor of the Penn School operations in the rural community.

Woofter, too, noticed the ways in which regulating religion was inte-gral to modernizing Black farming families at Penn School. The Penn School held chapel services for their students every day at noon. They extended the services to the wider community. Similar to Hampton Institute, the chapel or devotional services for students included bib-lical verses, religious songs, and a speech that usually related to cele-brating some aspect of agricultural labor. Contemporary scholars have argued that Cooley and House purposely tried to select spirituals that steered clear of excessive emotionalism.[67] Daily chapel services were held, along with Bible courses in the curriculum. What the chapel serv-ices, Bible classes, and devotionals at the start of community events show was that the school understood that religion was an impactful aspect of governing the Black rural landowners. The moral aspect of good religion was that it helped to motivate and discipline agricultural and domestic work habits and responsibility. Religion underscored how morality and industry complemented one another by showing that Blacks could be governed by modern moral standards. Woofter recycled UNC social psychologist Ernest Grooves's conclusions from his study of the praise houses. While Johnson pointed to the oral practices in the praise houses, Grooves and others highlighted their social function. They served as information bureaus where congregants heard news about community matters. For instance, Penn School officials sent news about tax deadlines, the boll weevil, and community events to praise house leaders, who in return sent it to the congregants. But more importantly, Grooves and other UNC social scientists highlighted an aspect about the praise houses that counter the ideologies of inherited black criminality.[68] The praise houses also operated as courts where the community settled conflict and adjudi-cated law and order. The praise houses kept crime to a minimum in the township. Woofter noted that "the people know of no crime wave, as there is little serious crime. . . ."[69] Woofter accredited the moral aspects mainly to community members themselves.[70] But he also acknowledged the Penn School's active interest for over 60 years in the promotion of moral order. The Black landowning community showed that they could be governed by civilizational standards of moral conduct and labor that could in turn benefit the entire agricultural/rural southern economy. And Johnson's research on the folk spirituals and broader religious practices confirmed that they had already assimilated into American culture in the first place, even at a lower stage of its development.

Conclusion

It is not clear that the Islanders were isolated. We have to call into question the trope of isolation that helped to fashion the rural farming community as static and suspended in a bygone time and place. The Sea Islands were not isolated by any stretch of the imagination. Throughout the twentieth century, the Island experienced the flows of a network of people, ideas, and resources that moved in and out of the Sea Islands. This is not to mention the droves of so-called modern scientists, folklorists, musicologists, colonial administrators, and educators who came to the Island and interacted with the Black farming communities. But St. Helena Islanders were mobile, just like other southerners after World War I. In fact, the population numbers had decreased since the 1890s. Graduate student Clyde Kisser noted that the numbers of the Islander residents in New York, Boston, and Savannah were relatively small before World War. But gradually residents (especially younger people) would migrant out of the Sea Islands to both southern and northern cities after World War I. Woofter noted that "St. Helena [was] a 100% rural community losing in population."[71] What was significant about their migration was that they often traveled back and returned to the Island to attend special events. Black migrants formed Penn Clubs in different urban cities in the United States. For instance, the Penn School Club of New York organized an "Address and Musicale" service at Abyssinian Church. The flow of migration of the Islanders actually challenges the myth that these people were cultural isolates and suspended in an American pastime.

This was also true with the spirituals. The folk category simplifies the variation of singing styles on the Island. The Penn School was always soliciting private funding to support their institution. In fact, both Cooley and House saw the St. Helena study as another marketing tool to publicize the moral and industrial work of the institution. But, like various educational institutions in the aftermath of the nineteenth-century Fisk Jubilee Singers, another marketing tool that Cooley and House used was the arranged spirituals by the St. Helena Quartet. The Quartet was invited to perform for predominantly white audiences, especially in the Northeast. The Quartet underscored another style of religious music while traveling outside the Island, only to return again. The movement of the Quartet highlighted that the Islanders were not isolated and therefore not folk. The school was trying to seize the market value of the spirituals by sending their Quartet to wealthy patrons, especially in the Northeast. The folk category ignored this phenomenon in identifying a so-called backwardness and isolation. Additionally, D. C. Washington supposedly gave way to a so-called middle-class homily on prohibition while he still almost performed the folk or fervent old-style preaching. This issue underscored that the yeoman farmers were never folk in the first place.

But Johnson's use of the concept was directly tied to the white southern liberalism at Chapel Hill. His political commitments were on full display in a later 1980 essay where he reflected on the St. Helena study. Although he mainly used the reflection to discuss the choices he made with regard to language, it still bore witness to the broader political import in his claims about the folk spirituals and overall Black American Protestantism. Addressing both Melville Herskovits's and Lorenzo Turner's previous claims about the distinct Gullah dialect on the islands, he faulted them for not adequately dealing with the history of Black and white contact in America. But his other rebuttal to their argument correlated to his political commitments. Lifting up examples of the deindustrialized urban context while ignoring the anti-apartheid struggles, he asked, "Does it help the black boy in the slums when we tell him about the genealogy of speech habits?" He further extolled that while scientists were interested in African customs, it had "little relevance to the practical problem to the dealing with substandard

English speech of millions of Negro Americans."[72] Johnson had rejected his advisor's racial biological theory of inherited race traits. But he nevertheless projected a hierarchy of culture more reminiscent of his progressive predecessor's idea of civilization (see Chapter 1) that contributed to his perspective that the Black yeoman farmers remained beholden to obsolete religious cultural practices. This hierarchy of culture (or civilization) circulated the myth of an American liberal and modern monoculture that Black southern people were not part of. The turn to culture still reified the myth of black inferiority. But his reading of the white roots of black folk spirituals and broader religious cultures was a testament that Blacks had the capability to fully acculturate into American modern culture. Moreover, sociologist T. J. Woofter further fleshed out the meaning of modern culture beyond religious orality. Using the model of "white civilization," Woofter described the Penn School as an ideal example of moral and agricultural governance that White state policymakers, local landowners, and business leaders should adopt for the advancement of Black laborers and consequently the rural southern economy. Johnson's reading of the songs was a perfect fit to how white southern gradualist liberals appealed for Black progress by focusing on the benefits to the regional economy. Not using racial equality as part of their platform, they simply tried to lift up the students and affiliates of the Penn School to show that Blacks had the capacity to be law-abiding, self-reliant, sanitary, and good landowning citizens that could help race relations and the poor South. They had the capacities to have the right conduct with aid from interracial cooperation by white bureaucrats and scientific researchers. Their focus on acculturation did not directly confront issues of Jim Crow segregation that shaped the economic and labor relations in the regional South. The Chapel Hill group disagreed with both the direct protest strategy of the National Association for the Advancement of Colored People (NAACP) and Southern communists. The Chapel Hill group thought that direct protest for racial equality caused racial friction and violence. They considered these political platforms and strategies to be counterproductive. But in the end, the focus on acculturative capacities only reinserted the subjugation of Blacks on political, social, and economic fronts. The use of "folk" in the study of religion and broader modern acculturation complemented the racial gradualism of the Chapel Hill while deflecting attention away from the role of racial segregation in race relations and regional economy. The folk category disclosed the paradox of white southern liberalism, more than it disclosed the religious and cultural practices of southern Blacks in the rural South.

3

Medicalizing the Folk

Superstitions, Family, and Germs in the Venereal Disease Control Program

> Anything seemed possible, likely, feasible, because
> I wanted everything to be possible. . . . Because I had no
> power to make things happen outside of me in the objec-
> tive world, I made things happen within. Because my envi-
> ronment was bare and bleak, I endowed it with unlimited
> potentialities, redeemed it for the sake of my own hunger
> and cloudy yearning.
>
> —Richard Wright, *Black Boy* (1945)

In June 1931, one of the four researchers from Fisk University interviewed Emma Morris, an elder farmer, in Hardaway, Alabama.[1] The researcher and Morris initially met at her daughter's house, then left and walked approximately 100 yards to conduct the interview at Morris's house.[2] The researcher described Morris as wearing a "ragged and dirty gingham dress," "scarf tied around her head," and without shoes to cover her "scaly feet."[3] As soon as the researcher and Morris entered her cabin, she immediately excused its appearance, grabbed a straw broom, and started to sweep the floor. While Morris swept, the researcher took note of the empty cans of salmon and sardines, and a basket of dried corn in the corner of the room. Minimalist in appearance, the main room only had an "untidy bed" and "two broken chairs." With a snuff brush in her mouth, Morris took a seat and discussed her daily experiences as a tenant farmer in Macon County's cotton economy.

To Know the Soul of a People. Jamil W. Drake, Oxford University Press. © Oxford University Press 2022.
DOI: 10.1093/oso/9780190082680.003.0004

Morris told the researcher that her husband was deceased and only two of her eight children were still living. The interview mainly centered around her daily transactions with the cotton industry of Macon County. She discussed how all her labor went to an absent landowner named "Mr. Glenn." As a tenant farmer, Morris stated that she worked approximately six to seven weeks—cleaning out ditches, planting, and hoeing cotton. In return, she rented her log-cabin house, two-acre plot of land, and, if lucky, earned a daily pay-rate of 50 cents. Instead of the 50 cents, though, her pay usually consisted of seeds to grow produce to eat, sell, and provide for her family.[4] When the researcher asked her about recreational activities, Morris responded that she did not have time for "pleasures" in her daily life because of her inconsistent wage earnings, endless debt, and rigorous labor demands. Church was an important aspect of her life. Morris stated that she was forced to miss the previous Sunday and all of last year's services because she did not have the proper attire. Cotton regulated every aspect of her entire life.

Morris was interviewed as part of the Julius Rosenwald Fund (JRF) and US Public Health Services (USPHS) mass venereal disease control program for rural Blacks that began in Macon County, Alabama, in 1930 (Figure 3.1). The study spanned the six county seats that comprised Macon County, including Tuskegee. She was one of the many Black farm patients in the program who received a regular 12-month treatment for syphilis.[5] Morris told the researcher that she had visited the clinics at the nearby Damascus Baptist Church and a local neighborhood school. Yet she had to quit treatment due to the pain that affected her daily labor productivity and compensation. Morris asserted, "If I wasn't working and could sit down and rest, [then] I would go." Morris and her daughter, Alder Smith, were one out of the 612 Black farming families whose interviews were compiled for Charles S. Johnson's *Shadow of the Plantation* released by the University of Chicago in the summer of 1934. The aftermath of antebellum slavery was still felt in the disproportionate racial demographic ratio that put Blacks at 12 to 1. At the time of the venereal disease study, Johnson was the director of the Social Science Department at Fisk University. With financial assistance from the Rosenwald Fund, under the presidency of Edwin Embree, the *Shadow of the Plantation* was intentionally published within the "timely significance [of] the National Recovery

Figure 3.1 A women receiving a Wasserman shot in the Venereal Disease Control Program in Macon County, Alabama.

Julius Rosenwald Archives, The Venereal Disease Control Program. Courtesy of Fisk University, John Hope and Aurelia E. Franklin Library, Special Collections.

Act affecting large sections of the South."[6] Both Johnson and his dear friend Embree undertook the study on Morris and other lower-class laborers with their sights on the Depression and welfare policy.

Edwin Embree's attention to the National Recovery Act (NRA) captured the historical backdrop of the transition of relief and welfare from private organizations to the state government with New Deal "alphabet agencies" during Franklin Roosevelt's first 100 days in office.[7] Passed in the summer of 1933, the NRA was designed to save business capitalism through establishing "fair labor codes," such as regulating work hours, wages, and unemployment (and granting unions). But for Black laborers, the NRA stood for "Negro Removal Act" as southern Democrats and business leaders adjusted the New Deal to Jim Crow governance.[8] The "fair practice codes" of the NRA, like the Agricultural Adjustment Act of 1933, did not extend to Emma Morris and other tenants and croppers in Macon County. Embree and Johnson were both proponents of the New Deal welfare state and its potential for racial and economic advancement for poor Blacks (e.g., tenant farmers and sharecroppers) and the wider antiquated agricultural South. Thus, the 1934 publication, *Shadow of the Plantation*, was a deliberate attempt to influence New Deal economic policies for rural Blacks in particular.[9]

Johnson compiled the interviews of Morris and other Macon County residents as data to refute what he called the "accepted social theory" in American social sciences. Contrary to "accepted social theory," Johnson argued that the interviews of Morris and other Macon County farmers actually confirmed that America did have a "folk social bloc." Morris, he argued, "represented an American type which can most nearly be described as folk, in so far as their lives were close to the soil."[10] Analogous to European peasants, the predominantly Black tenant farmers, according to Johnson, "were the closest approach to an American peasantry."[11] To further drive home his point, he stated that the claims about the nonexistence of a folk social class in American liberal democracy was not a "fact but an ideal." What was the category's importance in the medical demonstrations and venereal control disease in particular?

Johnson used the "folk" category to frame the social identity and experiences of Morris and the other 90% of tenant farmers in the 612

Figure 3.2 Charles Johnson pictured in Macon County during the
Venereal Disease Control Program in 1931.

Courtesy of Fisk University, John Hope and Aurelia E. Franklin Library, Special
Collections.

agricultural families within the JRF and PHS venereal disease control program for rural Blacks. Johnson's Macon County community study (Figure 3.2) showed that he was heavily invested in tracing out the cultural implications of poverty in the Jim Crow South. In the anti–venereal disease program, he placed just as much significance on the spiritual beliefs of the farmer-patients as he did on their material deficiencies in his overall assessment of syphilis and other diseases such as "tuberculosis, malaria, pellagra, and infant death" in Macon County and other areas in the Black Belt South.[12] His use of the folk category contributed to defining the lower-class religion based on their erroneous and irrational beliefs and customs. With the folk category, Johnson argued that the folk peasants' deficiencies were exhibited in their superstitions, otherworldly beliefs, and trivial social taboos. These deficiencies were pertinent to understanding and solving the high morbidity and mortality rates among rural Blacks. In the end, Johnson felt that the folk category contributed to classifying Black lower-class religion by its isolation from modern scientific and moral standards in medicine, hygiene, and state marriage and monogamy.

Against the backdrop of the Rosenwald Fund and Public Health Services, I argue that the folk category was part of a biomedical campaign that sought to reform the Black poor by studying and regulating their religious cultures. This reformist campaign sought to obliterate their spiritual beliefs and customs in order to subsume their religious cultures under moral and scientific controls. The goal of this biopolitical campaign was designed to transform the folk into a healthy and moral people by seeking to reform their beliefs to extend life expectancy, ensure labor productivity, and encourage strong nuclear familial relationship. Biomedical sciences did not erase religion from modern life. Rather, the Macon County campaign disclosed how religion was used in tandem with biology to identify cultural-behavioral problems, as well as ways to facilitate rural Blacks into scientific and moral knowledge and habits of disease and sex. This is why the Damascus Baptist Church was a site for one of the clinics. More importantly, we see how religion was part of the modern strategy of the cadre of racial liberals who emphasized the benefits of a healthier and efficient worker to appeal to federal, state, and private powerbrokers to extend healthcare to Blacks inhabiting the poor southern economy. This strategy sought to make appeals for racial equality by prioritizing the economy. The venereal disease control demonstration was an effort to extend public health to rural Black populations in the United States. The nature of this chapter is threefold. First, I will discuss Charles S. Johnson's work on race and religion before he arrived as chair of social science at Fisk University. We see how his use of the folk category in his work for the JRF and PHS was shaped by his early work with the Chicago Urban League and its subsequent national headquarters in New York City at the height of the Great Migration. His work on southern migrants was a product of the "Chicago School." Moreover, we see how his secular sensibilities came into play with his critique of the Protestant church and conjure cultures in the urban North. Second, I will narrate the history behind the JRF-PHS anti–venereal disease program. This aspect shows how the medical networks gave shape and form to the meaning of folk religion. I will also show the overall goal of Johnson and researchers from Fisk University in light of the relationship between race and medicine. At the time of the research, racial heredity was seen as a major factor in medical research on syphilis. Johnson's use of the folk category to frame the identities and experiences of Morris and others was a liberal move to emphasize labor and economic factors as the major contributors to the health conditions of Blacks. The liberal ploy of the research portion of the demonstration was to move away from the "Negro Problem" and connect Black health with the wider social and economic problems of the American South. Lastly, I will highlight the importance of the spiritual and/or superstitious belief system that Johnson presented in the research. We will see how religion factored into the liberal reformist project to govern the daily conduct of Black tenant farmers and sharecroppers through sex and familial values and hygiene. Sex and family were important aspects to liberal scientists and reformers.

Charles Johnson's Liberal Protestant and Scientific Biography

Johnson's deployment of folk to organize spiritual beliefs and practices was shaped before his tenure at Fisk University. Johnson grew up in Bristol City, Virginia, just three years before the Supreme Court handed down the decision of *Plessy v. Ferguson* that legislated the "separate but equal" clause in the southern states.[13] Bristol was a railroad town in southwest Virginia in the Appalachian Mountains that ran directly parallel to the Tennessee state line. In 1910, the town had a population of 4,579. Johnson's early view of religion was attributed to his Baptist household; his father, Charles H. Johnson, was pastor of a congregation that would become Lee Baptist Church.[14] His father named his son after the renowned nineteenth-century English Baptist preacher, Charles Spurgeon, otherwise known as the "Prince of Preachers." Charles Johnson later reflected that his parents were devout and earnest in their Baptist faith commitments. Johnson and his siblings were often required to participate in devotionals where they heard biblical passages read to them three times in the mornings. He would later appreciate his religious upbringing because he considered it a viable mode of social control that kept him out of trouble and harm's way. He would come to evaluate Protestant institutions in the rural South by their effectiveness at controlling the daily conduct of the parishioners according to new secular modern norms (e.g., family, sex, hygiene, and cleanliness) of industrial society.

Charles Johnson appreciated his father's religious orientation and how it shaped his own religious ideals and norms. According to Johnson, his father privileged education that supposedly separated him from the "typical Negro minister in Southwest Virginia."[15] Johnson's grandfather was enslaved in the Upper South by a Greek scholar and theologian who remained "aloof from the burning political controversies of the time."[16] The aloof classicist and theologian had educated his grandfather and father "without apology." According to Johnson, his father's experiences during the antebellum period stirred his intellectual curiosities and compelled him to pursue his education at Virginia Union college and seminary in Richmond. After completing boarding school at Wayland Academy, Johnson followed in his father's footsteps and received the "great tradition of learning and Christian piety" at Virginia Union. At Virginia Union, he fell under the scholarly tutelage of his Greek and English professors, Joshua Simpson and G. M. P. King. What he admired about his father's educated faith, and that of Simpson and King, colored his later analyses of the rural religious cultures of tenant farmers and sharecroppers in the Deep South.

Similar to many first- and second-generation social scientists, Johnson discarded his Baptist upbringing for Congregationalism. Later, in 1928, he would become a deacon at the Fisk Union Congregationalist Church during his tenure at Fisk University. Charles Johnson also became a vice moderator of the National Congregational Christian Church organization in the early 1950s. But he kept aspects of his early religious upbringing that influenced how he approached his career in science as a vocational endeavor. He would later apply his father's ability to translate his Christian faith into "social action." After leaving Richmond, his father reportedly sought to make his Christian message appeal to Black workers in "rowdy railroad labor camps" in the frontier town of Bristol. At Virginia Union, Charles Johnson recalled how his view of proper and right religion was further cultivated while he was "investigating needy applicants for Christmas baskets for one of the local charities."[17] His understanding of religion was gradually intertwined with his social philosophy that used empirical science to secure the public good. His preoccupation with religion and social action disclosed his dislike of supernatural reflections that he felt betrayed his empiricism. He later reflected that "[i]t is for this reason I early renounced the philosophies of escape, and pinned my faith to the power of life-experiences, guided by the highest ideals of my religious faith, to consummate the highest attainable human good." In fact, he later reflected that the divine was only empirically manifested in the moral conduct of human beings.[18] His renunciation of the "philosophies of escape" extended to his broader displeasure with formal systemic theology. Later reflecting on his attendance at the 1948 World Council of Churches' Amsterdam Conference, Charles Johnson noted that he preferred Reinhold Niebuhr, Visser T. Hooft, and Douglas Horton over Karl Barth, whose "philosophical position" was not as easily reconcilable to "social concern."[19] Johnson possessed the qualities of liberal Protestantism that supported a belief in the goodness of human nature, "this-worldly" social instrumentalism, and openness to natural scientific discoveries. Although he came to champion dispassionate objectivity in the social sciences, his liberal Protestantism shaped what he later deemed "bad folk religion" in Macon County.

Johnson's religious commitments were inseparable from his social philosophy. His social philosophy was deepened by his encounter with his future mentor, Robert E. Park, first at the University of Chicago in the Department of Anthropology and Sociology. Established in 1892, the department and the broader university had early roots in the American Baptist tradition. Supported by American Baptist John Rockefeller, William Harper was the institution's first president and saw to it that the university represented the best of social Christianity in its service to wider Chicago. Before World War I, the department housed sociologists who were trained clergy and had deep ties to liberal social Protestantism, particularly to the adult education program at the Chautauqua Institute in upstate New York. Before Johnson's tenure in 1917, the liberal Protestant sociologists filled the department, and merged their postmillennialism with the new sciences to promote social amelioration in urban cities. Maine native Albion Smalls studied theology at Andover Newton Seminary before he became founding chair in the department at the University of Chicago in 1892. Other liberal Protestants in the department and university were Charles Zueblin, Charles Henderson, and George Vincent. But social psychologist William Issac Thomas and journalist-turned-sociologist Robert Park later swayed the department away from Protestant social gospel influences to a more objective, natural, and male-centered scientific orientation in curriculum and research. But this transition to the hard and objective sciences had gender implications that reduced the sociological work of female sociologists, especially the professional and scientific women at the nearby Hull House, to the domain of social work.[20]

But, more importantly, the department's specialization in urban cities was rooted in its modern cultural evolutionary framework about the agrarian and rural life that preceded urban and secular life. In fact, W. I. Thomas's and Robert Park's urban science was predicated on a modern binary between rural and urban behaviors and social organizations. Park viewed the modern trends of science and technology, commercialism, and urbanization in industrial capitalism as natural and inevitable processes. And more specifically, he viewed these "modern trends" as separating the newly secular urban from the old sacred agrarian society. Johnson's liberal social Christianity, coupled with his evolving faith in rational and empirical sciences, set the stage for his later deployment of the modern category of folk in his study of the "outdated and agrarian" Black religion.

Johnson's field study of Black rural southerners and their religious cultures emerged out of his early research on southern migrants and urban proletraits. His professor, Robert E. Park, was one of the founding members of the Chicago Urban League. Johnson was one of the first of Park's students who worked as a research secretary assistant in the civic and social organization. Johnson's research opportunity was based on a tragedy at a beach on Lake Michigan in 1919. On July 27 white beach-goers started throwing stones at a group of Black boys whose raft had crossed over the invisible segregation line. A 17-year-old boy, Eugene Williams, drowned when he fell off the raft. The police chief's refusal to prosecute the culprits was the tip of the iceberg that led to the eruption of a three-day race war in which 23 Blacks and 15 whites died, and over 500 people sustained injuries. Chicago mayor Frank Lowder created the Chicago Commission on Race-Relations that included Black and white leaders and professionals, which included and Sears and Roebuck magnate Julius Rosenwald.[21] The commission decided "to . . . study and report upon broad questions of the relations between the races." A graduate student, Johnson was named the "executive secretary" of the report, and ended up being the primary researcher of the nearly 672-page document, published in 1922.[22] One of the social phenomena that he brought out in the study was the role of mass Black southern migration in the racial conflict in the midwestern city.

Johnson's work with the National Urban League prepared him for his later work in rural sociology at Fisk University. He was hired by the Urban League to head its Department of Research and Records in New York. Founded in 1910, the Urban League was a social work organization that promoted the social and economic advancement of Black southern migrants and proletariats in urban America. Arriving in 1921, the World War I veteran, Johnson lent his empirical social scientific methodology to quantifying the urban conditions of migrants and the poor in the areas of health, employment, crime, and housing. He recycled Park's racial-relations cycle theory that captured how the southern migrants had trouble adjusting (e.g. assimilating) to the urban environment. This trouble was labeled "social disorganization" since the so-called first primary social organizations of primitive populations (e.g., social relations that were homogeneous, direct, and

small) were not applicable to urban cities.[23] Their secular modern discourse in sociology highlighted that "social disorganization" occurred
among the rural migrants and immigrants when their previous modes
of social controls were not effective in urban environments. Johnson
replicated the Chicago view of rural and peasant mental and social life,
which he juxtaposed against more advanced modern urban mentality
and social organization.

Charles Johnson applied social disorganization to his early analyses
of the Black churches in the urban north. He acknowledged the power
of the church as a resource in Black life and history. Yet, he felt that
the Black churches (or "the Black Church") could no longer function
as the center of Black life due to the competing and viable social organizations in urban life. The secular view about the decentering of
Black churches in urban cities was prescriptive. In his early research,
he argued that the churches were not social centers that helped Black
migrants adjust to the complex urban environment. Churches were
"weak" centers of social control with regard to acculturating Black
communities, especially southern migrants, into modern society. For
instance, he noted that the churches were actually prohibiting Black
migrants from acculturating into urban life. His claim was based on
what he took to be the religious leaders' lack of support for the labor
unions in the industrial market.[24] The Urban League supported labor
unions for the advancement of Black employees in urban industries.
Johnson measured the viability of religion in accordance with his embrace of these secular standards of city life, such as social welfare. His
understanding of religion reproduced the modern rural and urban binary that he borrowed and reappropriated from the work with Robert
Park and William Thomas. Park asserted, "The culture of the modern
man [was] characteristically urban, as distinguished from the folk culture, which rest[ed] on personal relations and direct participation in
the common life of the family, the tribe, and the village community."[25]

In his research on southern migrants for the Urban League, he
began to delve more into the study of conjure (or, as Robert Park
described it, "magic"). The history of conjure was part of the African-
derived spiritual traditions through which enslaved populations
communed, interacted, and invoked unseen powers to satisfy specific purposes and overcome challenges that confronted them in their

immediate daily social contexts. As religious historian Yvonne Chireau notes, conjure was a source of empowerment in the quotidian worlds of Black life.[26] Conjure persisted in the early twentieth century in the American South in particular. But Johnson and other sociologists' Enlightenment-based rational and liberal commitments restricted their study of conjure to investigating its cognitive truth or falsity in nature. He cast conjure as folk superstition to show the difference between rural and urban behaviors and social organizations. Johnson was director of the Urban League's Research and Records Department and created and edited its monthly magazine, *Opportunity*. In the October edition of 1926, Johnson reviewed Niles Newbell Puckett's *The Folk Beliefs of the Southern Negro*. Born in Columbus, Mississippi, in 1898, Puckett was trained in sociology at Yale University after completing his A.B. at Mississippi College. At Yale, Puckett was advised by sociologist A. E. Keller, a former student of William Graham Sumner, who trained the former to approach folklore as a resource that traced the evolution of social behaviors and customs in modern society. A later sociology professor at Western Reserve University and affiliate of folklore societies, Puckett established his reputation in the professional world of folk sociology and literature, where he produced work on a range of topics from his field studies. He published work on folk southern churches; Black names and dialect; and riddles and tales. *The Folk Beliefs of the Southern Negro* was his dissertation research at Yale University that he published in 1926. He frequented the Mississippi (and Louisiana) Gulf, where he postured as a hoodoo doctor to acquire intimate information about Black conjure culture (Figure 3.3). Puckett understood the folk beliefs and superstitions as "normal stages of development through which all peoples have passed and are passing in their societal evolution." In his favorable review of Puckett's book, Johnson noted that "what these beliefs reveal is the fascinating interplay of advanced and backward cultures, of the absolute qualities of ignorance, of the stranglehold of superstitions on untutored minds."[27] He agreed with Puckett that the beliefs were found mainly with the "uncultured and backwards classes of society." Johnson agreed with Puckett that the folk most represented the beliefs and customs before the advent of modern science. Rural Black Mississippians, according to Johnson, revealed a world where the "light of science [was] blocked

Figure 3.3 Folk sociologist Newbell Niles Puckett standing in front of a hoodoo bag in Lowndes County, Mississippi. To get his materials on "black superstition," the Mississippi native pretended to be a conjure doctor.

Courtesy, Cleveland Public Library Digital Gallery.

out." But what Johnson most appreciated about Puckett's conclusion was that the white folk sociologist attributed "Negro superstitions" to Anglo-European traditions. For Johnson, this move warded against the use of superstition to racialize Black southerners. A familiar argument that he continuously made throughout his career, Puckett noted that folk beliefs and superstitions were as common among poor whites as among the Black poor in the rural South.

Charles Johnson's approach to conjure had recycled the Chicago School's view that rural and agrarian social life was steeped in tradition and authority that prevented folk populations from critical reflection or rational decision-making. He followed W. I. Thomas's 1912 premise that social, economic, and geographical factors excluded folk populations from stimulations and copies caused by the "high grade of the mind."[28] Conjure, in Johnson's estimation, was a part of the preindustrial and agrarian social order that did not free individuals to critically think for themselves, separate from the group and tradition. He felt that conjure was entangled in the web of agrarian and primary-social group contact and did not bolster the individual, rational, free subject suitable for liberal democracy. He privileged the Enlightenment-infused liberal tradition that filtered in the Chicago School's sociology of race and the city.

Johnson considered the study of beliefs to be a matter of life and death for Black communities. We see his interest in the spiritual culture of rural Blacks to be a broader social and secular study of Black health. In a secular and urban perspective, he considered the agrarian spiritual and material beliefs a public health problem. Johnson followed his review of Puckett's book with two short essays on superstitions. One of the essays was entitled "Superstition and Health" that was a precursor to his work in the venereal disease control program. Johnson concentrated on the various popular conjure-magical beliefs that defied what he saw as a "cause-and-effect" rationality in modern science. He explained how tea made with sheep manure was a treatment for scarlet fever. He repeated the "trinary negative reasoning" where he defined superstition in contrast to religion and science.[29] He discussed a southern migrant family who painted their child's face with "blueing" to reduce fever.[30] Fortunately, a doctor provided the child with a proper diagnosis of diphtheria and was able to cure him. Unfortunately, the child's siblings were not so lucky." For Johnson, superstition contributed to reducing the life expectancy of Blacks about five years less than whites. These beliefs were proof that revealed that rural Blacks were on a lower stage of mental development and needed scientific and educational reform. A budding liberal progressive, Niles Newbell Puckett used his sociological analyses of the Black folk superstition to make policy and programmatic recommendations. Puckett endorsed scientific educational reform (e.g. "training in biology, chemistry, physics, and other such sciences") to rid the Black southern mind of folk superstition.[31] Johnson's identification of the bad folk beliefs and customs were used to support health and medicinal reform policies for rural Blacks.

Charles Johnson was one of the secular social scientists who felt that religious institutions (particularly the "Negro Church") had lost their relevance due to the mounting social problems in a changing and complex industrial world. He was a secularist in the sense that he championed how other advanced knowledges, techniques, and apparatuses, and institutions in public health and medicine, should properly govern the daily habits and conduct of all humans, especially rural Blacks and their religious cultures. Moreover, he felt that the science and health institutions and practices could better usher a folk population into the complexity of modern life than could Protestant churches and conjure. At best, he supported a liberal American Protestantism that conceded to the secular authority of science, medicine, and hygiene. His classification of the preindustrial folk beliefs and customs animated his liberal-bureaucratic reformist logic that the latter venereal disease control program exhibited.

In the latter half of the 1920s, Fisk University's president, Thomas Elsa Jones, sought to implement a revitalization plan to put the institution on par with liberal arts education. Founded by the American Missionary Association, Fisk University was one of the various colleges targeted at Black people in American Reconstruction. Both Rockefeller and the JRF supported the plan within their initiatives to promote the sciences in order to meet the challenges and changes of modern society. Johnson had established a good reputation with both the Rockefeller Foundation and the JRF. These relationships would strengthen over the years, making him the first Black person to serve on the Board of Trustees at the Rosenwald Fund in 1946. With the support of the northern philanthropic organizations, Jones extended the invitation to Johnson to head and advance the Social Science Department at Fisk University. Jones picked Johnson over E. Franklin Frazier, who was highly recommended by university alum W. E. B. Du Bois.[32] Johnson's association with northern philanthropies presumably had a hand in his being hired to head the department. Johnson fully embraced the position as an opportunity to "inaugurate a broad social program in the South, where a vast majority of Negroes reside." He organized Fisk University's social science department on the desire to "get into the material of the Southern Negro,"[33] which he felt was lacking in the field of social science. Fisk was uniquely situated, with its "advantage in being located in the South where little has yet been done in the field." Fully supported by the JRF, Johnson, along with his renowned faculty, became a "research dynamo" on southern race relations and rural Blacks in the twentieth century.[34] Governments and philanthropic organizations consulted Johnson and the department for data in their reformist projects and programs. Johnson continued his health research that sought to know and reform the religious cultures of the folk. The JRF and USPHS venereal disease control program provided him with the opportunity to continue what he had started at the Urban League. But Fisk University provided him with an opportunity to build a research database from a firsthand account of Black rural communities in the lower South.

The Background of the Syphilis Venereal Disease Control Program

The JRF and USPHS developed out of the larger history of the anti-syphilis campaigns that were established at the turn of the twentieth century. The 1905 discovery of the *Spirochaeta pallida* (or *Treponema pallidum*) by zoologist Fritz Schaudinn and dermatologist Erich Hoffman contributed to anti-syphilis campaigns among moral hygienists and health practitioners in the United States and beyond. US public hygienists framed their anti-syphilis moral crusades as a battle to preserve white-American Victorian values and mores against the perceived threat of urbanization. The threat of syphilis was attributed to urban trends such as the influx of racial migration and immigration, leisure and alcohol, and "white slavery" (or, white prostitution).[35] At the outbreak of World War I, both executive and congressional branches intervened in the anti-syphilis crusade by legislating anti-prostitution laws, developing programs for soldiers, and procuring funds for state governments to establish preventive and treatment programs. During this anti–venereal disease governmental activity, Congress voted to transform Maine Hospital Services into Public Health Services (USPHS) and assigned it to take the leading role in combating syphilis via medical research, quarantines, and examination of populations.[36] Yet, these federally funded programs did not establish state programs that extended to the rural hinterlands where the majority of Blacks lived. Epidemiologist and director of the Bureau of

Preventable Diseases of the Alabama State Board of Health, D. G. Gill, celebrated the federally funded programs allocated to more industrial parts of the state, like Birmingham, but complained that the "solution for the program of syphilis amongst the rural Negro populations still awaits fulfillment."[37] Clinician O. C. Wenger, the USPHS's main liaison to the Rosenwald Fund, echoed Gill's sentiment when he explained to the director of the Rosenwald Medical Service, Michael Davis, that the "situation in Mississippi [was] perhaps no different from that of any other southern state where the public health problem of the colored population have heretofore been ignored."[38] In addition to the widespread neglect, rural counties tended to lack an organized health infrastructure comparable to that of the urban counterparts.

The widespread neglect of Blacks by state health programs inspired both the JRF and the PHS to organize a mass experiment to treat and control syphilis for rural Black populations, beginning in September 1929. The venereal disease control demonstration was an experiment on the "possibilities of mass treatment by determining the number of positive test results in a group of unselected rural negroes of all age groups . . . and [to] arrange treatment for all cases uncovered."[39] The mass venereal disease control demonstration first started with 2,000 "black cotton pickers," or what USPHS officials called "Plantation Negroes," in Bolivar County in Mississippi before expanding to five other rural counties in Alabama, North Carolina, Tennessee, Georgia, and Virginia in 1930.[40] Before the discovery of penicillin in 1940, the venereal disease control demonstration treated rural Blacks with free Wasserman testing and shots of neo-arsphenamine or mercury salve for a year. By the time the Rosenwald Fund pulled out of the demonstration in 1931, it was reported that approximately 40,000 Blacks had been tested and treated for syphilis in the six counties in the Black Belt South.[41]

The venereal disease control demonstration was part of a robust health initiative by the JRF. The Fund's namesake, Julius Rosenwald, had administered a mandate before his retirement that the Fund must distribute all of the total estimate of over $200,000 within a generation after his death to prevent philanthropic perpetuity and accumulation of wealth. This mandate compelled the new president and board of trustees to make health one of its top priorities for Blacks and low-income populations from 1928 to 1943.[42] The syphilis program was part of the Fund's Negro Health unit's commitment to provide Blacks with equal access to quality care, resources, and medical education within the bounds of racial segregation.[43] The Fund's Negro Health initiative separated it from other philanthropic organizations' health programs that tended to solely aid white population and acquiesce to Jim Crow segregation. Moreover, in addition to the Black health unit, another related, but distinct feature of the JRF was its medical service unit. Under the direction of a pioneer in the field of medical economics, Michael Davis, the medical service unit was charged with the task of making healthcare affordable for low-income populations in America. The venereal disease control demonstration was also designed to corral policymakers, corporate and private business owners, and land managers to assist with the reduction of health expenses for their workers. On the first anti–venereal disease site in Scotts, Mississippi, O. C. Wenger told Michael Davis that he was able to convince owners of the Delta and Pine Company to cover 50% of the health expenses needed for its predominantly Black labor base. Wenger further stated that he now only reserved hope that Mississippi legislators would pass "a suitable appropriation to uncover syphilis and make some arrangement whereby these patients can be treated at a nominal fee."[44] With the Macon County demonstration and its support of wider state apparatuses, I will later show that the anti–venereal disease programs were part of an effort to administer wider comprehensive state health policies and programs to effectively democratize medicine for rural Blacks.

The Macon County Venereal Disease Demonstration Study

Michael Davis recommended to the USPHS that a collaborative survey needed to happen in order to evaluate the health progress of the communities after a year of treatment. JRF spearheaded medical science research as part of its goal to "cultivate fresh fields through studies . . . leaving to society the support of new procedures and new institutions once their value was shown." Davis explained that the purpose of the survey was to evaluate the "methods used in the diagnosis and treatment of syphilis so as to judge the value of the medical results achieved and to suggest improvements."[45] In March 1931, Davis formally invited Johnson to join medical researchers from the American Public Health Association to provide "a social and economic study of the Negro populations." The emphases on the social and economic factors in the study captured the JRF's (and Fisk University's) desire to transform the perceptions of race and health in medical sciences and policies. Under Davis, the Fund deliberately established medical research projects that magnified the intersection of biological and social phenomena. In a later 1935 essay, Davis argued that "health involved the study of body and mind in the physical and social settings of the human species."[46] Davis's invitation to Johnson and Fisk University to participate in the anti–venereal disease program was intended as an opportunity to show the impact of the socioeconomic factors on the so-called disproportionate syphilis rates of Black communities in Macon County and the broader rural South. Laying out the scope of the study, Davis told Charles S. Johnson that he and his researchers from Fisk University would work alongside medical researchers from the American Public Health Association to provide a "social and economic study of the Negro population; with a view to bringing out [t]hose points which may have a bearing on the prevalence of syphilis." Davis leveraged the Macon County study to intentionally merge sociologists with "syphilogists" for the purpose of shedding light on the "economic relationships of the local medical practice to the treatment of syphilis."[47]

The Macon County study would be one of several surveys that Johnson and company used to tease out the socioeconomic factors in Black health. A year after he arrived at Fisk University to head its Social Science Department in 1928, Johnson participated in a JRF-sponsored epidemiological study on race and tuberculosis in Central Tennessee. Collaborating with epidemiologist Eldridge Sibley, Johnson provided quantitative and statistical data on social and economic conditions that Sibley relied on to bolster his argument that the social and economic differences between the races were responsible for the "differential mortality" rates in Central Tennessee.[48] Therefore, his deployment of folk category in the Macon County study refuted the prevailing idea that racial heredity and genes determined the poor health conditions of Blacks in the South and the broader nation. In an unpublished essay, "Health-Mortality Trends and the Transition from Folk Medium to Scientific Medium," Johnson asserted that the "history of Black [morbidity] and mortality [was] the story of the theories of racial differences successively altered or abandoned."[49] He was privy to the ways in which the professionalization of medicine in the United States was founded on espousing racial polygenetic thought in the early nineteenth century. He often recalled Louisiana physician Samuel Cartwright, one of the prominent medical ethnologists who used medical research to classify the Black race as a separate species with a different biological constitution. Cartwright used "southern medicine" to bolster his claim that slavery was a benevolent system in the nineteenth century. In Johnson's 1952 lecture delivered at the Tuskegee Institute, the same place where he had studied in 1931, Johnson asserted that the question of [Black] health was "bound up with the ... elusive facto[r] of political ideologies."[50]

Johnson understood the ways in which a racial polygeneticism filtered into the medical discourse around syphilis at the turn of the century. Contemporary medical historians Paul Lombardo and Gregory Dorr asserted, "the claim that infectious diseases like syphilis were endemic in Blacks because of racial differences was a cultural commonplace among physicians in the late 19th and early 20th centuries."[51] Blacks were depicted as a "syphilis-soaked race." At the start of his fieldwork in March 1931, Johnson was privy to how the history of medical statistics helped to mark Black people by their perceived natural susceptibility to syphilis, which confirmed their so-called inherited moral ineptitude in industrial America. Johnson often invoked individuals, such as Frederick Hoffman, a Prudential actuarial statistician, who relied on state and military data to argue that the dramatic growth of syphilis among Blacks after emancipation underscored their racial degeneracy and inherent moral and industrial incompetence. Hoffman used the purported disproportionate rates of syphilis and vital statistics to ground his claim that life insurance should not extend to Black populations. In his 1896 *Race Traits and Tendencies of the American Negro*, Hoffman noted, "For the root of evil lies in the fact of an immense amount of immorality, which is a racial trait, and of which scrofula, syphilis, and even consumption are the inevitable consequences."[52] Syphilis was a race science that was used to mark southern and eastern European immigrants by the late nineteenth and early twentieth centuries. After World War I, Congress used the USPHS syphilis studies to further racialize southern and eastern European immigrants at Ellis Island and to support the Immigration Act of 1924. The USPHS was at the forefront of race and medicine in the United States.

During the time of the Macon County demonstration in 1931, a strand of racial polygenism in syphilis research was amplified by the widespread popularity of eugenics in medical and social sciences and government in the second decade of the twentieth century.[53] By the 1930s, southern states added to their racial segregation laws the separation and sterilization of the feeble-minded.[54] Eugenics helped to bolster the common perspective that racial heredity accounted for morbidity (as well as intelligence and social behaviors). Prior to the Macon County study, University of Virginia, Northwestern University, Johns Hopkins University, and other medical departments and programs were at work on syphilis research to reveal the different hereditary variations of the races and sexes, particularly of Blacks and women. The Department of Venereal Diseases at Johns Hopkins embarked on several research projects that concluded that the Black population's (and women's, too) low rates of neurosyphilis, in contrast to cardiovascular syphilis, disclosed their naturally inferior brain and nervous system.[55] The fact that most of the PHS officials, at the time of the demonstration and study, were also affiliated with the eugenic organizations accounts for why the Macon County demonstration descended into an experiment on racial hereditary difference. For example, O. C. Wenger had suggested compulsory sterilization and birth control as possible solutions to curb the syphilis rates in Macon County. Inspired by the untreated syphilis experiment in Oslo, Norway, the USPHS was interested in teasing out the role of racial heredity in syphilis, which led to the infamous Tuskegee experiment beginning in 1932, after the Rosenwald Fund and Fisk University left the demonstration.[56] Johnson's sociological approach to syphilis was meant to contest the ruling on medical scientific and eugenic research agendas that proliferated and supported control of the growth of race(s) deemed to be scientifically inferior through containment and sterilization.[57]

Johnson's argument about the existence of a folk social bloc was to account for the impact of the staple-crop farming system on the health conditions of Black tenants and sharecroppers. There were disproportionate rates of syphilis, as well as tuberculosis, malaria, and pellagra, among Blacks, comprising 2,578 of the farming laborers with 2,258 or nine-tenths in the tenant class in Macon County. Out of the 612 families interviewed, 90% were tenant farmers. Johnson supported his research with his typical use of quantitative methods to maintain his objectivity. Johnson and his researchers also relied on their living "human documents" (or "life histories") to demonstrate the daily effects of the "old plantation system" on the health and everyday experiences of the Black farmer-patients. They deliberately organized the interviews around their daily transactions with the tenant and sharecropping system in Macon County.[58] Morris told a researcher that she had received $1.05 for 40 pounds of cotton the previous year. On average, Johnson reported that the cash handled by the average tenant family ranged from $72.00 to $90.00 in 1931.[59] One of the researchers recorded Minne Ivery's discussion about how she barely made rent due to the fluctuating cotton prices, coupled with the death of her husband in a labor accident in Tallhassee, Alabama. The researcher jotted down that Ivery "raised two bales of cotton" in 1930. One bale (500 pounds) went to cover her rent, while the other bale sold for $30.00, which was spent to cover her accumulated debt. Another researcher interviewed "Mrs. Edwards," who told them that her husband, George, a tenant farmer, divided his labor with the local sawmill plant for a daily rate of $1.25 during cotton off-season. The privileging of the cotton economy, the largest industry in Macon County, supported Johnson's argument that the "history of Negro [morbidity] and mortality in America [was] the story of economic factors . . . operating to limit their hold on life in the competitive struggle for survival. . . ."[60] It was their transaction with the soil that determined their "everyday" isolation and dull routine, endless debt and poverty, and complete dependence on external networks for basic sustenance—shelter, land, food, medicine, clothes, and farm tools. Their folk peasant status, according to Johnson, underscored a life of complete dependence on absentee landlords for basic sustenance of life.

He also noted that the unstimulated, everyday routine of ginning, mooting, sorting, preparing the grounds, planting, fencing, ditching, picking, and hoeing cotton hindered the mental and cultural development of the tenant farmers. Johnson noted that this unstimulated and monotonous work extended to adolescent life, too. Adolescents were often prevented from attending school in order to assist the family in the fields. Childhood labor laws were not enforced in Macon County. Cotton determined their lives and restricted them from the larger outside world. Johnson asserted, "[i]f these folk groups have a social life, it is unique and is due in large measure to the fact that they are cut off from the most direct channel of communication (e.g. radio, motion pictures, and mail-order catalogue, etc.) with the outside world and its interests through the economic system itself, which restricts economic negotiations virtually to their immediate white landlords."[61] As a member of the Minority Groups in Economic Recovery, Johnson noted that the "[t]enancy and the share system in the South developed as a compromise device, after the collapse of slavery with its completely controlled labor supply, to continue cotton culture." The health conditions underscored that Macon County Blacks were suspended in the "shadow of the plantation" of the antebellum period. The folk category reflected the antiquated and exploitative cotton economy that lagged behind rising corporatization, mechanization, and diversification of the agricultural industry in the Midwest and West Coast.[62] Johnson's privileging of the antiquated cotton economy in matters pertaining to health was meant to underscore that Black problems were part of the whole problem of the South. The rise of "[l]iberalism in the South," according to Johnson, situated the "Negro problem as a phase of the South's broader economic and cultural problems."[63] Johnson significantly and frequently pointed out that these problems also extended to poor white communities.

The tenant farmers did not need trained sociologists to explain to them the injustices of the old plantation economy. The farming-patients sought to leverage the interviews in the demonstrations to share their personal experiences as a way to challenge the race and economic conditions. Johnson and company's reference to the farmers' "religious and [social] fatalism" overlooked how they leveraged the interviews as a form of social critique through a retelling of their everyday experiences.[64] One of the residents noted to a researcher, "it seems like he could never break even."

The Problem of Folk Religion

The concept of the " folk Negro" was used to represent the lower-class position of Black tenant farmers in the rural South. It was a marker of class identity. In a "Folk Seminar" in the department, Johnson lectured graduate students on the shortcomings of the conventional upper-, middle-, and lower-class schema that overlooked the many subdivisions within class groups. He went on to note that the lower-class category ignored the "Folk Negro." The "Folk Negro" demanded an entirely different mode of interpretation and analysis than the "urban underworld Negro."[65] What separated the rural and urban Black lower class was that the former had a culture—meaning an organizational structure of values and meaning that governed their daily habits. He remarked, "the Negro folk group represented a type of subculture, with internal organization and cohesion and standards of value and meanings peculiar to the group which differ at many points from those of the larger American society."[66] Johnson understood the "Folk Negro" as more of a cultural concept than an economic concept.[67] The "Folk Negro" represented a "subculture." To put it more aptly, the "Folk Negro" was part of the "immediate legacy of the Great Depression for poverty knowledge [in] the social scientific study of how poverty was at once a cause and a consequence of psychological depression, [and] the distinctive values associated with lower-class culture."[68]

The folk category was responsible for framing the lower class as a social group with a distinct set of cultures and behaviors. Building on work by folklorist Mary Austin, Johnson argued that "to be shaped in the mind and social reaction, to some extent in character and finally in expression is to be folk."[69] Johnson understood that Emma Morris, Minnie Ivery, and other tenant farming families of Macon County were "folk" because they occupied an elemental and rudimentary stage of development specific to the American mind. Nowhere was the elementary stage of human development more apparent than in the metaphysical beliefs and practices of Macon County tenant farmers that ranged from spiritual visions, conjure, and beliefs in otherworldly phenomena. Johnson remarked that the "history of the Black [morbidity] and mortality in America [was] the story of the inheritance and persistence of folk superstition."[70] Committed to a developmental model of culture, it was no surprise that he categorized the metaphysical beliefs as "survivals"—meaning "proofs or examples of an older condition of culture" that transcended racial specificity.

Johnson's and the researchers' fieldnotes were replete with information on the spiritual, otherworldly, or magical practices along with income, labor conditions, and home and family dynamics. The term "metaphysical" is used to explain how the researchers classified and interpreted different yet similar beliefs and practices such as "waiting for heaven," superstitions, and spiritual visions that deified the "cause-and-effect" explanation of natural phenomena. Johnson and other researchers framed these metaphysical beliefs as folk data that disclosed the "mental antiques" in contemporary America.[71] They regarded the tenant farmers' reliance on spiritual and unseen forces to explain natural phenomena as superstitions. Johnson recalled an interview with an elderly woman who relied on a vision to cure her sickly granddaughter.[72] In the record, she was distraught that her self-made regular regimen of castor oil and dishwashing soap were not helping her "motherless thing." Yet, she had a miraculous dream come in the form of her deceased friend who appeared at night and stood near her bed and confirmed that the granddaughter would not die. The dream "from God" spurred her to continue to use her remedies that eventually led to her granddaughter's "resurrection." Other tenant farmers also attributed their health conditions to God. Another researcher interviewed a father who discussed the processes of relieving his daughter of tuberculosis: "God and myself worked, rubbed, and twisted her till she finally come 'round' . . . I tell you I believe in the Lord."[73]

Johnson also included reports on conjure, or what he called superstition—"half-magical and half practical practices."[74] The "half-magical and half practical practices" were revealed in one of the researchers' interviews of "Mrs. Edwards." The wife of a tenant farmer, Mrs. Edwards told the researcher that she was unable to work due to the painful boils on her body. But she took pride in her infant daughter, "Lille Gal," "ain't been sick since she been born." She attributed Lille Gal's health state to the leather string around her neck, as ordered by her midwife.

The Macon County study was a rare opportunity to detect how these beliefs provided a window into the behavioral and cultural patterns of the southern folk. As displayed in Ms. Edward's interview, superstitious beliefs were aided by the popularity of local midwives due to their rapport with the communities, as well as the high cost of local physicians. One of the researchers asked Rosa Lancastor about her knowledge as a midwife. Lancastor indicated that she just learned about midwifery by asking a former midwife. Midwives had various half-magic and half-practical measures, such as "placing a knife under the pillow" to prevent pain during delivery.[75] In another JRF and State Health Department study in rural Louisiana, a researcher from Fisk University jotted down the complaints of a state agent, Betsy Florence, about one of the midwife trainees. The researcher was observing a state certification program that Black midwives were required to attend. Despite the new state regulations that required midwives to attend the courses, one of the midwives openly continued to measure and supply doses of the patent medicine Kirby Miracle Water and her homemade herb concoctions. According to the researcher, Florence Beatty (a midwife trainee) "has her own peculiar notions and clings to them; for she frequently boasts that she can do more than the licensed physician for her patients by using her home-made moon-suggested and herb concoctions. She has many signs and notions that she holds are inviolate."[76] Dreams, superstitions, and cure-alls were evidence of the folk mind that supposedly attributed natural occurences to invisible forces and animate objects. Throughout the twentieth century, Johnson and Fisk University professors and students understood that the metaphysical beliefs were important to their sociological enterprise of studying Black populations in the Black Belt South. Metaphysical beliefs were depicted as the result of rural poverty and consequently were attributed to European superstitions, like witchcraft. In his book *Shadow of the Plantation,* Johnson used Puckett's argument that the superstitious beliefs of southern Blacks were "borrowed from whites . . . their folklore is scarcely distinguishable from that brought over from Europe by the early colonists. . . ."[77]

Aside from the "supernatural" and "premodern" beliefs, the researchers also examined the Protestant churches in Macon County. According to the report, the Black religious demographics comprised mostly Baptists, then Methodists, with a few African Methodist Episcopalians and Methodist Episcopalians. Out of the 612 rural families, only 17 were not affiliated with one of the churches. One of the churches, Damascus Baptist Church, was in a secluded area in Hardaway. It was a gray wooden box with a bell on top of the gabled roof. The interior was described as having three wooden pews with a picture of Abraham Lincoln and a crayon portrait of a former pastor plastered on the white walls in the sanctuary. Johnson and company replicated familiar tropes that interpreted the Protestant culture as reflecting the revival strain from the Second Great Awakening. He perceived that "during the heyday of their camp meetings and revivals at the beginning of the nineteenth century that patterns of religious expressions [of the Black folk] were made."[78] He goes on to suggest, "it was the time of the ecstatic shouting, screaming, falling, rolling, laughing, jerking, and even barking of mass hysteria under the stress of religious enthusiasm, now most commonly regarded as characteristically Negro emotionalism came into vogue." The religion of the black folk underscored how the function of the church was a conduit of expressions that bound rural Blacks together over a scattered distance. Similar to Guy Johnson (see Chapter 2), he highlighted the typical expressions such as the "shouting with [the] sudden sharp groans of spiritual torture, [with] screams of exultation," as the preacher launched into his climax of the sermon that discussed God's intervention in the plight of Paul and Silas in a jail in Jerusalem.[79] The demonstrative and ecstatic faith was characterized in the study as a form of escape from the daily hardships of life. According to Johnson, he did not see the political and social possibilities of spiritual beliefs and concluded that the revival faith spurred a kind of "religious fatalism" that generated a hope in the "bye and bye." In other studies beyond Macon County, Johnson characterized the demonstrative and expressive dimensions of the church as characteristic of the "plantation church" after World War I.

But Johnson remained preoccupied with the folk mind and described the social taboos of the tenant farmers. The taboos, documented in the report, included prohibitions against card-playing, baseball, frolics, and motion pictures. These taboos were described as essential to the respectable values among the rural farming community. They depicted the prohibitions as "outmoded doctrinary [sic]" restriction that led to tension in the community without relevance to social relations. He and other researchers ascribed importance to the church because they considered it a significant agency of control and regulation in the community.

The Macon County study was meant to show the best of quantitative methodology that Johnson privileged in the social science research. Johnson and his team of researchers studied the religious and metaphysical beliefs through empirical and scientific methodologies such as interviews, questionnaires, participatory observation, and statistics. Yet, his and his researchers' description of the metaphysical beliefs—superstition, magic, and otherworldly—were circumscribed within the larger aims and goals of the JRF and USPHS anti-venereal demonstration to curb syphilis and other maladies. The assignment of the folk category was determined by the 90% of tenant farmers whose metaphysical beliefs and practices were not informed by the "modern conception of disease." Johnson argued that the persistence of superstitions (and other metaphysical beliefs) "were not merely interesting survivals but actually continue to play a part in the illness and mortality of rural blacks."[80] Johnson's use of the modern conception of disease harkened back to Louis Pasteur, Richard Koch, and other chemists, physicists, zoologists, and physicians who had helped to advance knowledge about diseases by discovering microorganisms in their experiments on infections in the mid- to late nineteenth century. This "bacteriological revolution" helped to move the understanding of disease from the zymotic conception that attributed disease agents to the chemical agents that sporadically arise in atmospheric environments.[81] By the turn of the century, the microorganism was widely accepted among the broader American public and sparked a widespread "gospel of disease" that sought to reignite a pre-existing "revolution in personal and domestic behavior" in the late nineteenth and early twentieth centuries.[82] This gospel of disease was filtered through various print media that sought to instruct the wider American public on the everyday practices of sanitation: household cleaning and architecture (plumbing and indoor toilets), storing food, proper ventilation, handling the sick, and the assignment of proper sleeping arrangements and utensils (e.g. dipper, combs, toothbrushes, cups, etc.).

The modern conception of disease was the barometer used to measure the spiritual religions of the Black folk. For Johnson, they did not translate into sanitary and healthy habits: pasteurizing milk, opening windows, the use of individual toothbrushes and beds, a vitamin-supplemented diet, covered water wells, using contraception, and cleaning privies to curb communicable diseases and malnourishment. The tenant farmers' outdated religious cultures were folk in light of the perceived fact that, as O. C. Wenger noted in his fieldwork, "sanitation was a word that did not exist among them."[83] Folk religion was directly connected with unsanitary habits of tenant farmers at "private" homes. This accounts for why the researcher documented the empty cans of salmon and sardines and the untidy bed in Morris's cabin house while she swept the floor. In addition to documenting her midwifery services, the researcher also recorded Rosa Lancaster's refusal to sleep with her windows open at night for ventilation to air out germs.

More specific to syphilis, Johnson, similar to physician H. L. Harris, also noted to Davis that the farming-patients were still clueless about the cause of the venereal disease. In his memorandum from his fieldwork in March 1931, Johnson said that the farming-patients attributed syphilis to a natural case of "bad blood," like "bad teeth" or "bad lungs." They thought that syphilis was hereditary. He further stated that the colloquialism of bad blood demonstrated their ignorance with respect to communicable diseases. Johnson criticized the evangelical Protestant churches in Macon County on the basis that their "social taboos and gossip" did little to stigmatize syphilis and cultivate the stable nuclear family. Instead, the preoccupation with metaphysics and the minutiae of social taboos only spurred what he observed as the matriarchical family structure and "illegitimacy." He asserted, "Actually, there is less stress placed by the churches upon illegitimacy as a social sin than upon card playing, ball playing, and begging."[84] He felt that rural Baptist and Methodist churches were complicit in the "quasi-family" structure and illegitimacy of the folk. Johnson argued that rigid and "outmoded doctrinary [sic] restrictions" prevented the congregants from understanding the "social implications of the clinics" established in the churches.[85] His use of "quasi-family" structure and illegitimacy was a reference to "the amount of sexual freedom, the frequency of separation and realignment of families, and the number of children born out of formal wedlock."[86] Regarding marital union, Johnson stated that numerically out of the 612 households, there were approximately 404 married couples or couples living together in common law. Yet, the majority of the multiple marriages were the result of the Folk Negro's confusion around divorce. Divorce in folk thought was simply a matter of leaving a spouse and crossing state lines. One researcher jotted down a woman who had remarried: "My husband done cross and I don't hear nothing. He may be living or dead. Ain't dat divorce?" The folk family conflated separation and divorce without knowledge of the state's legal institution. Another researcher recorded an unnamed farmer: "They say when you separate from your husband, you already 'vorced." Generally, the purported folk pattern of divorce was often granted through a strip—a handwritten note that included the divorce status. While Johnson celebrated that orphans did not exist in Macon County, he still found that illegitimacy sometimes translated into biological parents not caring for their children. Rather, they recorded that many children were cared for by grandparents or somebody in the community.

No doubt, Johnson was insinuating that syphilis was partly the result of this quasi-family structure through multiple remarriages and lasciviousness. Understanding the controversy behind the topic of the history of sex among Blacks in US history, he made sure to maintain his argument that the quasi-family structure was attributed to their "amorality"—meaning their ignorance of state marriage and divorce procedures that was result of cultural and geographical isolation from the modern world. What is interesting about Johnson's analyses of the quasi-family of the Folk Negro was that he lost sight of the larger racial and economic apparatus that animated his discussion about cultural habits, like sex and marriage. For instance, he recorded Emma Morris's statement that "I aint want no husband myself, and I don't care if Alder (her daughter) marries or no." To be sure, her statement was followed by her refusal to marry Alder's dad and suspicion of her daughter's partner, Willie's, philandering ways. But her personal statements about her disgust with marriage did not include the loss of her partner, a migrant worker, in a labor accident. Countless interviews underscore the impact of adverse economic circumstances on the marital and relational structure in rural and southern Black communities. Beyond that, Johnson and researchers standardized the patriarchal familial structure that measured what he termed the "illegitimacy" and "casual" relationships among Macon County farming families.

Johnson was not confident that the Protestant church was an institution that could fashion Blacks into a modern people. He asserted, ". . . there is a widening gap between doctrine and behavior which leaves the traditional doctrine empty and unconvincing in relation to the normal currents of life."[87] However, Johnson and other bureaucrats affiliated with the demonstration knew that any attempt to reform the conduct of Black farmers had to find a way to incorporate religion. Johnson mentioned the importance of churches in mobilizing the farming families to collectively participate in the venereal control demonstration. The importance was clearly demonstrated with the adoption of different strategies used to solicit more participants in the community. For instance, Johnson recorded that health practitioners unsuccessfully tried to solicit families to participate in the demonstrations through the method of door-to-door canvass. Rather, they quickly found out that visiting churches proved more effective in recruiting Black families to the venereal disease demonstration. Researchers and bureaucrats working with the demonstrations attended religious services to establish rapport with the families involved in the study. After communicating that he was a deacon at his church, Columbus Holmes, a tenant farmer, mentioned to the Fisk researcher that he saw the researcher at Sunday service during "tithes and offerings." Additionally, other researchers and participants visited churches to make announcements about the demonstrations. "Mrs. George" said she listened to one of the researchers who gave an announcement in one of the local churches. Researchers encouraged Protestant ministers to incorporate modern health—such as notions of the modern family structure and germ theory—into their sermons and teachings. Another strategy they used to solicit participants was to establish demonstrations in the churches. This explains why Emma Morris, the Edwards, Rosa Lancaster, and others frequented the Damascus Baptist Church to receive regular examination and treatment for syphilis. Johnson confirmed that "[t]he presence of these stations in church . . . draws [the farmers] within the circle of group approval."[88] Clinics were organized in the churches to facilitate the process of altering the faith of the Folk Negro into a scientifically informed religion. In *Shadow of the Plantation*, Johnson still argued that the clinics were not effective in church due to the otherworldly and outmoded folk beliefs and practices that could not make practical connections between religion and health.

A key component of the Macon County syphilis control demonstration was the emphasis on scientific education. Education was a common tool that other public health officials used to inform the wider audiences about the importance of sanitation and hygiene. After his visit to observe the Macon County sites in March 1931, Johnson made a recommendation to the Fund that "there should accompany such demonstrations a deliberate health education campaign." He further suggested that the health plan should be "suited to the intelligence of the families, and employing pictures, lectures and home instruction."[89] Johnson assumed that exposure to biology and other natural sciences would stimulate and consequently promote development from a folk to a scientifically informed religious orientation.

Health and State Governance

The JRF understood the limits of medical philanthropy. The venereal disease program exceeded mere charity and philanthropy, especially due to the policy that required the JRF to spend all the money within 25 years of Julius Rosenwald's death. In this sense, the JRF funded the demonstrations with an eye to developing a comprehensive state health program for rural Blacks. The chief aim of the demonstration was to corral and incite policymakers, health practitioners, state and county bureaucrats, corporations, and private landowners to collaborate and establish sustainable programs and policies to guarantee the health of its predominantly Black labor base. This was evident in the first demonstration in Scotts, Mississippi. Wenger proudly reported to Michael Davis that he had convinced Delta and Pine Company and legislators to fund part of the cost of the demonstration for their predominantly Black cotton-pickers. He also mentioned that he had convinced the Tunica Board of Supervisors to agree to purchase 5,000 Keidal tubes used for the Wasserman blood testing in the demonstration. He would later speak to the Mississippi state legislators about a devising a "suitable appropriation to uncover syphilis and make some arrangement whereby these patients can be treated at a nominal fee."[90] Through its Negro Health and Medical Service Departments, the Rosenwald Fund was effectively attempting to engineer what southern skeptics termed "socialized medicine." Through the JRF, Davis would work to influence health legislation by reducing the cost of medicine. Various tenant farmers were provided bad or fraudulent health insurance plans; the Fund's president, Edwin Embree "[recognized] that a major problem of medicine was to get its benefits to the masses of the people at a cost they could afford to pay."[91] Through the JRF, Davis helped establish the Research in the Social and Economic Aspect of Medicine that pushed to include health insurance in Relief Emergency Programs and the Social Security Act.[92] The overall aim to engineer a state health program was the reason why Macon County was selected for the study. Not only did Macon County have the reported highest number of cases of syphilis in contrast to the other sites, but it also had a surrounding structure of state and local governments, hospitals, and colleges. The Macon County Health Department, Alabama Childhood Welfare Services, Tuskegee Institute, J. A. Andrew Hospital, and the VA Hospital all supported the demonstration. Macon County presented an "administrative control [that] is more favorable to this type of social experiment than one usually finds in southern counties."[93]

It is important to mention how the researchers sought to appeal to the majority white southern powerbrokers to invest in Black health on the grounds of its economic advantages. Throughout American history, Black health has been considered in light of labor efficiency and economic progress. Johnson and other affiliates perpetuated the logic of the benefits of a healthy labor force within a struggling economy. Johnson briefly mentioned that an adequate healthcare program must have the interest and support of landowners and should show them the superior economic advantages of healthier workers. He further told Davis that the "number of working days has actually increased following treatment at the clinics." In his effort to persuade state legislators, private corporations, and landowners, Wenger told Davis that the white group "realized that black health was one of the important factors in the economic life of the community and production of cotton." He further explained how they were feeling the economic pinch due to the mass exodus or "Great Migration" in the interwar period. Folk religion was also used to mark specific beliefs and practices that did not cultivate health and labor efficiency. In the end, the use and meaning of folk within the Macon County demonstration was a biomedical campaign to encourage state apparatuses to create sustainable legislation and programs to care for the Black worker. It was a campaign that relied on the power of religion in the lives of the Black tenant farmers to convert their souls to the modern habits of health to ensure their longevity, happiness, and productivity.

Conclusion

Charles Johnson was correct. Emma Morris and other tenant farmers were largely excluded from medicine and health. Historian Edward H. Beardsley noted that "health and medical professions and its political leadership . . . moved even more haltingly in developing the will to change the system of life that bound Black [southerners] to their fate of ill health and early death."[94] The widespread medical neglect of Black southerners was not lost on the tenant farmers and croppers interviewed for the Macon County demonstration. In fact, Emma Morris and other tenant farmers were already making the connections of their economic plight to their health conditions in Jim Crow Alabama: "If I wasn't working and could sit down and rest, [then] I would go [and receive my treatment]." Morris and other laborers were fully aware that their economic plight controlled every aspect of their life. Morris, Ivery, Edwards, and other tenant farmers challenged low to no wages, lack of labor protections, and exploitations in the cotton economy in their interviews. In fact, Emma Morris named a "Mr. Glenn." Johnson overlooked the tenant farmers' courage to share their stories about their daily living conditions in the tenant farming systems. Some Black tenant farmers and sharecroppers were enthusiastic to share their experiences with interviewees in hopes that "experts" and bureaucrats would see the need for transformation in the Depression and New Deal period. The religion of the so-called folk did not blind them from their actual conditions: Emma Morris said she missed church for a year because she did not have anything to wear. In fact, Morris and other farmers shared stories that actually aided Charles Johnson's "modern" sociological analysis of health and poverty in his *Shadow of the Plantation*. What the folk concept ignores is the "modern" knowledge and aspirations of laborers that shaped their religious cultures and other choices within arrangements of racial and economic domination and exploitation.

But Johnson's use of folk religion said more about him and his liberalism than about the people under study. Johnson remained committed to espousing a "culture of poverty" through documenting their spiritual cultures. For him, his idea of folk religion underscored how Black tenants and croppers were suspended at a lower stage of cultural and moral development. Johnson's use of folk religion sought to prove that they were removed not only from commercial society of newspapers, transportation, mail order catalogues, and movies, but also from the scientific and moral cultures of modern society. In the Macon County Syphilis Demonstration, he deemed the folk beliefs and customs to be "bad" religion. Folk religion was not under dictates of modern science (medicine and hygiene) and morality (e.g., sex and nuclear family). In end, the Macon County demonstration showed the importance of folk religion as used by liberal-minded social scientists, like Johnson, to identify the distinct cultures and behaviors of the Black poor in liberal thought. Moreover, the demonstration also disclosed how obliterating folk religion (and managing religion in general) was equally an essential component in liberal reform in the rural South. The importance of managing religion accounts for why physicians and field researchers on behalf of the Rosenwald Fund and Fisk University engaged the churches to solicit more participation in the syphilis treatment from the rural community. They engaged the so-called folk religion in hopes of altering their religious cultures in accordance to modern standards of knowledge and conduct.

But Johnson's use of folk was a distraction from his sociological study. His preoccupation with religious and moral deficits hindered his challenge to the regional southern economy. For instance, Johnson discussed how the tenant workers did not adhere to appropriate forms of marriage and sexual relationships in accordance to Protestant, scientific, and state status. Their so-called removal from these standard practices foreclosed the significance of the labor economy in the familial arrangements, such as migratory male workers, multiple jobs of females (e.g., growing cotton, laundry, digging ditches, and household work), and child laborers. For instance, the folk category cannot explain Minnie Ivery's situation in the loss of her husband in a labor accident in another town in Alabama. "Folk" was a moral and cultural lens that idealized and extracted the "nuclear family" from the actual political economy. The nuclear family was an "economic entity" used to govern the distribution of labor. The nuclear family was also used to create good and bad religion for the sake of the maintenance of racial difference and hierarchy. In this sense, the moral and cultural deficits fed into the racial logics used by white powerbrokers to govern Black workers in the Jim Crow system.

Lastly, Johnson framed the advantages of Black health within the white southern power bloc's desires and wishes for Black laborers. By emphasizing rural Blacks as folk laborers, he framed Black health within the fortunes of the [white] South. In this sense, the appeals to the state-based Black health and modern development was cast in a utilitarian-industrial logic that only fostered the exploitation that he was seeking to earnestly combat. In the end, classifying the lower-class religion was a common strategy used to illuminate how Blacks could be assets to economic development of the southern and the broader national economy. The scientifically and morally informed Protestantism would help extend not only the longevity of rural Blacks, but also their labor efficiency. His attention to religious and moral behaviors undermined his earnest and "practical" political strategy. In this sense, Johnson's emphasis on the economic utility of Black health revealed that he, too, was trapped in the "shadow of the plantation." This was the irony of his pragmatic southern liberalism.

4

Saving the Folk

Cultural Lag and the Southern Rural Roots of the Religion of Poverty

> The fundamental character of these efforts and their result have been to diffuse American middle-class norms to the uneducated and crude Southern folk Negroes, emerging out of the backwardness of slavery.
>
> —Gunnar Myrdal, *American Dilemma*

> This [Negro lower] class is Southern in origin and character.
>
> —Gunnar Myrdal, *American Dilemma*

After visiting a Holy Communion Banquet at one of Father Divine's "Heavens" in Harlem, the Swedish economist Gunnar Myrdal wrote a memo about his experience to the Carnegie Corporation's president, Frederick Keppel. The economist stated that "a person [more] acquainted with the problems and techniques of abnormal psychology" would be more equipped to understand Black religion.[1] Myrdal's memo expressed how he was overwhelmed with the "religious hysteria" at the banquet. He would later consult psychiatrists in his study. But he would mainly rely on his research deputy, Guy Johnson, to guide him on questions about Black religion for the Myrdal-Carnegie Negro Problem Study.

In September 1939, Guy Johnson also attended one of the banquets with Guion, Fisk University sociologist Nelson Edward Palmer, and "Mrs. Palmer" in Harlem at 11 p.m.[2] The banquet was located at one of "Heavens on Earth" at West 126th Street between Harlem's

To Know the Soul of a People. Jamil W. Drake, Oxford University Press. © Oxford University Press 2022.
DOI: 10.1093/oso/9780190082680.003.0005

Seventh and Lenox Avenues.[3] As soon as Johnson arrived, he immediately took note of the interior of the large rectangular-shaped main room that included balconies and several long tables arranged in a U-shape format. Johnson and company were offered seats in the cramped balcony that he said was "exceedingly uncomfortable" and caused them to perspire. Johnson focused mainly on the predominantly "black middle-aged female congregants" who were engaged in "hand-clapping, foot-patting, swaying [their] bodies and sometimes, a sort of shuffle dance, well into the midnight hour." With the sounds of the "orchestra," the congregants reportedly sang 30 to 40 songs that ranged from popular love tunes, like "Sweetheart Waltz," to shout songs, and old-time hymns, like "Draw Me Nearer," that were accompanied by the hard-like rhythms popular in music of the day. Johnson was no stranger to this type of Black religious expression found in the banquet service. Yet he was astonished "by the rise and fall of the emotions and energies" of the congregants in the banquet hall. This, according to the Johnson, lasted three hours. Johnson asserted, "They would sing heartily, almost hysterically, for a while then there would be a lull during which there was either no singing or only half-hearted singing with many of the people seeming to be almost asleep, and the tension would mount again and rise to another climax of singing, hand-clapping, etc."

He made special note of the erotic nature of the religious expressions exhibited by the Black women who "accompanied their songs by looks and gestures of adoration, flirtation, surrender, ecstasy, etc." He further noted, "[t]hey would look at the large photograph of Father Divine, throw kisses, smack their lips, make gestures of embrace, and make such exclamations as "Father, you are so sweet," "Father, I love you so," "Father, I know you belong to me, etc." But the congregants erupted when Father Divine entered the service around 1:15 a.m. Johnson documented that the emotional level reached its "hysterical climax," the songs were "lusty," and the "phrases of adoration were heightened." In a problematic description, Johnson noticed that when Father Divine glanced in the direction of one "very black, ugly, woman, . . . she gave out a loud shriek, held her hands in the air, trembled all over, then made a whirling movement and collapsed in the arms of women standing around her."

But Guy Johnson's fieldwork left out what his other colleague, Palmer, a research assistant for the Myrdal-Carnegie Negro Problem study, witnessed in an earlier visit to one of the late-night banquets in August.[4] Palmer's descriptions shed light on other factors that could have contributed to the growing popularity of the Peace Mission. Palmer described the different banners on the wall that illuminated the political ideologies of the religious organization. One of the "oil cloth banners" had words in red, white, and blue letters:

No True Follower on Relief
20,000
Since 1932,
Father Divine Saved the City of New York.

Another banner also read:

Father Divine Has Kept the United States Out of the War

Additionally, Edward Palmer also jotted down how one of the white angels read Divine's words about the "Anti-Lynching Bill" coupled with his denunciation of "slave, earthly names. . . ."[5] The message highlighted the "virtues of [the] new, evangelical names." Palmer captured elements of the Peace Mission's Righteous Government platform that supported racial equality. Divine described the Peace Mission as a religious organization that adhered to and championed legal and cultural democracy. Like Myrdal, Johnson's field memorandum focused primarily on the religious expressions of the "black lower-class" congregants at the expense of acknowledging other factors that contributed to the Peace Mission's popularity. Their neglect suited their aims to explain lower-class behaviors and culture in the urban North.[6] Certain factors were foreclosed in the making of lower-class religion. Later folklorist and anthropologist Arthur Fauset tried to add more texture to the study of the "cults" in urban life by highlighting how they compensate for the social, political, and economic lack in de facto segregation.[7]

Early twentieth-century racial liberalism culminated in the Myrdal-Carnegie study. The Myrdal-Carnegie report supported abolishing racial inequality and championed that Black Americans fully assimilate into democratic life. The Myrdal-Carnegie Negro Problem study initially emerged from a recommendation that the Carnegie Foundation should explore new directions in addressing the race problem during the Depression. Although Myrdal was the primary author of the study, he employed nearly 31 of America's top social researchers to submit research projects on specific areas of America's Negro Problem. All social researchers mentioned in the previous chapters submitted research memos to Myrdal except Howard Odum. Charles Johnson and Guy Johnson were part of the study's core researchers who first met in New York in the summer and fall of 1939.[8]

But the Myrdal-Carnegie study also revealed the familiar culture problem at the crux of American racial liberalism. Gunnar Myrdal continued the liberal logic that sought to outline the impact of economic factors on cultural behavioral patterns. The Myrdal-Carnegie study helped to lay the foundations for the later "culture of poverty" idea.[9] More importantly, the study also continued to perpetuate arguments that framed Black "sects and cults" within the contours of lower-class cultures in American life. Moreover, Johnson and Myrdal's description of the Peace Mission disclosed the culture problem in liberal thought. Social scientists generalized the Peace Mission movement and the other "religious hysterica[l]" congregants to bolster their argument that Black lower-class culture was a "distorted development and the pathological condition of the general American culture."[10] To be sure, Johnson added to the culture problem in the study. He attributed the "religious hysteria" in the Peace Missions to migrants' encounter with "cities of destruction" that contributed to their "loneliness, emptiness, and frustrations."[11] Gunnar Myrdal depicted the Peace Mission's banquet service as an opportunity for the Black lower class to simply "let off steam." Yet, as I will show, they felt that lower-class religion did not really directly impact the urban social and political situations. The religious organizations did not uphold higher principles and values of the American Creed, such as individualism and autonomy, and were tagged as "compensatory." By Myrdal's lights, these compensatory organizations hindered assimilation and the broader struggle for racial democracy. His discussion of religious organizations was a microcosm of his political critique of Black leadership and institutions.

What was interesting was how the regional South figured into the narration of lower-class religion in urban America. Social scientists in the comprehensive study referenced the "backward" agrarian South in their analyses of the popular "cults and sects" in New York and other northern urban environments. Johnson, Myrdal, and other social researchers tried to account for the rising "sects and cults" by situating them within American lower-class religious (typically Protestant) history. Both Johnson and Myrdal sought to make these "sects and cults" legible by highlighting their origins and popularities in the poor regional South. In his memorandum on the Peace Missions, Johnson asserted that the "singing, hand clapping, shouting, etc. [were] all in keeping with the sort of thing which [was] found in the religious behavior of lower-class Negroes and whites, particularly in the South."[12] He said that Father Divine's Peace Mission and other sects and cults were extensions of the "old revivalistic religions" of the camp-meetings and the subsequent "restoration groups" in the nineteenth century.[13] Myrdal recycled Johnson's history of lower-class culture by arguing that these movements "gained headway, perhaps, among the poor whites and the Negroes of the South."[14] In short, they attributed the rise of the sects and cults to the backward rural and poor southern migrants. Their knowledge of the archaic and primitive stage of mental and cultural development in the South contributed to their construction of lower-class religion. These racial liberals espoused a developmental view of culture that recycled their progressive predecessors' ranking of beliefs and practices in a hierarchy. In the end, regional or folk southern culture and history were used as devices to explain lower-class religion in broader America .

Myrdal used the folk category in his discussion of the Black southern poor in the agrarian South. He used the prefix to reference backward, isolated, agrarian, and poor culture in the rural areas in the lower South. By his lights, the backward, isolated, and agrarian southern environment conditioned the "uneducated and crude folk Negro."[15] The Swedish economist repeated Charles Johnson's claim that the "Folk Negro" had a "low degree of assimilation in modern American standards."[16] Myrdal also used "cultural lag" the same way he used the folk concept. He was not invested in the folk category like Howard Odum per se. But folk and cultural lag were both a part of the liberal nomenclature used to represent rural Black populations and their cultural behaviors in the 1930s and 1940s. Guy Johnson noted in his research memorandum on Black religion for the study: "As such the [Pentecostals] represented a cultural lag which is usually characteristic of folk or lower-class religion" in the lower South.[17]

Myrdal relied on Johnson and other social scientists to provide knowledge about Black southern religion to support his claim about the deficient cultures of the Black lower-class. Myrdal and these racial liberals turned to southern social scientists to explain the southern roots of Black and American lower-class religion. He relied on Guy Johnson's and Guion Johnson's two-part memorandum on "The Church and the Race Problem" for the study. Additionally, he also invited social anthropologist Allison Davis to submit research. In 1939, sociologist Donald Young told Myrdal that he should visit Yale University's Human Relations Institute (HRI) to meet with social psychologist John Dollard and Allison Davis. At the time, Davis was a professor at Dillard University, but was on a fellowship leave at Yale's HRI. At Yale, Davis had completed a manuscript with Dollard on advancing ideas on culture and personality in their life history study of Black youth in Natchez, Mississippi, and New Orleans, Louisiana. Davis's work was an extension of his position as director of the Southern Urban Division of the American Youth Community (AYC).[18] The AYC was a New Deal program dedicated to assisting youth during the Depression. Although Myrdal took him to be a caste and class dogmatist, he was impressed with Davis and extended an invitation to him to join the study and submit research on Black southern religion and lodges in the Lower South.[19] Davis was a social anthropologist who was a part of the "caste and class school," and came to the study after wrapping up his field study in Natchez, Mississippi, with his colleagues.[20] Davis also had his former student John Gibbs St. Clair Drake participate in the Myrdal-Carnegie study as a research assistant.[21]

Allison Davis did not use the folk prefix to classify the religion of the lower-class Black southerners. He stayed away from using the category in his research. He may have avoided the category due to its connotations in the field of cultural anthropology. In Davis's graduate student days at Harvard and the London School of Economics in the early 1930s, he was prepared to study the African influences on "Negro folk-life, in certain isolated sections of the lower South."[22] By the time he joined the Myrdal-Carnegie study, he used "cultural lag" to discuss Spiritualism, Holiness/Pentecostalism, and Mainline Protestantism in the Lower South. "Cultural lag" had been another familiar term in the American social sciences, particularly sociology. Popularized by American sociologist William Ogburn, cultural lag was a concept that simply highlighted that some aspects of culture did not change at the same rate and speed as others in industrial and modern society. Davis applied how certain aspects of the Black religious cultures in the Deep South had lagged behind other cultural and material changes in more advanced industrial society. In this sense, Davis's use of "cultural lag" still shared the same conceptual terrain as the folk prefix that presented southern lower-class religion as suspended in a historical and cultural time warp. Not only did Myrdal's, Johnson's, and Davis's knowledge about the folk and/or lagging southern religion contribute to the construction of the deficient lower-class religion. But their concepts of folk and lagging southern religion also were the precursors to the formulation of the "culture of poverty." But Myrdal, Davis, and Johnson used folk or southern religion to bolster their support for scientific and bureaucratic governmental planning to advance the social and economic conditions of Blacks, and the Black lower-class in particular. They collectively felt that the scientific and bureaucratic planning in state government (e.g., New Deal government) would save the lower class by transforming their socioeconomic environment, which would change their conduct. What this chapter will underscore is that the folk prefix in lower-class religion (particularly churches) was cast as morally weak and politically inept in the struggle for racial democracy, otherwise known as the "American Creed." The lower-class church institution in the Myrdal-Carnegie study acquiesced to the antidemocratic caste-and-class racial inequality that contributed to the material conditions and cultural standards of the Black southern poor. The study perceived that these institutions fostered dependency. Moreover, the construction of folk religion was a product of the liberal (and more leftist) secularization thesis which argued that religion could not foster rational, self-reliant, and civically involved moral liberal subjects. They argued that folk religion was entangled in the "vicious cycle" of white prejudice and discrimination. But folk religion supported white prejudice and discrimination and contributed to cultural lag or "lower standards in health, education, manners, and morals."[23] Manners and morals were just as important to Myrdal as his emphasis on health and education. Davis's fieldwork on Spiritualists and Pentecostals in Natchez was evidence of the "vicious cycle" of white supremacy and lagging standards. Folk religion was considered a conservative orientation that succumbed to compensatory strategies that hindered full assimilation and integration into democratic and capitalistic society. Moreover, Myrdal-Carnegie's evaluation of the folk religion of Black rural and semi-rural southerners led to their belief that science and the democratic welfare state would save Blacks by cultivating higher manners and morals and access due to greater access to quality education, health, and working conditions. As a consequence, lower-class faith could not save the Black southern poor from the vicious cycle of prejudice and discrimination. With this said, the Myrdal-Carnegie study contributed to the making of Black folk and lower-class religion.

This chapter has three sections. First, this chapter will lay out the origins of the Myrdal-Carnegie study. Additionally, it will briefly examine the study's attention to the poor South. Myrdal's analysis was shaped by the political environment, which was determined by the Depression. In this environment, Franklin Roosevelt was trying to mobilize a New Deal contingent against the opposition from southern Democrats. Roosevelt's campaign to mobilize a voting bloc for the New Deal existed alongside the political radicalism flourishing in the Dixie South. This environment complemented the Swedish economist's focus on the intersections between race and economic issues in the South. Second, I will discuss how Guy Johnson complemented Myrdal's class analysis by treating Black religion as a product of American economic conditions. This class analysis sought to implement poor southern whites in the equation of independent Black organizations and practices, particularly with the emerging "sects and cults." Lastly, the chapter will deal with Davis's ideas about the so-called lagging Spiritualism and Pentecostalism from his previous fieldwork in both Natchez, Mississippi, and New Orleans. Despite spiritualism and Pentecostalism's challenge to Jim Crow boundaries, Davis mainly affirmed Myrdal's view that the lower-class Black religious leaders were lagging in democratic values and principles due to their acquiescence to caste and class structures in the South.

The Origins of the Myrdal-Carnegie Negro Problem Study

The Carnegie Foundation of New York's comprehensive study on the Negro Problem was initially recommended by trustee Newton Baker at a board meeting on October 24, 1935.[24] The 64-year-old Baker took the floor and asserted that the foundation needed to alter its conventional approach to the Negro Problem. His mentioning of the conventional approach was a reference to the trend initially set by the foundation's namesake, Andrew Carnegie. The 75-year-old steel magnate and philanthropist had established the foundation in 1911 to relieve him of the duty of distributing funds to various projects in promoting the advancement and diffusion of knowledge. Carnegie had an acute interest in education and personally invested in promoting Black industrial and liberal-arts schools in the early 1900s.[25] The steel magnate's support of education was to position Blacks to help themselves. Newton Baker felt that the conventional approaches to funding Black colleges and universities did not adequately address the racial problems specific to the Depression period.

The son of a former Confederate soldier, Baker had served as mayor of Cleveland before joining Woodrow Wilson's Cabinet as his Secretary of War during World War I. As Secretary of War, he had to deal with the mounting Black protests concerning racial segregation and tension in the armed forces. In the aftermath of World War I, there were a series of "race riots" across urban cities that James Weldon Johnson tagged "Red Summer." At the time Baker asked the board members to rethink its approach to the race problem, he had his sights set on the "dependency" of Black workers on the New Deal "relief rolls," compounded by their persistent migration to urban cities. He thought that a comprehensive study would provide answers to the race problem. The Carnegie Foundation's president, Keppel, considered the suggestion a wonderful opportunity to remake the philanthropic foundation in a different image from its namesake. Moreover, the Carnegie Foundation would follow Edwin Embree, president of the JRF, who had singlehandedly positioned the Fund at the forefront of Black struggles. The JRF had established programs and fellowships that sought to address racial struggles by forging a Black professional class to aid the urban "masses" and the rural "folk." Under Embree's tutelage, the JRF led the way in causes for Black education, health, and science. Davis benefited from the fellowship due to his close relationship with Embree, who leveraged his presidency to support his graduate educational pursuits and involvement with New Deal bureaucratic organizations, like AYC.

The former director of the Laura Spelman Rockefeller Memorial Fund (LSRM), Beardsley Ruml recommended to Keppel and the Foundation that they should consider Gunnar Myrdal to lead the comprehensive study. The Foundation's Broad of Trustees unanimously voted for the Swedish economist to lead the study. The Board's endorsement was threefold. First, Keppel insisted that the head researcher come from another country outside of the United States. The Foundation president felt that American social scientists were too close to the race issue to have any critical distance to perform an objective study. Keppel noted that there was no lack of "competent scholars in the United States," but he felt that they were too "charged with emotion" to generate fresh and innovative ideas on the race question. Second, as reported, Myrdal was from a Western country that had standards of high intellect and scholarship. With the cultural anthropologist Melville Herskovits's recommendation, he was picked because his native land, Sweden, was not an imperialist country. Lastly, and most importantly, Myrdal had a distinct résumé in academic and public life by the time he accepted the invitation to head the comprehensive study. Erudite social psychologist Alva Myrdal shaped her husband's acceleration into the higher echelons of the academy, banks, and, most importantly, the Social Democratic Party in Sweden. He and Alva were instrumental in implementing welfare state reforms during Sweden's depression. Alva Myrdal pulled her husband toward a "greater concern for equality and issues of social welfare."[26] Myrdal felt that the welfare state would usher in science and egalitarianism in democratic societies. On this note, he detested the growing leftist radical sentiment in America that showed a lack of faith in formal political processes and institutions.[27]

Myrdal was tasked with bringing "fresh ideas" to the old and ongoing American Negro Problem. The Negro Problem, according to Myrdal, was the result of a moral tension between the "American Creed" (i.e., democratic ideals of individual dignity, human equality, and inalienable rights and opportunities) and racial prejudice in the minds of white America.[28] He noted that the tension was actually a moral dilemma for whites. To his credit, Myrdal interpreted the Negro Problem as fundamentally a white problem. Myrdal was optimistic that the American Creed would defeat racial prejudice.[29] He believed that the government's social engineering in the economy would lead to racial integration.[30] Myrdal was part of the "liberal consensus" that emphasized racial prejudice and its effects on both individuals and the entire nation.[31] Moreover, he emphasized how racial prejudice induced a "vicious cycle" that contributed to the low standards of health, education, morals, and manners of Blacks. Although he framed the race problem as a moral and psychological problem, he was still keen on showing the economic impact of racial prejudice in American life. Thus, he considered that the New Deal state government was heading in the right direction toward undermining racial prejudice with its centralization of labor and the economy. He believed that state intervention in the labor market could consequently improve health, education, and other areas in the lives of Black Americans.[32] As an economist, his view of race coincided with other liberal-minded social researchers who sought to leverage the New Deal economic policies and programs to solve the race problem. Professional social scientists had a significant role to play in the bureaucratic state and rationalizing all aspects of American life, and so-called Black lower-class culture in particular. Many of the social scientists—Charles Johnson, T. J. Woofter, Howard Odum, Allison Davis, and Guy Johnson—each lent their scientific expertise to, and participated in, some New Deal programs. The New Deal era had a profound impact on how social scientists teased out racial prejudice through labor conditions and economics. For them, racial prejudice and discrimination spelled poverty for Blacks, especially for Black southerners.

The New Deal, Southern Poverty, and Black Radicalism

Gunnar Myrdal's first of many tours to the American South shaped his view of American labor and the economy in the aftermath of the stock market crash in 1929. His visits to the American South dramatically informed his economic critique of the Negro Problem. Not long after he and his family arrived and settled in their lavish Manhattan suite, Myrdal left on tour for the American South accompanied by his trusted colleague, Richard Sterner, a Swedish economist, and the Rockefeller's General Board of Education's agent, Jackson Davis.[33] After his first assigned trip to the southern states with Davis, he told Keppel that "without it our later studies should have had no concrete points at which to be fixed."[34] Davis organized the trip intending to help the Swedes understand the Negro Problem by giving them opportunities to converse with local and professional southern leaders and educators. However, the Swedish welfare economists were more interested in visiting the "plantation fields and farms, coal and steel mines, textile mills, tobacco factories, bars and pools," to obtain an intimate knowledge of the Negro Problem, through the everyday experiences of the "black masses or common people." According to Myrdal, "the workers and farmers . . . were so amazed by the unique opportunity of meeting somebody overseas that they talked, so we thought, with less restraint and conscious self-control than they were accustom[ed] to do."[35] Myrdal observed much more closely than if he had simply talked to professional leaders and educators about the actual socioeconomic conditions of Blacks plagued by ill-health, poor housing, and overall poverty. He concluded that their livilehoods were not compatible with any modern concept of "minimum health[ly] standard of living."[36]

Moreover, the Swedish economist was appalled by the rural conditions of Black southerners. In a letter to a colleague, the Swedish outsider communicated that he was overwhelmed by "these sick, undernourished masses of people, and their depleted soil, and poorly-conserved resources."[37] He later wrote in *An American Dilemma* that the "economic situation of the Negroes [was] pathological."[38] He used pathology to describe the few property ownership opportunities, low and irregular incomes, and dilapidated houses, and inadequate goods."[39] Most Blacks were concentrated in the South, where they disproportionately worked in agriculture, which had become a depressed industry. Similar to UNC white sociologist Rupert Vance, Myrdal argued that the regional culture contributed to the economic and natural conditions of the agricultural South. Unlike Vance, Myrdal played up racial inequality in his analysis of the poor southern regional economy. Racial segregation and inequality contributed to the poor southern economy. According to Myrdal, "[t]he explanation for the economic backwardness of the South must be carried down to the rigid institutional structure of the economic life of the region which, historically, is derived from slavery and, psychologically, is rooted in the minds of the people."[40] Myrdal felt that the twentieth-century southern economy gave way to a revised form of slavery. A consummate liberal, Myrdal thought that changes to the economy (equal opportunity) would alter race relations in the South.[41] As historian Walter Jackson argued, Myrdal thought that "improving the efficiency of the southern economy was key to the solution to the Negro Problem."[42] Myrdal's racial liberalism was based on his support of state governmental intervention and equal opportunity in the marketplace.

Myrdal's research took place within the New Deal welfare state and its special attention to the southern states. When Myrdal took his first southern tour in September, the National Emergency Council (NEC) had released the "Report on the Economic Conditions of the South" just a month earlier.[43] The Myrdal-Carnegie research project coincided with an intense focus on the economic conditions of the American South. Just before Adolph Hitler invaded Poland, Myrdal's research was caught in the political maelstrom that led southern Democratic and Republicans to protest against the New Deal administration. After winning the election, Franklin D. Roosevelt felt his once popular New Deal policy declining with the onslaught of criticisms and disapproval of southern Democrats that spring of 1938. In 1937, southern Democrats had claimed that FDR courted oppositional and radical politics that caused them to partner with some Republicans to block New Deal initiatives, such as the Fair Labor Standards Act. They interpreted the New Deal legislation as too "radical" an intrusion on certain free-market and economic liberties. Southern Democrats also believed that the legislation would indirectly upend Jim Crow governance. A southern romantic, FDR felt compelled to make a deliberate appeal to mobilize White southern voters to campaign for New Deal candidates in the primary elections. He sought to mobilize this southern political contingent by stressing the New Deal's impact on the rural South in particular. Georgia native and white liberal Clark

Forman, an official at the Interior Department of the New Deal, recommended a report that showed the tangible benefits of the New Deal on the South to inform a white southern voting bloc. While Roosevelt welcomed Forman's recommendation, he suggested that the report exclude New Deal benefits and simply focus on presenting "facts" that revealed its regional needs. The NEC's director, Lowell Mellet, explained that the 64-page report "presents in only a small degree the manifold assets and advantages possessed by the South, being concerned primarily not with what the South has, but with what the South needs."[44]

In a release of the 10,000 copies, the report was published as a pamphlet which explained the economic needs of the South. It was designed to show that the South was "the nation's #1 economic problem." The NEC pamphlet explained that the impoverished South was attributed to the lack of economic resources that would generate wealth for its population: poor soil, inadequate public water infrastructure, illiteracy, and underpaid and unskilled labor force, to name a few. The lack of a solid manufacturing base, according to the report, forced the South to "sell its agricultural products in an unprotected world market and buy its manufactured goods at prices supported by high tariffs."[45] Additionally, the report was part of the New Deal administration's support of Keynesianism that was premised on the logic that low wages stymied economic growth because the majority of workers did not have the purchasing power to contribute to the struggling regional economy. Race was not highlighted as a factor in the South's economic conditions. Since FDR arrived in office in 1933, he had courted racial segregation and violence in order to push his New Deal agenda among white southern voters and policymakers. In August, he also made a southern tour to appeal to white southern voters just before Myrdal's and Sterner's trip with Jackson Davis. His pandering to both de jure segregationists, mob terrorists, and all-white union representatives compelled Blacks to claim that the New Deal was actually the "Raw Deal." To be sure, these critiques gave rise to a leftist contingent in Black America.

The political landscape was already ripe for Myrdal's economic analysis of race and the agricultural South. His study took shape against the backdrop of the popular front in the Dixie South.[46] The Depression, coupled with the "Alabama Scottsboro Nine" case, publicly unearthed coalitions between Black, liberal, and leftist organizations. By the time Myrdal began to travel below the Mason Dixon line, there was a vibrant southern leftist popular front that included communists, socialists, Black farmers and industrial workers, and liberals who challenged Jim Crow. In his first southern tour, Myrdal, accompanied by Richard Sterner, saw firsthand the popular front coalitions when he visited the Southern Conference Human Welfare Conference (SCHW) in 1939 in Birmingham, Alabama.[47] With a Communist organizer, Joseph Gelders, at the helm, the SCHW Conference was an interracial and popular front organization that emerged out of an effort to unite the South's economic problems with its history of racial discrimination.[48] With approximately over 12,000 attendees, the SCHW Conference represented all persons across the liberal and progressive spectrum, including Eleanor Roosevelt, Pauli Murray, Virginia Durr, Charles S. Johnson, Myles Horton, and C. Vann Woodward, to name a few. During the Depression, the Communist Party had been transformed into a racial working-class movement with its struggle for Black self-determination.[49] Black farmers united with the Communist Party U.S.A. to confront racial and labor suppression in the agricultural South. The eclectic southern popular front profoundly impacted social researchers, such as Ira De Augustine Reid, who traveled to Moscow during the 1931 Scottsboro trials. In fact, the Myrdal-Carnegie study was preceded by a kind of political radicalism that had been pioneered by younger Black social researchers and leading activists who rubbed shoulders with socialists and communists in the 1940s. Historian Jonathan Holloway noted how these younger social scientists and leaders were more economically driven and sought to incorporate Black struggles within the broader grassroots labor struggles.[50]

This radicalism was notable with regard to younger people's orientation to American Christianity. During this period, Benjamin E. Mays and other race leaders noticed that younger Blacks had "repudiated God" for "Marx, Lenin, and Stalin."[51] In the Myrdal-Carnegie Report, an unnamed Congregational Black minister noted that the young Black people had lost faith in American Christianity. Instead, the minister noted that their faith was directed toward Russia.[52] Meanwhile, Guy Johnson said that communism held no mass appeal for Black religious communities. Yet, the issue of left-leaning politics was a source of ideological tension in the Myrdal-Carnegie study. For instance, Myrdal's closest confidant and friend, political scientist Ralph Bunche, who was a part of the "Howard [University] boys," represented this new and younger generation who believed in grassroots interracial labor organizing. These struggles underscored Myrdal's more Enlightenment-infused liberalism that championed a top-down social engineering within formal political processes to address the race and class problems in America. Myrdal's interpretation of the American Creed (what he originally called "American state religion") revealed his own faith in liberal democracy and centralized welfare capitalism. He equated Bunche and other leftist researchers' and activists' focus on the strategy of the interracial labor grassroots struggle to a form of political fatalism.

More importantly, Myrdal was just as preoccupied with the pathological consequences of poverty in Jim Crow America.[53] In his mind, economics determined behavioral and cultural dispositions. Myrdal and other American second-generation social scientists were not solely focused on the material conditions that highlighted the abject poverty of Black southerners in particular. Myrdal followed social researchers who were invested in teasing out the behavioral implications of southern and regional poverty. The culture of poverty was very much visible within the lives of the Folk Negro. The culture of the Folk Negro was a mere reflection of the backward southern economy. Committed to Enlightenment rationalism and individualism, Myrdal noted how the southern (and northern, too) poverty stifled "resourcefulness, self-reliance, and sense of individual dignity." Moreover, Myrdal noted that the "lower-class Negroes have kept more of the mental servility and dependence of the slave population." The racially tinged economy did not cultivate rational and free liberal subjects. This culture of poverty manifested itself in various examples, which I have already laid out in the previous chapters, that resurfaced in the study. Therefore, Myrdal's *American Dilemma* recycled how the Folk Negroes succumbed to family disorganization, dishonesty, lax sexual mores, and laziness. Moreover, they had behavioral and cultural traits that were not held in high regard in American democracy with its liberal principles. Strangely, Myrdal made his claims about the anti-democratic conservatism of Black religion while postulating how the American Creed had developed out of its unique Protestant roots of religious individual freedom, anti-authoritarianism, and moral-civic postmillennialism. Behind his political evaluation of Black religion and his interpretation of American Protestantism lay his own secular commitments to orthodox liberalism, which he saw first in private charity and consequently realized in the New Deal welfare state.[54]

The folk southern religion was a cultural category in the liberal social sciences responsible for reproducing ideas about lower-class behaviors. Myrdal and American social researchers turned their attention to the religious behaviors of Black southerners to mark their distinctly lower-class status during the New Deal era. Myrdal's turn to the religious dimensions of poverty were part of a broader intellectual trend after World War I. Myrdal had entered a preceding American social scientific milieu where "doctrine and dogma" and expressive practices (e.g., songs, sermons, "frenzy," testimonies, prayers, and sacraments) supposedly communicated something about the effects of the socioeconomic environment on human personality and culture. At the time of the Myrdal-Carnegie study, several social researchers had turned their attention to how the "cities of destruction" had ignited the popularity of the "small church movement" and the "cults" that flooded the urban centers of America in the interwar periods. They inaugurated the study of the so-called cults and small church movement(s) by showing their "pathological" development. During this period, social researchers had framed these religious institutions and cultures—Pentecostalism, Holiness, and Peace Mission movement—as lower-class organizations that reflected their material urban lack. But these so-called lower-class religions were mainly attributed to southern folk migrants and their cultures. Sociologist E. Franklin Frazier noted that southern migrants sought to recreate their folk rural cultures to ward off the "social disorganization" in urban America. These studies associated southern, rural, and religion as folk and lower-class cultural behaviors in New Deal and World War II eras. Myrdal continued to study southern and folk religion to frame the culture of poverty. The Swedish economist's religious research portion of the Myrdal-Carnegie study continued the intellectual trajectory in the social sciences that had preceded it. In other words, he continued to associate what he pejoratively dubbed "religious hysteria" with the social and economic deficits of the Black lower class.

But Gunnar Myrdal's evaluation of the folk religion of poverty was shot through with his own liberal idealization of Protestantism in American history. The Myrdal-Carnegie study articulated folk religion of poverty in relationship to the so-called higher standards of Protestantism in liberal democracy. He juxtaposed Black lower-class religion (along with White bigoted religion, too) against the standard democratic forces in American Protestant churches that compelled it to "greater tolerance and ecumenical understanding [and] greater humanism and interest in social problems."[55] I will show how he used Davis's and other social scientists' observation of folk religion to show how the study perpetuated the political view that the Black lower class did not have an invested interest in addressing social and civic problems.[56] He considered the lower class to be docile and passive. Addressing social and civic problems was considered among the higher democratic ideals of American religion (Protestantism, in particular). Additionally, the emotionalism among the folk or lower-class congregants did not reflect the higher ideal of humanism, scientific rationalism and civic engagement (e.g., community organizing). Folk religion was framed as opposite to the higher values and principles of the American Creed in the Myrdal-Carnegie study.

Poor Southern Whites in the Study of Black Religion

The Myrdal-Carnegie project recycled the prevailing ideas about the religious cultures of the Black lower class. Before Myrdal visited the Peace Mission banquet in 1938, social researchers were uncovering the class differentiation within Black life.[57] Myrdal noted that the Black upper and educated class preferred Episcopal, Congregational, or Presbyterian churches, where both education and strict puritanical codes were stressed.[58] Black Catholics were presented as representative of the upper and middle classes. Although Myrdal understood that churches defied strict class logics, he still nevertheless reified the class divide in his assessment of lower-class religious behaviors and practices. In *American Dilemma*, upper and professional classes supposedly did not engage in the "frenzy" or succumb to beliefs considered outside the realm of rational and natural science (e.g., divine healing or divination), like their lower-class counterparts.

Just as Myrdal had his sights set on the backward and antiquated agricultural South, he equally gave attention to its folk or lagging religious expressions and institutions. In *American Dilemma*, he noted that Blacks, southerners, and lower-class demographics were more religious than the rest of the nation. In his chapter on the "Negro church," he further explained that "[lower-class] blacks together with some poor, isolated groups of whites [were] lagging about a half century behind."[59] Yet the lower-class "shouting churches" were evidentiary data that revealed the psychological impact of the "caste and class" system in the Jim Crow South (and North, too). Myrdal debunked knowledge about inherited religious emotionalism or Africanism that he felt was used to rationalize Black inferiority and to sanction Jim Crow governance. Here, Myrdal pointed to the pathologies of poor Whites and their folk religious cultures in the South to refute ideas about innate Black difference and inferiority.

Myrdal consulted Guy Johnson. Johnson was the perfect scholar to direct the portion of the study that dealt with Black religion, especially due to his liberal view about religion and culture. Guy Johnson and Guion Johnson wrote a two-part memorandum on "The Church and the Race Problem" that influenced Myrdal's discussion of religion in *American Dilemma*. Guy Johnson was also in charge of organizing other research memoranda and field notes on Black religion. By the time he joined the Myrdal-Carnegie core staff in New York City in 1939, Johnson had established himself in the social sciences and philanthropic organizations as a voice in the chorus of racial liberalism, regarding questions about race, culture, and acculturation. Guy Johnson's take on religion and culture assisted Myrdal's claim about the all-too-American character of Black religion, even in its lower-class "pathological forms." And, most importantly, Johnson's interpretation fed into Myrdal's liberal strategies that supported the assimilation of the Black lower class into mainstream (or "middle-class") American culture. In the study, mainstream America was implicitly rooted in predominantly white middle-class values.[60] Moreover, Johnson leveraged his research memorandum to further extend his previous arguments about Black folk religions from the St. Helena study and subsequent research (see Chapter 2). Johnson helped Myrdal advance his liberalism by minimizing race traits and privileging the role of economics in the study of Black religion. Myrdal rehearsed Johnson's argument in the memorandum that argued that Black religion "adhered closely to the common American patterns."[61] Johnson certainly added to this view in Gunnar Myrdal's attention to so-called small and independent religious movements.

Guy Johnson used his position in the study to reassess the nature and function of Black independent religious organizations. He acknowledged that religious life in America was divided along racial lines. Johnson noted that "the separate Negro congregation is the dominant pattern throughout the United States."[62] Both Guion Johnson and Edward Palmer provided the history that gave rise to Black Protestant churches and subsequent denominations after American independence. Guy Johnson (and Palmer, too) provided summaries of the reasons that led to the formation of independent Black religious movements. Johnson (as Myrdal would learn) wrote his reasons in the memorandum with an understanding that religious differences was used by white scientists and critics to rationalize racial difference and inferiority. In Part Two of the memorandum, Guy Johnson provided a broad sketch of the different arguments in the scholarly literature on the factors that gave rise to independent Black religion. He outlined arguments in scientific and religious texts that attributed the religious independence of Black people to "forces" unique to them, such as inborn instincts or African heritage. Johnson further noted that other arguments in the scientific and religious literature interpreted the formation of independent Black religious institutions as mainly the result of white prejudice, particularly in Christian churches.[63] Johnson characterized the aforementioned argument as attributing religious independence and difference among Black people to race-relations, particularly to slavery and segregation in American society. To be sure, many social scientists offered a combination of both opposing arguments in their assessment of the origins of independent Black religious communities.

But Johnson had his sights set on challenging certain studies of Black religion in late nineteenth- and early twentieth-century sociology and psychology. He criticized the persistence of the "old mechanistic theory of racial instincts" used to account for the independent "Negro Church" in particular. To be sure, Johnson had his UNC advisor-turned-colleague Howard Odum's view of the folk mind as he challenge the Darwin and Spencer-laden old theory in the study of Black religion. He mentioned Odum's folk mind that had been an extension of his training under Frederick Giddings and Thomas Bailey (e.g. "consciousness of kind" or "social communion"). Based on the concept, Johnson summarized that the old theory found that "the Negro church was peculiarly Negro because it was managed by the Negro themselves; that is, racial traits differ in degree as well as kind."[64]

But Johnson knew that he was participating in the Myrdal-Carnegie study at the height of the emerging so-called Black "sects and cults" in urban America. Moreover, Johnson's memorandum followed Mark Fischer's plea that the US Bureau of Census should include these religious "sects and cults" in the 1936 Census of Religious Bodies.[65] He summarized how the argument that attributed the urban "sects and cults" to "residual" African cultural patterns in the broader diaspora. He noted how this argument was most attributed to cultural anthropologists, like Melville Herskovits, who actually worked behind the scenes of the Myrdal-Carnegie project. Additionally, he also saw these arguments exhibited in claims by W. E. B. Du Bois, Carter G. Woodson, T. J. Woofter, and John Dollard about the persistence of African heritage(s) in the formation of Black religion in the United States. But the argument about Black religion in the Myrdal-Carnegie studies was in the research memorandum submitted by Jewish cultural anthropologist Ruth Landes. Landes submitted a research memorandum on the "new" or "independent" religious "sects and cults" in the broader Atlantic world. As deputy of research, Johnson directed Landes's research memorandum, "The Ethos of the Negro in the New World." After graduating from New York University in social work, Landes pursued her doctoral degree in the Anthropology Department at Columbia University in 1931. While pursing social work at New York University, she became fascinated with former Garveyite choir director Arnold J. Ford and the Ethiopian Hebrews at Beth B'nai Abraham before she studied Black female candomblé priests in Bahai in 1937–1938. While

performing her fieldwork on candomblé, Landes's research memorandum made preliminary arguments about the "intra-cultural phenomena," where the Black peasantry retained African traits, both
universally and locally.[66] Although Landes noted that West African
forms were not as pronounced in North America, she noted how
the homologous African forms manifested themselves in the "shout
religion." She noted that the Black shout religion in America was
similar to the African forms of religious trance and mediumship in
South America and the broader diaspora. She also included that the
Africanisms manifested themselves in the political power of the supernatural. The African sense of the supernatural and politics was
displayed in the charismatic leadership of Marcus Garvey, Father
Divine, and candomblé female priests in Bahia, Brazil. Another distinct trait in these religious movement was economic cooperation in
the religious organizations in Harlem and Brazil. Johnson situated
the "intra-cultural phenomena" within the arguments about Black
religious difference that highlighted distinct culture patterns over
and against white prejudice and discrimination.

Guy Johnson's summary in his research memorandum provided
resources for Myrdal to disregard Landes (and Herskovits) in order
to amplify his liberal interpretation of the origins of Black religious
movements. His memorandum provided the Swedish economist with
the perspective that Black "sects and cults" arose out of race-relations
in American society. He claimed that the historical force of white prejudice contributed to the formation of independent Black religions.
Johnson noted that white prejudice enforced religious segregation and
served as the impetus that led to the formation of Negro Protestant
churches and other religious organizations. Through Johnson's research, Myrdal used Johnson's argument (and those of Benjamin
E. Mays and Joseph Nicholson, too) in his discussion of Black religion,
particularly the "sects and cults." Both Johnson and Myrdal perceived
that Landes's memorandum and broader Boasian-laden cultural anthropology field had no relevance to the practical political matters
pertaining to acculturation of Blacks into American mainstream culture. Moreover, they also thought that the racial and religious logics in
cultural anthropology were indirectly used by racists to further rationalize racial prejudice and Black inequality.

Yet Guy Johnson doubled down on his claim that independent Black religions showed strong parallels to white religion. He felt that white religion was often overlooked in the research on Black religion in American life. The parallels were most striking among Protestant mainline denominations. He noted that both Black and white Protestants were similar with regard to creed, theology, and worship: for instance, Black younger intellectuals espoused the same Christian socialism or Social Gospel as their white counterparts; or, Free Will Baptists had the same creed, theology, and polity across racial difference. Agreeing with E. Franklin Frazier and John Dollard, he also claimed that middle-class and professional Black Protestants had the same low regard for emotional practices as their white counterparts. Johnson noted that middle-class and professional Black and white Protestants both showed a disregard for the so-called lower-class instruments of the "tambourine and guitar" used in so-called "sects and cults." Moreover, he noted that the differences in American Protestantism were "insignificant." Johnson noted that the African Methodist Episcopal Church was only different in polity from their white Methodist counterparts in order to maintain Black leadership.

But more importantly, he extended his claims on the religious similarities to the Black "sects and cults." This argument provided Myrdal with the information to argue that class played a more important role than race in American religion. In this sense, Johnson's note on both Black and white sects and cults worked its way into Myrdal's argument that religious pathology was not bound by distinct racial traits and tendencies. Rather, the sects and cults were depicted as a lower-class phenomenon. Myrdal called attention to how otherworldliness, emotional "hysteria," biblical literalism, and divine gifts were pathologies that included both the white and Black poor. Guy Johnson drove home the point that the arguments about distinct racial instincts or African patterns ignored the white poor. He noted, "[i]t has been assumed, for example, that fanatical religious behavior is not peculiar to the Negro, for to make such an assumption would be to deny the long history of religious fanaticism among whites in this country."[67] Johnson noted that the discussion of the religious extremism postulated by Elder Michaux's Church of God, Daddy Grace's United House of Prayer for All People, and Father Divine's Peace Missions overlooked the "white fanatics and crack-pots" in lower-class religions, like the "rattlesnake cults of Tennessee." Moreover, he drew parallels between the Black sects and cults and the white Pentecostals. He noted that white Pentecostals—Apostolic Faith Missions, Metropolitan Church Association, and Assemblies of God—also exhibited religious pathologies in their exaggerated otherworldliness, biblical fanatical and literalism, emotionalism, and personal taboos (e.g., no smoking, narcotics, alcohol, or sex). The emotionalism that characterized the Black sects and cults in the cities (and orthodox bodies in isolated rural areas) was also heightened among white Pentecostals. Johnson perpetuated the history that Holiness and subsequently Pentecostalism reflected lower-class religious bodies and behaviors. This view obscured the middle-class and aspiring Pentecostals in the South and broader America.

Guy Johnson contributed to the idea of a lower-class religion by utilizing his argument about folk religion in American history. To be lower class was a behavioral category that suggested that one was assigned to obsolete behaviors and lagging practices. Similar to his work in St. Helena, Johnson saw that these class-based interracial religions were products of the American Revivals or the "religion of the heart." Johnson went so far as to claim that Blacks, both in the rural church and in the lower-class churches in urban areas, have retained certain characteristics of religious worship which were prevalent in the white churches, especially in the South of the antebellum and Reconstruction periods. Showing the folk or southern roots of religious poverty in isolated rural and urban areas, he equated the "rousing sermons, biblical literalism, spirituals, and emotional behaviors" to the white camp-meetings in the antebellum South. Myrdal rehashed his argument that Black religious communities were already acculturated in (white) American life, and borrowed from white religious cultures, like the "emotionalism" in the anachronistic revivals. Johnson's narration of folk religion in the South played a part in the comprehensive study that identified how pathological religious subcultures were not relegated to the Black poor. This "class over race" thesis in Black religion correlated with how the study fomented the southern (and rural) origins of lower-class religion in America life. For instance, Guy Johnson traced the emerging Black sects and cults in urban America to the biracial revivals of the nineteenth century in the South. Johnson mentioned the religious extremism within white rattlesnake cults in the South. He inspired Myrdal's assertion that the "emotionalism" that characterized lower-class Black religious orientation was an adoption from poor white folk during the antebellum period. But Johnson's argument about the significance of white lower-class religion provided an avenue for Myrdal to frame his liberal "pathology thesis" for a multi-racial lower-class demographic and their religious cultures. Since Johnson believed that Black lower-class religion was an offshoot of white religious cultures, he further noted that the former mimics the otherworldly compensatory traits of white religionists that prevented it from involvement in democratic struggle. Johnson concluded that the spectacular folk remnants of sects and cults (and the bourgeois middle-class Negro church too) jeopardized the place of Black religion in liberal democractic politics.[68] Myrdal lacked the faith that Black religious institutions could serve as resources in the struggle for racial democracy. Davis added to the Swedish economist's lack of faith in the democratic potentiality of Black religion, especially in its so-called lower-class forms.

Allison Davis on the Cultural Lag in Black Religion

Allison Davis (Figure 4.1) presented a different alternative to the field of cultural anthropology in the Boasian school as exhibited by Melville Herskovits, Ruth Landes, Zora Hurston, and countless others. Later, in a 1941 book review of Franz Boas's *Race and Culture*, Davis commended the German Jewish anthropologist for pointing anthropology and the study of culture in the right direction of historical particularity over and against natural evolutionism. He championed Boas's efforts to make anthropology an empirical science with attention to the environment. But he further argued that Boas had overlooked how individual groups were under the stresses of the [dominant and macro] culture in which they lived."[69] In short, Davis noted that the pioneer of American anthropology presented a "narrow view of the sociocultural environment" and ignored race and class norms and customs in Jim Crow America. Although Myrdal considered Davis a "class and caste" dogmatist, he still considered Davis's social anthropology more

Figure 4.1 A later picture of Allison Davis as a professor at the University of Chicago, a position he held from 1942 to 1978. He was the first African American to hold full faculty status and to be tenured at a predominantly white institution.

Courtesy of University of Chicago Photographic Archive, Hanna Holborn Gray Special Collections Research Center, University of Chicago Library.

useful to his own political claims about Black culture in *American Dilemma* than cultural anthropology. Moreover, Davis was a product of the class and caste school in social anthropology that came to Harvard University and the University of Chicago by way of British anthropology. Davis's advisor, William Lloyd Warner, looked to Alfred Radcliff-Brown and subsequently Bronislaw Malinowski to ground his anthropology in a study of social structures and its assortment of norms and rules that enabled society to function and the human group to act. These social structures were enacted in patterns of social behaviors. Davis added caste to his advisor's analysis of class within the broader anthropological exploration of American social structures and its functions. Warner had launched a school of social anthropology that "felt justified in being just as much interested in the life of our modern American communities as some of our colleagues are in the peculiar practices of the polyandrous Toda."[70]

Allison Davis came to the Myrdal-Carnegie study after completing a two-year collaborative participatory-observation study of the novelist Richard Wright's hometown, Natchez, Mississippi.[71] While finishing the manuscript, Davis submitted a research memorandum to the Myrdal-Carnegie study from the field study of Natchez, as well as new research on New Orleans that he was doing for the New Deal's AYC. Natchez was situated on the Mississippi River in the Delta region. In 1930, Davis noted that Natchez had 7,159 Blacks and 6,255 white. The Black lower class, according to Davis, constituted more than 90% of the Black population in Natchez. The main engine of Natchez's economy was the cotton industry that underscored its dependence on the surrounding rural counties. The farmers in the surrounding rural counties serviced the mills in Natchez. Davis highlighted the plantation economy where a disproportionate number of Blacks were tenant farmers and sharecroppers inhabiting rental property.[72] He noted in his research memorandum for the study that the average daily income for Black families was $1.00. Additionally, poor whites did not fare much better in the planation cotton economy, at a daily rate of $2.50. Blacks (and whites) were suspended in a low standard of living due to their dependency on the cotton crop and tenant farming system. The reduction of cotton acres, depreciation in cotton prices, and the boll weevil and other natural disasters (e.g., flood in 1927) compounded the lived experiences of Black southerners. He also noted that poverty was reflected in the old two- or one-room cabins and "lean-to kitchens." In the end, Davis sought to bring to light the caste and class structure in Natchez and the broader county (and New Orleans as well).[73] This research bolstered Myrdal's argument about the backward and stagnant southern economy.

For Davis, the social structure was enacted in the rules and customs of the residents. Natchez, like the Deep South in general, was a caste system on the basis of its endogamic sanctions that prevented Black and white marriage. He noted that the "[caste sanctions] prevented legal recognition of family life between Negroes and whites, denied legitimate sexual contact, and made impossible legitimate issue of Negro-white sex unions."[74] Davis used caste to imply the sheer permanency of race relations that structured black inferiority and white superiority. In a caste relation, Blacks and whites could not change their caste status. Myrdal used caste in his assessment of social stratification in the American South.[75] But his use of the term was not doctrinaire, as it was to Davis.

Caste was intertwined with class in American social structures. Davis's understanding of class was social in character. He defined class by group associations or clichés, and consequently their perceptions and attitudes toward one another in a given social system. Social class was reflected in both intimate and informal relationships, such as "visits, teas, the taking of meals together in the home, dances, receptions, and large informal affairs."[76] While both caste and class intersected in a given society, the latter was not a closed and rigid system like the former. Davis noted that "[w]hereas [persons] may not marry or associate intimately outside [their] caste, however, he may change his class position during the course of his lifetime."[77] Class systems, according to the social anthropologist, allow "upward or downward social mobility."[78] Davis outlined in his research memorandum that Natchez had five social classes within its rigid caste system. Although Myrdal did not subscribe to the social anthropologist's view of class, the latter's view of social classes complemented the former's classification of behaviors, attitudes, values, and sensibilities. To be sure, this was the case with the study of Black religion, particularly the Holiness, Pentecostal, Spiritual, Episcopalian, Catholic, Baptist, and Methodist congregations in the Delta and Gulf states.

Davis's research on Black religion complemented Johnson and Myrdal's arguments that attributed the character and function of Black religion to white racism or the caste system. Davis's study of the "Negro church" was a larger critique of the "white church" in the Lower South in the states. The white Catholic and Episcopalian churches in Natchez (and New Orleans) accommodated the caste system and espoused white control. In Natchez, the "Universal Church" had barred Black Catholics from the procession ceremonies on "All Saints Day." The dozens of Blacks who appeared at the gravesite saw the literal back of the white bishop during his sermon and officiation of the events at the white-only cemetery. Davis recorded his white colleagues' interview of an Episcopalian bishop who mentioned the separate seminary for Blacks training for the priesthood. Acknowledging the southern system, the bishop reiterated that "it would stir up too much criticism. People would say we were teaching equality."[79] The theological dogmas reflected and enforced the caste system. His argument was a perfect complement to Myrdal's claim that the Negro Problem was a white problem. In the Myrdal-Carnegie study, American religion was a caste phenomenon.

Davis's field report highlighted how Holiness and Spiritualist churches challenged the strict caste sanctions that led to arrests, fines, and penalties in Natchez (and in New Orleans). He observed that the caste sanction proved the weakest in these lower-class churches. For instance, a Black male Spiritualist leader was warned by police to not allow white women to congregate at his church. According to Davis, the leader "persisted in reading the future for white women" and was arrested by the police and fined by the municipal courts.[80] He also noted that several Black mothers in the Spiritualist church had ordained white mothers.[81] The laws against Spiritualism correlated with the sexual governance in the Jim Crow South. Folklorist Zora Neale Hurston was fully aware of the tension between "religious outsiders" (e.g., Spiritualist and conjurers) and law enforcement in the Gulf states. These religious outsiders stood against what she referred to as state religion or the "theology of the nation." This is what happened when she arrived at the "aging pink house of the 70-year-old Hoodoo spiritualist, Luke Turner" (or "Samuel Thompson" in *Mules and Men*).[82] Turner rejected her initial request to work under him as an apprentice and undergo a process of initiation of spiritual empowerment. She was aware that the many municipal ordinances against fortune-tellers, hoodoo doctors, and the like contributed to his distrust. She even noted that the leader's appropriation of the spiritualistic name on churches [was] a useful device of protection coloration."[83]

But Davis did not linger with this state policing of Black Spiritualism and Holiness in the Lower South (and the Caribbean, too). He did not consider the democratic possibilities of these churches that partly challenged the caste system that he was against. Although Davis may have been agnostic, he nevertheless privileged the Christian standard of "brotherhood," which he did not extend to congregations that conflicted with state law enforcement in the southern caste system. Rather, he wrote them off as lower-class practitioners who were not deliberate or conscious of their acts. His lower-class designation was used to ignore the complexities of the religious organizations that had to navigate the state caste system that sought to manage religious conduct. Yet, his lower-class designation actually reified the "theology of the nation" that help to supplant the caste system that he protested.

Davis confirmed in his study that Black churches accommodated the caste sanctions of white supremacy and Black inferiority. They were not dependable institutions for democratic reform. Davis's assertion was primarily a critique aimed at Black male leaders. He considered them responsible for managing matters of life and death. In the 17 counties that comprised the Mississippi Delta, whites lynched Blacks more than twice a year between 1900 and 1930.[84] During his study, Mississippi was the leading state for Black lynching. Davis shared one story where a Black minister stood in front of a congregation to protest against white men sleeping with Black women. A son of a local Black leader in Natchez had to stave off the white mob who had planned to inflict violence on the minister. Davis heard a sermon where the minister preached to his predominantly lower-class congregation about preventing hostility toward whites. He recorded that the minister's sermon was a response to the lynching of two Black men. The minister, according to Davis, said "We ain't no more than a coon with a collar 'round his neck! That's all! You know I am right!"[85]

Davis alerted the Swedish economist to the significance of white patronage in the function of the caste system. Myrdal repeated Davis's claim that poverty caused Black congregations to depend on whites. The accommodation of Black churches to the caste system was related to white money. The caste system was predicated on the gift exchange. He noted that there were economic incentives that shaped the decisions of Black ministers and congregations. With the surrounding plantations, Black ministers and congregations were dependent on white patrons for economic security, such as paying for their pastor's salary or building. Davis even found Black ministers endorsing farm tenancy from their pulpits because they worked in white-owned county stores during the week.[86] To be sure, Davis extended his critique to the Black middle classes. White planters had the Negro Business League frequent Black Protestant churches to make appeals to congregants to stop urban migration from the plantation fields. He also mentioned how educated and middle-class Blacks had to compromise their skill and education to perform the white dogma of the humble, meek, noncompetitive, and emotional religious subject in return for financial support of their events and institutions. The upper- and middle-class religious churches had perform the "cultural lag" for social and economic status, and remained disconnected their interests from the plight of the lower-class folk. Davis noted that "the greatest controls and pressures [of the dominant white group on black churches and organizations] were in areas where populations is small, with a relatively simple social structure, and where the economic control of the Negroes by whites is the strongest [33-4]." Myrdal picked up on Davis's view of the conservative nature of the church in the face of White racism.

Davis's perspective on what constituted lower-class religion complemented the folk concept that social scientists had used to refer to the Black poor in the American South. To be sure, he understood that the "Black Church" was not a rigidly classed institution. He further noted that Black religious organizations most effectively integrated diverse social classes and minimized the disintegrative class hostilities. Yet, rarely did he find any upper- or middle-class demographics congregating with the lower classes. In this sense, he maintained that these institutions also perpetuated the different "class antagonisms." He witnessed one of the mothers of the Spiritualist churches espouse "hostility" toward formally educated and higher-class congregations. Moreover, Davis articulated that social class still "modified" dogma, ritual, aesthetic adornment, behaviors, and taboos in Black churches. For this reason, he associated the Spiritualist, Holiness, and mainline Protestant organizations with lower-class religions.

His classification of lower-class religion was based on his participatory-observation in Natchez. Also, his classification was based on his observation of the different social classes' perceptions of each other. But Davis was not left off the hook in his analysis. His classification was shot through with his own principles and values. Davis's interpretation of the dogma and rituals of "lower-class religion" reflected his personal biases. To be sure, he considered the cultural lag evident in the "fortune-telling" knowledge that Spiritualist leaders and practitioners practiced.[87] In Natchez, practitioners were paying 25 to 50 cents for their fortune-telling. Why he considered this practice lower-class should be called into question. In the surrounding planation districts, he had data where upper-class white women visited Spiritualist practitioners to have their fortunes told. One white female informant told Davis's white colleagues that she visited a fortune teller who was right with their predictions. She noted that other white upper-class women visited Spiritualists to have their fortunes told as well. Although Spiritualism took different forms across race, class, region, and political ideologies in American religion, Davis associated the Spiritualism (prophecy, healing, or seances) with lagging traits that defied modern knowledge. To get his point across about the cultural lag of these lower-class religions, he used the pejorative "otherworldly" category for Spiritualism and other lower-class religious forms. More than likely he probably assigned the otherworldly category to theology of sanctification that was upheld by Black Holiness and Pentecostals. He noted that the Spiritualist and Holiness churches unconsciously reified the white dogma of the humble, noncompetitive, child-like, and superstitious Black subject. Since Davis associated the lower-class populations with ignorance due to their education and unskilled labor, he noted that the lower-class churches were also not aware that they were performing the white dogma of the Black religious subject like their middle-class counterparts. But he described how the otherworldliness of lower-class congregations reinforced white dominance. He noted how converts in the revivalistic Protestant churches authenticated their spiritual visions in their conversion experiences by confirming a "white person or object in their vision."[88] Interestingly, he recorded a Spiritualist who faulted these revivalistic churches for seeing "Jesus as a white man." He noted how these lower-class Protestant faiths divinized whiteness. Davis did not complicate these various religious communities that he tagged lower-class in light of the white dogma. Instead, his classification of the lower-class religion based on the otherworldly and spiritual lag indirectly reified the white dogma that he was protesting against.

Similar to Guy Johnson's folk religion concept, Davis also associated emotionalism with lower-class communities. He discussed the lower-class "chanted" sermons with their "intoning and sobbing techniques" (also called "gravy sermons"). Yet, he overlooked both Benjamin Mays's and Joseph Nicholson's comments on how educated Black preachers were increasing their religious and cultural capital and popularity through their chanted sermons. These techniques, according to Davis, were complemented by the revivalistic shouting, ecstatic jerking, and yelling members. The emotional characteristic was depicted as the psychological function of the Black lower-class faith. But he also considered the emotional faith to be the persistence of the religious lag from past revivals. His description of the lower-class faiths matched Guy Johnson's description of the revivalistic underpinnings of the Black and white Pentecostals and cults in American life. Moreover, his description of the Black Protestant church was similar to Johnson's view of folk religion as a relic of an America pastime, remnant of past revivals, first in the eighteenth century, and then in the nineteenth.

Allison Davis grew up in a middle- and professional-class Episcopalian church in the nation's capital.[89] Yet, his son later recalled that his dad was not a church-goer. Nevertheless, his ideals on what he considered good, proper, modern religion shaped his research memorandum. He acknowledged the contradictions between the caste system and Christian "brotherhood" that Black ministers knew in their hearts. The lower-class faiths (and upper and middle classes, too) did not subscribe to the ethical doctrine. He concluded on the same note as Guy Johnson that the Black church faced a serious dilemma because it was not a viable institution of social reform. On one level, Davis attributed this dilemma to the majority of church leaders and professionals who were fully invested in "making a status-gain through their leadership in the church." He noted that the "chief problem [was] that of making accessible to these mobile individuals those skills and ideologies which will contribute to effective reform of their society."[90] Yet, he did not mention the so-called lower-class organizations and their place in "effective reform." Rather, his description of their cultural lag in otherworldliness, emotionalism, and conservatism (biblical literalism, efficacy in conversion, fire-and-brimstone faith) played into the white dogma of the Black religious subject. By his lights, they were not considered viable institutions for challenging the caste system. Underneath his view, he indirectly felt that social and economic reform came from outside lower-class communities. Therefore, he considered these lower-class religions to be compensatory and accommodationist.

The Welfare State over and against Religion

Myrdal was intent on showing that the Black churches were generally conservative. By conservative, he meant that the churches accommodated and conformed to Jim Crow segregation.[91] Both Guy Johnson and Allison Davis confirmed his understanding. He further argued that the institutions encouraged dependency, passivity and sought to dissuade congregants from challenging caste and class arrangements. Myrdal visited a church in the Upper South, probably Virginia, and noted that he heard a preacher tell his congregants to forget about the importance of "real estate, automobiles, fine clothes, learnedness, prestige, and money."[92] After he asked the minister about his sermon, he replied that the main objective of the church was to help make the "poor Negro satisfied with their lowly status."

To be sure, St. Clair Drake followed the same reasoning about Black religion as Myrdal in his research memorandum. With a father who was a Garveyite Christian minister, Drake was critical of the lower-class religion in the agricultural South. Yet, he held on to his faith of a more activist religion that caused him to later encourage a young Martin Luther King and the Southern Christian Leadership Council.[93] Yet Allison Davis had resolved that the churches were accommodationist, which Myrdal cited to justify his own view in *American Dilemma*. The church (and lower-class religions) was to "moderate the violent antagonisms between the two castes, [and offer] ultimate sanction to the caste and economic systems." In fact, Davis examined the material incentives and advantages when ministers, in general, "sanctioned" the caste and class system, like a Black treasurer who leveraged his relationship with a landlord to finance the church and lodges in a plantation economy.[94]

Davis understood the complexity of the caste and class system and how it impacted the behaviors and activities of the Black religious community. Davis and Myrdal both noted how the economic plight kept Black male religious leaders dependent on white male benefactors. They also called attention to the significant role of violence and intimidations in these orientations.

Both Davis's and Myrdal's perspective on the conservative nature of religious institutions reflected a larger trend in the world of social research and reform. Political scientist Ralph Bunche, who traveled with Myrdal to the South in 1939, also concluded that the Black religion, mostly Protestant, was conservative. While in Savannah, Georgia, Bunche who noted that a substantial number of Black male preachers had protested against other clergy who were engaged in the fight for voting rights.[95] A part of the younger leftist social scientific generation, Bunche leveraged his analysis of Black political leadership and organizations to support the Myrdal-Carnegie's conclusions concerning the political conservatism of Black Protestantism and religion in general. The claims about the docility and passivity of Black communities contributed to the folklorization of southern lower-class religion and broader culture.

Overall, the Myrdal-Carnegie study's construction of folk or lower-class religion was, for the most part, intended to support what they hoped to be the decline of the religion in Black life. Myrdal noted that the rising protest from congregants were forcing the churches to change. He, like other racial liberals such as Charles S. Johnson, pointed to younger Blacks to demonstrate the decline of the folk, rural, and/or "plantation church." Davis noted how a few young boys stood outside of the church poking fun at the preacher and a person praying. Echoing racial liberals, Myrdal noted that the church has "lagged when viewed from the advanced positions of Negro youth. . . ."[96] According to Myrdal, increasing rates of education and exposure to modern amenities were inspiring youth to be "critical of the shouting and noisy religious hysteria in old-time Negro churches and new cults."[97] He cited Benjamin Mays's and Joseph Nicholson's claims in *The Negro Church* that greater exposure to the broader modern world contributed to the decline of the "revival meetings." The claim concerning the folk or lagging religious institutions in the American South correlated with his description of the modernization of the younger Black populations.

Gunnar Myrdal's dismissal of Black religion was related to his faith in social welfare democracy. He held out a glimmer of hope for Black southerners and the broader American Creed in the South.[98] He was self-reflexive about his own presentation of the illusions that the South was static. The Swedish economist believed that Howard Odum's discussion about the resistance of folkways and mores (à la William Graham Sumner) to "stateways" was more relevant to a "regional religion" than social reality. He retained his bureaucratic liberal faith in social democracy. He held out faith in scientific and governmental engineering to ensure American democracy for Blacks. He felt that social democracy and welfare capitalism were most embodied in New Deal liberalism. To be sure, he acknowledged the limits of New Deal liberalism in its catering to the caste system in the South in particular. But he also noted that the "liberal New Deal" was steadily undermining southern folk practices.[99] The economist attributed this undermining to economic benefits for the poor region, coupled with the strength of the labor and Black voting blocs in the North.

Myrdal considered the New Deal a popular movement. He felt that the New Deal was popular with the Black and white lower class that gravitated to the social welfare assistance and economic reform. Although he said social welfare democracy was "spoon-fed from above," he took the spirit of the New Deal to have trickled down to the working poor in their communities. The New Deal had stimulated and compelled them to organize among themselves in civic activities such as "county planning and other agricultural groups, in 4-H clubs, in credit associations and cooperatives, in religious reform groups, discussion, forums, fact-finding, committees, parent-teacher associations, interracial commissions, etc."[100] Moreover, he said the spirit of the New Deal in the South had done what other national welfare governments had not done: educate the "masses." He noted that the "Farm Security Administration had educated the masses for a fuller and more efficient life."[101] This education from New Deal organizations and bureaucracies was moving the "South toward a higher level of general education and cultural participation"[102] in civic life. But New Deal liberalism had used the paternalism and dependency of the Black poor to develop them into the democratic ideals of independent, rational, and self-reliant subjects. In Myrdal's mind, the New Deal state was able to do what folk or lagging religion could not do. Yet, Myrdal's liberal faith underestimated the racism of white lower-class populations in particular.

The decline of folk and lower-class religion underscored Myrdal and the racial liberals' faith in the social engineering of federal policies over and against the lagging religious organizations. And social engineering privileged social researchers and bureaucrats over and against religious leaders in saving the Black folk. Welfare programs of the New Deal state, coupled with federal civil rights legislation (e.g., judicial and legislative branches mandating the Fourteenth Amendment), would facilitate the salvation of the Black poor because these measures would generate their acculturation into mainstream America. He surmised that New Deal economic policies and the post–World War II global context would significantly alter the racial and economic landscape in the United States. With the rise of the modern civil rights movement, Myrdal later acknowledged that he had underestimated the significance of Black religion in his study. He enlisted social researchers to help with federal governmental planning to legislate full employment; birth control and agricultural programs; public housing and social security; and vocational and adult education. Myrdal's policy proposals were based on assumptions that the New Deal would inspire social and economic reforms that would alter the conduct of poor Black southerners.

Conclusion

The Myrdal-Carnegie study generalized Black religion as conservative and accommodationist. This was partly due to the religion's cultural lag and/or folk character (and bourgeoisie neglect from upper- and middle-class churches). This cultural lag was southern in character— meaning that these were extensions of folk Protestantism that gained prominence in the antebellum period. This economic lag of the agricultural South hindered the religious development of Black southerners. Religion underscored the moral and social lag of lower-class Blacks. This lag was attributed to the regional socioeconomic environment.

The Myrdal-Carnegie study made southern folk religion part of its arguments about the culture of poverty.

What did the folk (or cultural lag) category in the Myrdal-Carnegie study foreclose? Social researchers in the study mentioned some notable exceptions that undermined how they understood lower-class Black religion in the agricultural South. They reduced the complexity of the Black lower class in order to bolster their claims about their so-called folk religion. Guy Johnson briefly mentioned the complex fundamental, ecumenical, and social Christianity and radical politics of Owen Whitfield and farmers throughout the South and Midwest.[103] Whitfield symbolized one version of the educational and political aspirations of the lower-class rural Blacks that the folk category in religion foreclosed. The world of Whitfield leads to a composite of groups associated with the "agrarian radicalism"—Garveyites, Sharecroppers Tenant Farmers Union, and the Communist Party in the agricultural South. Johnson's folk category ignored the subtle interclass conflict of rural Blacks with landowners, business managers, and/or residents. For instance, Johnson's brief discussion in his memorandum on C. T. Boyd, a Black Church of God in Christ (COGIC) pastor in Chapel Hill, North Carolina, focused on his and the congregants' "emotionalism," coupled with their beliefs in "divine healing," "sanctification," "biblical literalism," and "disapproval of personal sins."[104] He noted that the noise in the church caused white residents to complain. He mentioned how white employees complained that their domestic servants were "too sleepy" to perform their work after nightly service at the COGIC church.[105] Guy Johnson used the emotionalism category to extend his argument about the folk-history of the persistence of the revivalistic religious orientations of the nineteenth century. Similar to fieldwork in the banquet in the Peace Mission movement, he also focused on the emotionalism of Boyd and the congregants to underscore the moral "weakness" of lower-class religion. What if the attendance and practices in the late-night services at the COGIC church were ways in which Black female domestic workers subtly contested or challenged their white employers?

I do not want to impose the protest motif on Black religion in the early twentieth century. Maybe the domestic workers were actually tired and did not feel like working. But the folk category that renders them docile, passive, or accommodationist fails to capture the complex layers of religious institutions and practices in relationship to the Jim Crow economy. The folk (or cultural lag) category obscures the complexity of Whitfield, the domestic Black female Pentecostals, or even Father Divine's deliberate rejection of the New Deal welfare state to static liberal and scientific categories, such as emotionalism, otherworldliness, and superstitious. Additionally, his reduction of Pentecostalism to a lower-class faith could not account for the "few of the respectable Negroes" who converted to the COGIC church in Chapel Hill. Additionally, the scientific category did not account for the work of sanctification in the social world that congregants, especially women, inhabited. Contemporary American religious historian Anthea Butler argues that sanctification was not a form of religious compensation or escapism. Rather, COGIC women's beliefs in sanctification filtered into their social involvement in education, war, civil rights, and other civic issues.[106]

This challenge also includes both Davis and subsequently Myrdal. The "cultural lag" idea reduced the complexity that limited what they understood as lower-class religion. Similar to Johnson, Davis also reduced certain "emotional, cathartic" orientations to lower-class religions. Davis's explanation does not account for the visiting preacher who "successfully" used the revivalistic technique—shouting, moaning, even weeping—in sermons to attract older and upper-class Blacks in the agricultural city of Natchez. Davis attributed the success of revivalistic technique of the visiting preacher to the older and upper-class Blacks' close contact with lower class. Yet his argument does not logically follow his claims about how socioeconomic status determines religious comportment and styles. Whatever he considered old-time religion could not be confined to economic position (or formal education). Also, some lower-class congregants may have preferred to associate with the upper- and middle-class communities for a variety of reasons.

Just as there were churches colluding with white landowners and businessmen working to support caste and class subjugation for complex reasons, they were also lower-class communities supporting the Communist Unemployment Councils or Huey Long's "Share-the-Wealth" policies in the Deep South. The choices that certain southern

Black people made were guided by their "modern" aspirations and needs. The folk category and cultural lag concepts in the Myrdal-Carnegie study that sought to represent lower-class religion simplified the religiously and politically complex landscape of Blacks in the Deep South.

5

Preserving the Folk

Folk Songs and the Irony of Romanticism

In the sweltering summer of 1941, the Library of Congress's Alan
Lomax and Fisk University sociologist Lewis Jones attended a state
Baptist convention to record a religious program at the First African
Church in Clarksdale, Mississippi.[1] Located in the Yazoo-Delta region,
Clarksdale was a trading "city" in Coahoma County. Clarksdale's own
population was nearly 48,333 people, with Blacks comprising 37,267.[2]
According to the 1940 census, Blacks comprised 77.1% of the total
population in Coahoma County. Incorporated in 1882, Clarksdale was
on Route 61 and located 70 miles southwest of Memphis.[3] Jones and
Fisk University graduate student Samuel Adams referred to Clarksdale
as the "New World" with its vibrant commercial district that boasted
of "fifty-one food stores, twenty-two eating places, twenty general
merchandise stores, twenty-four clothing stories, eleven automobile dealers and garage."[4] Seated in the top balcony, Lomax set up his
government-loaned equipment, which included a huge microphone
and recording machine that he held over the pulpit in order to capture
the various sound impressions. His excitement was fueled by his new
state-of-the-art amplifier, microphones, acetate, and recording machine that had the ability to capture every sound effect for a significant
duration of time. Lomax noted, "In the past I had tried to capture the
lambent sound of Black congregational singing and had always failed."[5]
The failure was attributed to the earlier portable equipment that "could
not cope with a church full of Black Baptists singing their hearts out,
improvising harmonies and swinging round a perfect beat."[6]

Alan Lomax's recording experience that evening was a disappointment. The conventional hymns performed by the robed choir compelled him to turn off the advanced machinery in disgust. During one
of the arranged hymns, a visibly agitated Lomax turned to Lewis and

To Know the Soul of a People. Jamil W. Drake, Oxford University Press. © Oxford University Press 2022.
DOI: 10.1093/oso/9780190082680.003.0006

asked, "What is this?" Amused by the frustrations of Lomax, Lewis grinned and whispered, "It's the latest thing. They call it gospel." Most likely at Lomax's recommendation, they left the service for a "breath of fresh air." Lomax felt that the choir had not mastered certain pitches and harmonies standard in arranged musical selections. He noted, "It is hard to tell which was more out of tune, the pianist or the choir." His disappointment was largely based on his presumptions about what southern Black Baptist churches *should* perform. Lomax noted that he could not believe he was in a southern Black Baptist church without the performances of the "great hallelujah spirituals."

Alan Lomax thought that gospel music was desperately trying to imitate conventional European tradition, with its emphasis on formalized composition. While catching fresh air, his ire was further heightened when he saw "Reverend Martin" selling gospel sheet music outside the convention.[7] Martin told Lomax: "You see, in the modern Baptist church, we are trying to move past the wonderful old cornbread spirituals and sermons." To add more to his frustration and Lewis's amusement, they later attended a local juke joint where the Library of Congress agent was confused to see a couple "slow dragging" their bodies, "erotically" against each other to Duke Ellington's "In the Mood," that played on the neon-green, electric juke box.[8] Lomax said that the jazz sounds transformed the setting more into a club in Harlem or Southside Chicago than the Mississippi Delta.

On another separate trip in 1942, his expectation was satisfied when he and Fisk University musicologist John W. Work III frequented the Stovall plantation, where they interviewed and recorded blues musicians. One of these musicians was a shoeless guitarist, McKinley "Muddy Waters" Morganfield. And Lomax finally heard the more "heroic and noble" folk spirituals, which he preferred to what he called the "defeatist disposition" of gospel music. The Arafat Baptist Church on the King and Anderson Plantation on Route 61 provided the authentic and pure folk songs that resisted the encroachment of the outside modern commercial world. The irony was that Muddy Waters and the folk churches were just as commercialized as Thomas Dorsey, Mahalia Jackson, and other blues musicians and gospel choirs after World War II. Lomax ironically helped to facilitate the commodification processes of these so-called resistant, pure, authentic, and premodern art forms.

Commodification of artworks in market industry was not lost on Muddy Waters and other so-called folk religionists in rural and urban Mississippi. The commodification process of producing, selling, and consuming goods contributed to the "folk" songs. Additionally, the exchange-value of the folk songs was not lost on the informants who performed songs for Lomax. Black informants sought to negotiate certain needs and wants for the performance of the folk songs that Lomax sought to record and collect. Folk songs were a far cry from anything natural or authentic.

The history behind the Library of Congress and Fisk University Coahoma Study was further complicated by the power dynamic behind the scenes. Contemporary scholars Robert Gordon and Bruce Nemerov have provided a revisionist history of the origins of the collaborative study that countered Lomax's selfish and romantic narrative. Both Gordon and Nemerov rightly argue that the origins of the research study highlight how the collaborative study actually emerged from the work of Fisk University's musicologist, John W. Work.[9] Work initially planned to record and study the folk music in the aftermath of the 1940 fire at a social gathering at the Rhythm Night Club in the commercial district of Natchez, Mississippi. On April 23, 1940, while the Walter Barnes Orchestra of Chicago played before a packed house, which included civic leaders and middle- and working-class Blacks, an electrical fire erupted that killed 209 people. Work's original plans to record folk songs about the fire were interrupted by Fisk University president Thomas Elsa Jones. A white paternalist, Jones invited the Library of Congress to join the study, which expanded the project and shifted management from Work to Lomax due in part to the latter's governmental position in the Library of Congress.[10] Lomax's narrative about the origins of the Coahoma Study ignored Work's creative plan and involvement in the study. Lomax noted that he approached "Fisk University, the Princeton of Black colleges, with the idea of doing a joint field study with my department at the Library of Congress in the Mississippi Delta counties."[11]

The Coahoma Study never came to fruition due to a confluence of personal squabbles and the interruption of the United States' entry into World War II after Pearl Harbor. Fisk University sociologist Lewis Jones was drafted into the army. But what was more interesting was

Lomax's critique of the Fisk social scientists. His critique alerts us to the tensions in the idea of the folk category in Black religion, as exhibited in his disagreements with Jones. Lomax noted that while Fisk's fieldworkers were highly skilled at situating the oral lore in their proper social context, they nevertheless failed to account for the highly creative cultural forces of Black lower and working classes in the Delta region. His dream to establish an "active South-wide folklore work" in the Social Science Department at Fisk University was diminished due to what he described as the faculty and students' cultural prejudice against the religious vernacular traditions of the unlettered and poor people."[12] This dream ignored the graduate Folk Seminar and other community projects that were already an important part of the master's program since the department's inception. Samuel Adams accredited the late Robert Park for pointing him to the legitimacy of folklore in rural and southern sociology.

Alan Lomax might have been partially right about the cultural prejudices operative in the objective and empirical studies in the social sciences at Fisk University. Zora Neale Hurston, who almost joined the faculty at Fisk University, shared the same sentiment with her folklorist colleague.[13] Chapter 3 of this book already demonstrated how Charles S. Johnson's deployment of the category underscored his faith in secular modernity within his pragmatic southern liberal program. Although Johnson was the consummate empiricist, he adhered to liberal moral narratives of modern progress that privileged sanitation, family values, and scientific rationality to govern the daily Black tenant farmers and croppers. But, Lomax's and other folklorists' "antimodern modernism" represented the other side of the folk coin that shared the same logics as racial liberals, which simplified rural Blacks as premodern.[14] At the forefront of national romanticism and cultural pluralism of the New Deal programs at the Library of Congress, Lomax's characterization of black folk religious expressions still classified uneducated and lower-class southern Blacks as stuck in a natural and primitive state apart from the so-called artificialities of industrial and commercial culture. He noted that these authentic songs sharply contrasted with jazz, or concert spirituals of soloists and college glee clubs.[15] Again, his work with the Library of Congress replicated the myth that the lower working class and their religious practices were in isolation from mainstream America. Or, put another way, the implications of his romanticism were that the enclosed rural area was their natural habitat. If anything, Jones and later Adams's work in the Coahoma Study attest to the idea that Black lower-class workers had the same aspirations that underscored their knowledge and interaction with the cultural industry and market. No wonder Muddy Waters asked Lomax for his check after he completed the field interview and recording. We can learn about the artificiality of the idea when we consider the disappointment of American folklorists, including Hurston, just as much as that of the racial liberal scientists and reformers that I discussed in previous chapters. The disappointments said more about the expectations of the romantic fieldworkers than about the actual Black southern community. Early in her fieldwork, Hurston had a couple of disappointments in Louisiana and the Florida Everglades with regard to collecting folk material. In her first fieldwork, Hurston wrote to Franz Boas that she was finding it hard to collect materials because Blacks were tuned into their phonographs. The celebratory intentions of romantic preservationist contrasted with the liberal reformist tradition. Alan Lomax and other romanticists still reproduced the same modern knowledge that reduced Black poor southerners and their religious and cultural aspirations. Like the liberal counterparts, Lomax also projected that the Black lower-class southerners were isolated from modernization.

Before I tackle the Coahoma Study, I will delve into his first field recording trip with his father, John Lomax Sr. We will see the beginnings of Alan's anti-modern romanticism that later culminated in his collaborative work with the Fisk University Social Science Department.

Anti-Modernism and Recording the Religious Songs of Black Prison Laborers

At the time of the Coahoma Study, Alan Lomax was officially the assistant in charge at the Library of Congress, beginning in 1937. But his work with the Library of Congress extended back to the early 1930s at the height of the Great Depression. His career with the Library of Congress was accredited to his father, John A. Lomax, Sr., who was an official folklorist with the Federal Writers' Project. Both John Sr. and Alan were part of the Washington-based bureaucratic folklorists who contributed to redefining American national identity during the New Deal era.

Alan Lomax's early field trips with his father would shape the contours of his understanding of the black folk. Alan was enamored with the labor strikes and protest movements that put him at odds with his more conservative father after World War I. Despite their different political ideologies, they both shared the same "anti-modern modernist" perspective about the meaning of folk in Black culture. In 1933, 18-year-old Alan went on his first recording expedition with his father on behalf of the Library of Congress. At the time, Alan was an undergraduate in philosophy at Harvard University, before he transferred to the University of Texas–Austin. At the time, the 64-year-old John Sr. had fallen on difficult times with the death of his wife and the economic pinch that ensued in the Depression.[16] Alan and his older brother, John Jr., convinced their father that he should revisit his first love—folk song—to revive his poor financial and psychological state. Alan's and John Jr.'s recommendation of their father's first love recalled his early interest in the cowboy ballads of his home state, Texas. John Sr.'s first love was cultivated in the Harvard English department where professors Barrett Wendall and George Kittridge encouraged and provided him with resources to advance his fieldwork on cowboy ballads on the Southwestern frontier region.[17] Theodore Roosevelt praised John Lomax's work in the frontier cowboy ballads. John Sr.'s expedition led to the publication of *Cowboy Songs and Other Frontier Ballads* in 1910. Roosevelt asserted that the songbook framed the "back country and the frontier" and that the "crude home-spun ballads" resonated with his masculine politics of authenticity, as he sought to counter the industrial "feminine" over-civilization of American society.[18]

John Sr. had a book contract from Macmillian Publishing Company, with funding from the new archive of folk songs at the Library of Congress. The book contract and funds enabled John and his restless son to embark on a four-month southern trek from Texas to Virginia, before heading to the nation's capital to transfer the aluminum and celluloid disc to the Library. This expedition solidified the Lomaxes' long professional relationship, albeit contentious, with the Archive of American Folk Song at the Library of Congress. John Sr. organized the 1933 expedition around his lifelong interest in recording the folk sounds of southern Blacks. He noted, "the main object of this journey was to record on aluminum and celluloid disks to deposit in the Library of Congress, the folk-songs of the Negro."[19] The collection from the first trip made up the first of many folk song collections catalogued at the Library of Congress. The collection was published in their 1934 *American Ballads and Folk Songs*.[20]

John Sr. and Alan wanted to test the 350-pound Dictaphone machine before toting it on their southern expedition. They encountered a "skinny little black woman" who set the standard for Alan's view of what constituted folk songs and the "old-time" Black Protestantism. Thirty miles outside of Dallas, Texas, in Terrell, the woman took a break from washing clothes and decided to sing a baptismal song, "Wade in the Water," for the father and son folklorists. John Sr. characterized the woman's voice as high-pitched with a "liquid softness that made the [sound] effect beautiful and moving."[21] Alan supposedly was said to be in total amazement: "She was full of shakes and quivers as the Southern rivers. She started slow and sweet, but as the needle scratched her song on the whirling wax cylinder, she sang faster and with more and more drive, clapping her hands and tapping out drum rhythm with heel and toe of her bare feet."[22] After the performance the informant broke out in tears and repeatedly exclaimed: "Lord, Have Mercy." According to John Sr., this first recording compelled Alan to put his undergraduate degree on hold temporarily and to dedicate his life to collecting ballads. This first field expedition piqued his curiosity about folk songs in what they called "old-time religion." They considered folk songs central to "old time religion" in the South.

But what was most interesting about his first expedition was the significance the father and son imposed on prison farms and state penitentiaries. In their expedition, they visited a total of 11 prisons and communicated with approximately 25,000 Black inmates. What is more astonishing was their ironic romanticism that compelled them to painted the prisons in a sort of glowing light. John Sr. remarked that the southern penitentiary was our best field. Alan later asserted his father's sentiment that southern prison farms were the "richest stores of Negro folk material."[23] This sentiment about the prison farms and state penitentiaries provided a window into what Alan understood to be folk songs and consequently authentic southern and "old-time" Black Protestant culture. Both John Sr. and Alan were part of a group of folklorists who frequented prisons to record folk songs and other materials. But contemporary anthropologist John Szwed noted that "no one before the Lomaxes had appreciated the richness of creativity within prison life, and none had sought [it] out with such, dogged persistence."[24] They frequented prisons well into the 1940s and 1950s.

The penal system was an important mechanism of racial governance in the wake of slavery. Ex-Confederate states enacted segregation laws and arrangements designed to punish Blacks to forced labor in order to restore and revitalize southern infrastructure, collect revenue, and to manage the formerly enslaved and their progeny. By the 1870s, these states leased their predominantly Black convicts to private employees and corporate managers for a fee. In 1899, a British journalist for the *Anti-Slavery Reporter* noted how business bidders paid southern states for Black convicts to work on large cotton, corn, and wheat farms, turpentine distillers, saw mills, brick yards, phosphate mines, coal and iron mines, and railroads.[25] Thus, industrial capitalists and entrepreneurs monopolized Black forced labor to generate profit and industrialize the postbellum South and broader nation. Southern states and counties capitalized on the penal system by leasing convicts out to private companies and farms to work in the late nineteenth and early twentieth centuries. In the wake of antebellum slave labor, the Black convict laborers continued to industrialize the postbellum South.[26] Prison reformer W. P. Thirkied decried the "convict leasing system because the underlying motive of both State and Lease is not morals, but money, not reformation, but exploitation of criminals of gain."[27] At the time of the 1933 expedition, John Sr. casually stated that the "penitentiary Negroes" played an instrumental role in establishing the New South infrastructure by "clearing the land, working its plantations, building its railroads, loading steamboats, raising levees, and cutting its roads."[28] At the turn of the century, Louisiana leased 90% of its Black laborers to levee contractors. Beginning in the late nineteenth century, state and county municipalities and private business, such as railroads, all had a vested interest in the convict-leasing system. The convict-leasing system replaced the old slave system of the antebellum period. A cadre of progressive reformers—white populists, civil rights reformers, criminologists, muckraking journalists, and social scientists—contributed to the slow but gradual end of the convict-leasing system. Yet, government continued to manage Black convicts by sentencing them to state-owned prison farms and chain gangs in the long twentieth century. Mississippi sought to abolish its convict leasing system in 1890, giving rise to Parchman Prison Farm in 1901.

The Lomaxes recording expedition mainly took place on prison farms. In addition to labor exploitation, prisoners were subjected to various forms of cruel and unusual punishment on these farms. For instance, Joe Savage and Walter Brown, two Black informants, told Alan about the state-approved instrument of discipline: "the broad leather strap on the bat."[29] At the infamous Parchman Prison Farm, these state mechanisms drew "blisters from the bare flesh with each blow." Joe Savage discussed, "They [prison guards] whupped us with big wide straps. They didn't whup no clothes. They whupped your naked butt. And they had two men to hold you down."[30] Violence and exploitation formed the backdrop of the field recordings.

In Alan's first trip with his dad, they transformed prisons and penitentiaries into living and breathing archives of religious folk songs and oral cultures. These spaces of confinement were presented as sites that protected Black prisoners from so-called modern influences. Alan recycled his father's romantic portrait of prisons and the "penitentiary Negro." While they were totally dependent on technology and science to preserve black folk songs, John Sr. felt that modernization was damaging the pure black folk cultures by creating new sensibilities and motivations of Black southerners. He argued that modern (cosmopolitan) culture was structured on a specific type of Black–white contact that threatened natural and local black folk songs. His view of anti-modern knowledge idealized Jim Crow segregation: "They [Black and white prisoners] are kept in entirely separate units; they even work separately in the fields. Thus, a long-time Negro convict, guarded by Negro trusties, may spend many years with practically no chance of hearing a white man speak or sing."[31] He furthered noted, "Such men slough off the white idiom they may have once employed in their speech and revert more and more to the idiom of the Negro common people." John Sr. felt disdain toward the "modern New Negroes" with their education, cosmopolitanism, and disregard for the folk religious songs of the unlettered and rural black folk. Alan recycled his father's thought about the New Negroes in his critique of Fisk University's Lewis Jones and social scientists in the Coahoma Study.[32] John Sr. said, "At each [prison] camp I heard spirituals hitherto unknown to me. The convicts came from every part of Mississippi, and the best songs of many communities survived among these singing black men." What both John Sr. and Alan overlooked was that their romanticization of the "penitentiary Negro" repeated the very same modern logic that standardized forced Black labor for their production (e.g., extractive and crop products or folk songs). They were dependent on the modern logic of black containment and labor production for the so-called natural and premodern folk songs. The prison farms (and chain gangs) were very much a continuation of the modernization that placed Black labor at the heart of mainstream society through their work in extractive industries and agriculture.

What Alan personally experienced while recording religious songs and customs in small rural small churches, labor camps, and homes were equally duplicated in prison farms and state penitentiaries. What he understood as authentic Black southern churches was shot through his first encounters with the emotional, creative, polyrhythmic, and improvisational prayers, sermons, and spirituals in the state prisons. John Sr., like Alan, highlighted the affective quality that transformed the recording field sessions into an emotive experience that both father and son were not shy to mention in their reflections. For instance, one of their first prison recordings was a "rousing or gravy sermon" at the Darrington Convict Farm, nearly 30 miles outside of Houston. Alan latter referred to "Sin Killer Griffin's 'singing sermon.'"[33] Rev. Sin Killer Griffin was a 75-year-old state chaplain for Black prisoners in the Texas Penitentiary System. When John Sr. notified Griffin that he had permission to record his sermon for present and future generations to hear at the Library of Congress, Griffin responded that he was going to preach his "Calvary sermon." Stationed behind a pulpit between two huge corridors where the inmates were "caged," Griffin pained a creative portrait of the crucifixion: "Lightin' played it limber gauze/ When they nailed Jesus to the rugged Cross;/The mountain began to tremble/When the holy body began to drop blood down upon it/Each little silver star leaped out of its little orbit." John Sr. was captivated by the "force of his voice, the intensity of his appeal," and the enthusiasm that transformed a penitentiary into a religious space through the immediate call-and-response from the inmates: "So-nuff, Sure!" "Amen!" and "Oh, yes!" After listening to his Calvary sermon on the recording machine, John Sr. noted that Griffin responded, "for a long time, I'se been hearing that I'se a good preacher. Now I knows it."

Yet, the singing Black women and men in the Mississippi prison system elicited the most visceral reaction from John Sr., and especially Alan. After they discovered the self-proclaimed "king of de twelve-string guitar players ob de world," Huddie "Lead Belly" Ledbetter, in Louisiana's Angola Prison, both John and Alan arrived at Mississippi State Prison on Sunday where they recorded the "best spirituals" for the federal archive.[34] Arranging the equipment in a large dining hall, the Lomaxes were struck by the "powerful moving" spirituals of the inmates. John Sr. noted, "These faces, some cruel, some crafty, some of them older, all, without expectation, had rapt expressions of intense devotion." John Sr. attributed the beautiful and powerful spirituals to the raw emotions unique to the southern Negroes. These songs were devoid of "self-consciousness and artificiality." Indeed, John noted that his son, Alan, stood "blinking back tears while his body swayed with the rhythm of the songs." His emotional attachment to the folk songs and cultures was constant during his field experience. In the preface of his autobiography, Alan noted that the field recording experience was a "magical moment opening up in time."[35]

Both John and Alan's emotional attachments were extended to the sewing rooms among Black female inmates at the infamous Parchman Prison Farm. John Sr. noted that the soul-stirring songs, e.g., "Hearing My Mother Pray Again," "Motherless Child," and "So Soon, So Soon, I'll Be at Home," erased any trace of "evil" implied in their alleged acts of murder.[36] According to John Sr., the Black women sang old-standard hymns in a peculiar long meter rhythm that was punctuated by low moans held to "breathless length." The exhausted axe- and hoe-toting male inmates also encapsulated the folk idiom in their singing of "Hell and Heaven": "I been 'buked an' I been scorned,/Childrens, I been 'buked an' I been scorned,/Childrens, I been 'buked an' I been scorned,/I been talked 'bout sure as you're been born." Not a stranger to heart-stirring spirituals and hymns due to his experiences with "zealous [white] Methodists" in summer camp meetings in his Texas community, John Sr. said he had never heard the spirituals that were performed in the Mississippi State Prison and Parchman Prison Farm.[37] After these visits, both father and son concluded that the best spirituals came out of the Mississippi Delta.

The recording expedition in 1933 piqued Alan's fascination with what he later called "old-time religion" among southern rural Blacks. This first expedition disclosed how Alan's interest in the religious songs and experiences of Black rural southerners was initially cultivated by his father's own Old South pastoral romanticism. Raised on a frontier farm in Bosque County, Texas, John's pursuit of these informal religious expressions was prompted by his romantic yearning for an idyllic rural or agrarian paradise. Like many Americans whose lives were disrupted by the rapid industrial change beginning in the nineteenth century, his father's nostalgia privileged these agrarian settings—plantations, prison farms, and lumber camps—over and above the artificial urban environment. His pastoral romanticism accounted for his association of the religious sounds of rural Black southerners with uncontaminated natural locations. After listening intently to a "handsome mulatto" sing "Deep River," he noted, "To me and Alan, there were a depth, grace, and beauty in this spiritual; quiet power and dignity, and a note of weird, almost uncanny suggestion of turbid, slow-moving rivers in African jungle."[38] John's listening habits were part of a larger American tradition in which primitive, rural, and strenuous living functioned as a pathway to distinct authentic national culture. But more importantly, John's "anti-modern modernist" pastoralism was also deeply tied to Old South romantic portrait by singing Black prisoners and white guards and law enforcers in rural regions.

To be sure, Alan was influenced by his father's Old South pastoral romanticism and cultivated a disdain for the impact of modernization on the religious experiences of Black laborers in the American South. This is not to mention that both John Sr. and Alan were representative of the very modern culture that they seemingly deplored, especially with their technological equipment and commodification of the music in discs and books. John Sr. and Alan established market relations with the prison singers that commodified the folk songs through selling

books, records, and concerts. Moreover, the technology and commercialism were both prone to debates regarding the recording and
sale of folk sounds. John W. Work extended the debates about musical
production and technology when he complained that phonograph record companies modified the folk sermons for "light entertainment"
purposes.

What John Sr. and later Alan often overlooked was how their field
recordings of folk religious songs in these supposedly remote prison
farms were "artificially" arranged within modern forms of power and
domination. There was nothing pure or unmediated about their field
recordings. Historian Alex Lichtenstein reminds us that since Radical
Reconstruction, both carpetbaggers and old planters were united
in their use of Black prison laborers in their plot to industrialize the
New South. But both John Sr. and Alan accentuated the natural, un-
consciousness, raw emotion of spirituals, betraying intricate power dynamics and relations in their fieldwork. Father and son ignored how
their professional affiliation with the federal Library of Congress gave
them access to the prison farms and state penitentiaries that normally
others could not access. They could gain entrance by flashing their
signed documents from the federal government. The signed federal
documents gave them power that actually shaped the arrangements of
the recording exercises. With their federal support, the prisoners were
often *forced* to perform the so-called folk religion and blues. There was
nothing natural or unself-conscious about the folk spirituals. At the
Parchman Prison Farm, inmates were actually forced to sing so-called
natural folk songs for the Lomaxes in the late night hours after a full
day of labor in the fields that usually began at 4 a.m. John described the
Parchman prisoners: "The male convicts work from 4 am until dark.
"Thus our chance at them ["Negro male convicts"] comes only during
the noon hour and at night before the men are sent to their bunks for
sleep, at nine o'clock." He remarked that the men were "timid, suspi-
cious, and sometimes stubborn."[39] John stated, "In other instances,
a guard forced an inmate to sing the devil music after the guard was
told that the inmate did not know any blues or 'reels'" to protect the
inmate's relationship to his Protestant faith. For instance, the prison
guards forced "Black Samson," a prisoner, to sing "sinful" tunes for
John and Alan despite his insistence that he "got religion." Before he
sang the sinful work tune, he "closed his eyes and prayed: Oh Lord,

I knows I'se doin wrong. I cain't help myself. I'se down here in the worl', and I'se gotter do what dis white man tells me. I hopes You unnerstan's the situation an' won't blame me for what I gotter do. Amen!"[40] On another note, focusing on these remote environments that supposedly helped to preserve natural folk song allowed them to ignore the many reasons why Black inmates decided to sing into the recording machine in the first place. The prisoners rarely benefited from their performed spirituals and other songs. The motives of the prisons actually showed that they were never folk in the first place. Often Black prisoners were under the impression that if they sung in the recording machine for the "big Washington men," they would be released from prison. After beginning his 21-year sentence, "Black Samson" performed the "sinful song" and asked John Sr.: "Boss, cain't yo help git outa dis place [prison farm]." Due to John and Alan's status with the Library of Congress, the field experience and consequently the folk religious songs were everything but remote and natural. The folk religious and blues songs were manipulated in conditions of state power that both father and son extended in their fieldwork. Prisoners also sought to advance their motives and desires in their participation in the exchange with the father and son folklorist duo.

The listening habits and preservation activity of father and son also revealed their stark political differences. Alan's anti-modern sentiment in his hunting for folk songs was deliberately wedded to his leftist politics. Influenced by the labor strikes in Harlan, Kentucky, Gastonia, North Carolina, and Birmingham, Alabama, and the emerging working-class movements and popular front, 18-year-old Alan had already started to draw a connection between the power and beauty of the religious songs and experiences of Black southern workers and the misery caused by white supremacy. Reflecting over his state of mind on his first recording expedition, he noted: "the powerful voices of the convicts blended and lifted their song like a black marble roof tree raised upon shining columns of onyx harmony. They were singing out of abject misery and utter despair, yet the sound was so majestic." He imagined that the so-called [Black] "murderers, rapists, and gunmen were individual gestures of protest against the harshness and deprivation of black life in Niggertown and in the quarters." Of course, he had to keep these opinions hidden from his father, who "had sympathy for the Negro prisoners and a genuine concern for Black welfare, [but he] believed in the overall beneficence of the Southern system." Yet his father definitely knew that his son, like most college students, appreciated Marxism and had developed an interest in labor unions and protest movements, especially the coal miners' strike in Harlan, Kentucky.[41]

During the recording expedition in 1933, a frustrated John noted that his poor son wanted to set all the Black inmates free. It was after his first expedition that Alan sought to extend his father's understanding of the "folk or the real people, the plain people, devoid of tinsel and glamour" to the concept of the proletariat.[42] This merger was made particularly plain when both father and son traveled to a small dirt-floor church at the Smithers plantation and a sharecropper "spoke into the recorded horn." "Now, Mr. President, you just don't know how bad they're treating us folks down here. I'm singing to you and I'm talking to you so I hope you will come down here and do something for us poor folks here in Texas."[43] Reference to the newly elected Franklin Roosevelt and subsequent New Deal programs captured the historical spirit in which Alan merged his passion for the authentic folk songs of the southern Black Protestant culture to his left-leaning politics in order to re-establish the "official" American cultures through the lives of what Roosevelt called the "forgotten man." While John's love for the old-time spirituals underscored his attachment to the old planta-tion South, Alan's attachment was indicative of the political climate, sparked by the Depression and World War II. But despite their political differences, both father and son had a shared cultural knowledge that colored what they deemed the real folk songs and cultures supposedly removed from modern culture. They both fell prey to a romantic prim-itivism that produced a historically static and isolated population in their view of the fixed and standard modern monoculture. John Sr. and Alan represented modernization in reverse.

Southern Black Protestantism and New Deal

Alan Lomax continued to work for the Library of Congress and added to its archive. He formed a constitutive part of the Washington bu-reaucratic folklorists and culturalists that included his father, Sterling

Brown, B. A. Botkin, Charles Seeger, and others. After his 1933 expedition, Alan joined both Columbia University English professor
Elizabeth Barnicle and famed folklorist Zora Hurston on an expedition to Georgia and Florida, where they collected Black folk songs
and cultures. He continued to enhance the archives at the Library of
Congress with his hunting of ring-shouts, children's game songs,
chanteys, rushing songs, anthems, sermons, and prayers from the Sea
Islands, Belles Glades, Nassau, and Port-au-Prince. Although Alan
Lomax emphasized the American nature of Black folk cultures, in the
later twentieth century, he gradually grew more and more certain that
songs and cultures were part of the broader African diaspora. By 1937,
he was appointed to assistant in charge of the Archive of American
Folk Song at the Library of Congress, which solidified his status as
America's foremost authority on folk music. Moreover, his authority
extended to the wider cultural apparatus. While in charge of the collection, he was chief producer on folk music series for the American
School on Air with the Columbia Broadcast System in 1939, as well as
the Rockefeller-funded Experimental Radio Project in 1941.

   Alan's folk-song hunting was made possible by New Deal cultural nationalism. The Roosevelt administration extended the Works Progress
Administration (WPA) to the artistic, musical, theatrical, and literary
fields (otherwise known as Federal One). This extension gave rise to
the various cultural bureaucracies, such as the Federal Arts Project,
Federal Writers' Project, Federal Theatre Project, and Resettlement
Administration. Even with the 1933 Public Works Administration, art
and culture played a fundamental role in New Deal America. For instance, the visual arts—particularly photography—was a major part in
the Farm Security Administration, designed to personalize the effects
of the Depression and to provide a snapshot of the intimate worlds of
the ordinary working communities on farms and in factories.[44] On
one level, these cultural bureaucracies were simply designed to employ
budding actors, painters, writers, and musicians. Local branches of the
Federal Writers' Project extended the "writer occupation" to librarians,
typists, white-collar professionals (e.g., lawyers), and students who
contributed to the State Guide Series books. But on a deeper level,
these cultural programs played an important part in New Deal liberalism that sought to rethink American national identity away from the

Anglo-Saxon and Protestant nativism dominant in the Progressive era. Although Alan has been associated with the Popular Front, he contributed to the New Deal cultural nationalism by focusing his folk collection on the creativity of the multi-racial and lower working-class group who stood in dire need of state welfare. He extended American cultural nationalism and music to the dustbowl ballads of Woody Guthrie, the mountain songs of Aunt Molley, the blues songs of Lead Belly, and the spirituals of the original Soul Stirrers in Texas farm fields, the levee, turpentine, and labor camps, and wooden domestic shacks and churches. Even Franklin and Eleanor Roosevelt personally contributed to the New Deal cultural liberalism. In the summer of 1939, President Roosevelt and the First Lady hosted King George VI and Queen Elizabeth at the White House for an evening of American folk songs, such as the Black spirituals, cowboy ballads, and Appalachian mountain songs. Alan Lomax joined the festivities by singing cowboy ballads. The *New York Times* reported, "A broad composite picture of the music Americans love and sing was presented in a widely diversified program for King George and Queen Elizabeth at the White House musicale tonight."[45] The reporter's concentration on the songs of the miners, farmers, lumberjacks, and workers of all kinds illustrated the discovery of the folk roots of American culture and a celebration of its diverse demographic. This symbolic celebration "had become the new basis for a new style of patriotism celebrating America."[46] Moreover, the methods of oral history and field ethnography were part of the documentary impulse and took on new meaning in the New Deal administration's commitments to the ordinary or forgotten populations in "remote" and "poor" places in the South.

Southern folk songs and broader culture played a significant role in the Roosevelt administration's aims to shed light on the "forgotten man." Following Sterling Brown and other culturalists, Alan took pains to show the broader white public that these folk songs underscored how Blacks, in particular, contributed to the American national culture. During the New Deal, the federal cultural programs sought to redefine American cultural nationalism on the basis of the multi-racial, ordinary lower- and working-class population(s). According to historian Jerrold Hirsch, a cadre of individuals, composed of a liberal American intelligentsia, sought to revitalize national American culture through an embrace of cultural difference beyond provincialism.[47] These culturalists were involved with New Deal cultural programs and helped espouse a romantic cultural nationalism that was grounded in a kind of pluralism. Moreover, these liberal intellectuals earnestly thought these federal cultural and artistic programs could significantly alter the racial perceptions of the American white public. With a faith in the power of culture, these bureaucrats understood these federal arts and cultural programs to be representative of New Deal racial policies.

This is why the documentary of religion took on new forms in New Deal America. Building on cultural modernism, the focus of New Deal liberals, as well as the Popular Cultural Front, on forgotten and marginal populations helped to expand how religious cultures were located and assessed. The heavy emphasis on the working-class populations in these local regions sought to validate and democratize religion beyond conventional settings, authoritarians, and abstract or formal theologies. In fact, we might say that the documentary impulse under New Deal America gave way to a preoccupation with local customs and practices over and against doctrine and national religious structure. Alan's attention to authentic rural Black southern Protestantism was part of the documentary impulse in which different state bureaucrats gave their attentions to what might be considered folk or marginal religions—Spiritualists, Holiness, Pentecostals, conjure, and others—in the American South, especially. In *Picturing Faith*, Colleen McDannell argues that the New Deal and World War II created a bridge between the unchurched and the churched. Alan, like other federal workers, documented and consequently gave religious minorities an honored place in the national story. For instance, the Louisiana Writers' Project covered Black Spiritualism in New Orleans. The Georgia Writers' Project examined the conjure coupled with the Peace Mission and United All House of Prayer in Savannah. Alan Lomax was linked to a cadre of unchurched secular humanists who were not necessarily affiliated with any traditional faith-based community or a set of conventional religious commitments. Rather, he, like other "secular humanists," remained interested, and somewhat moved, by what the religious expressions and experiences communicated about the spirit of the lower- and working-class Black communities in rural settings. In fact, the lines between religious and nonreligious often broke down

in the field, as Alan was moved to tears, goosebumps, and other physiological affects while recording the religious expressions of rural
Blacks in the South. Like other federal workers, Alan documented
and consequently gave "religious minorities an honored place in the
national story" by housing their practices in the federal archives and
published books.

Alan Lomax's focus on the songs and emotive religious experiences
of rural Black Protestantism was deeply informed by his progressive,
left-of-center political commitments. Michael Denning and other
leftist historians often overlooked the role of religious songs in the
ways in which the cultural left shaped their collection of the cultures of
the folk.[48] Alan argued that the religious expressions were not merely
compensatory or fatalistic, like Charles S. Johnson and other racial
liberals opined. Rather, he wanted to communicate that the religious
experiences of rural farmers were deeply relative to how these communities confronted their exploitative environments and maintained
their vibrant religious cultures. Later, in 1941, at Arafat Church, which
was on the King and Anderson Plantation, Alan recorded an old-time
spiritual about Daniel in the lion's den. Before the spiritual, Brother
Joiner, an informant, remarked, "It takes Daniel for a reference. Daniel
went through the same troubles that we are going through down here.
Daniel was persecuted, put in the lion's den." In this sense, Daniel became a symbolic medium for the sharecroppers, representing the
abject poverty of the Mississippi Delta. Although the sermon was entitled "Payday in Heaven," informant Rev. Savage's guttural and roaring
sermon, according to Alan, was a protest against two main problems
ailing his congregants: "the racial caste system and poverty, rooted
in segregation and dishonest economic system." Alan interpreted the
highly emotive quality of old-time religion as a direct response to the
conditions of race and class exploitation in the rural South.

Yet the federal archive of rural Black religious and cultural songs was
shot through with his romantic "anti-modern modernism." Alan's se-
lection of which songs made it into the archive was based on his subjective criteria of what constituted pure and uncontaminated folk songs.
Unlike folklorist B. A. Botkin and, more like his father, Alan ascribed
to the modern binaries of rural and urban, natural and modern, that
defined how he classified the folk Protestantism of rural Black workers.

His replication of modern binaries recycled the common view that rural Black workers were static, homogenous, and marginal to the "urban" mainstream. If he was seeking to preserve the vibrant, resilient, and beautiful religious songs and experiences of the rural Black southerners, he nevertheless rehearsed the modernization project of the folk category that differentiated rural and urban, lower and professional populations on the basis of perceived styles, behaviors, and cultures. Again, his romanticism slipped into a misrecognition of the rural Black religious cultures that linked him to the liberal reformers that he later criticized. Alan's replication of the anti-modernism that he picked up from his dad was most evident in the Coahoma Study with Fisk University in 1941 and 1942. And his anti-modernism explains his disappointment with the religious cultures of Blacks who, in his mind, had abandoned their natural and authentic southern Protestantism for a modern faith.

Alan Lomax's Disappointment in Clarksdale

The Coahoma Study began in the summer of 1941, and it ended in an ideological clash about the "Plantation Blacks" and their cultures. Alan Lomax, Lewis Jones, John W. Work, Samuel Adams, and Ulysses Young all worked together to study Black communities in Coahoma County. But the center of the disagreement between Alan Lomax and the affiliates of Fisk University revolved around the issue of modernization in the northwest region of Mississippi. Specifically, the source of tension was the secularization or urbanization of Clarksdale and its impact on what they collectively called the "plantation Negro." Clarksdale had won the battle of the county seat in Coahoma due to the establishment of railroad transportation that transformed the county into a trading and commercial center. The presence of the railroad beat out the other counties, like Sunflower, whose transportation and trade were still organized by the river. But the coming of the railroad, coupled with land loans, connected Coahoma County's Delta cotton to urban markets in Memphis and New Orleans. Building the railroads helped to generate a commercial and entertainment district that included the Savoy Theatre, Sander's Drug Store, Messenger's

Pool Room and Café, and Dipse Doodle, on Fourth, Issaquena, and Sunflower Streets. Also, Jones and his advisee Adams documented the class division within Black life, such as a petit-professional and business class. The Black business district contributed to a new "consciousness of race" after World War I. The different fraternal lodges were part of the race consciousness of Blacks in Clarksdale: Pythians, Order of Todor, and the Odd Fellows. But both Lewis and Adams also noted how the building of the highway furthered modernized the Blacks and consequently the obliteration of their so-called old folk culture.

Lewis Jones and Fisk University students' primary aim was to examine the processes of social change in the Mississippi Delta. They collectively described these processes of social and cultural change as the acculturation of plantation Blacks into urban society. Under the advisement of Jones, Adams later stated in his master's thesis that the "[s]outh [was a] more integral part of the national economy, the old plantation system is rapidly collapsing."[49] Acculturation was most evident in the labor conditions on the neighborhood plantations. In the fall of 1941, Adam and anthropology fellow Young stayed on the King and Anderson Plantation for a couple of months. Established at the height of the cotton boom, the King and Anderson Plantation was one of the largest plantations in the Mississippi Delta region. The plantation was 7,000 acres. Owned by white owners, J. W. King and J. A. Anderson, the plantation included an agricultural high school, commissary, churches, community centers, and one- and two-room cabin homes for the predominantly Black tenant farmers and sharecroppers. During the 1940s, both King and Anderson were worried because their predominantly Black workers were leaving the cotton fields for Jackson, Chicago, or other urban cities. At the time of the study, Adams paid close attention to the changes of the labor conditions on the plantation. In the aftermath of the New Deal state, the plantations were engaged in mechanized agricultural labor, with tractors, flame weeders, and air spray. Additionally, Adams also noted that plantations were accessible to the county agricultural and home demonstration agents. Lewis Jones highlighted how mechanization created more time for leisure in Clarksdale's entertainment district. Leisure was made possible by the move from labor-intensive to capital techniques in the farming industry. Alan Lomax made sure to note that elderly Blacks were dissatisfied with the mechanization. Although he was on a different plantation, Phineas Maclean, a sharecropper informant, complained, according to Alan Lomax, that the tractor "machine broke [his] land, plant[ed] it, plow[ed] it," and left him standing around with "nothin to do."[50]

But Fisk University sociologists were more invested in outlining the impact of urbanization on Black Protestantism in Coahoma County. They saw that access to Clarksdale (and its broader urban markets) decentered the primacy of the church in community life. Adams argued that the "development of science," coupled with "places of amusement," impacted the traditional status of Black churches in the social community. In fact, he used the phrase "secular transition" to note how the "city ecology and social forces" signaled a movement away from the "sacred."[51] Here, they recorded how ministers were leery of social change that reportedly threatened their authority. Fisk University sociologists noted that religious leaders were decrying that "secular institutions" (e.g., burial societies and places of amusement) were decentralizing churches. Samuel Adams asserted that one pastor was against the agricultural farm agent's method that bred new hogs. They reported how city life expanded their access to other public institutions, which Blacks were selecting over Protestant membership. Adams documented that 20 of the 100 families on the plantation were not affiliated with a church, and that "not all families on the church roll participated in the church programs actively." For instance, an informant noted that she was part of the burial society against the Protestant church because the society actually enforced the laws and regulations. But the secularization was also documented in the ways that younger people "satirized" the church in their songs. In the end, sociologists championed secularization because they believed these processes expanded the mental and cultural horizons of Black laborers. In short, secularization, these Fisk crew felt, ignited their social and cultural development.

Lewis Jones, Samuel Adams, and John W. Work all noted that the folk songs, especially spirituals, were fading from the cultural life of the tenant farmers and sharecroppers in Coahoma County. Both Jones and

Adams argued that the folk songs gave way to the secular blues songs in that the blues directly addressed the changing urban environment. The writers based their observations on the informants who made a distinction between the folk spirituals and blues as they pertained to the latter's lifestyle. Muddy Waters said he had a desire to "join" a church, but the idea of having to give up the so-called devil's instrument (his guitar) was not a sacrifice he was willing to make. Yet he also knew that the Saturday night revelers also attended Sunday church service, too. As products of the Chicago School, Fisk University social scientists replicated Robert Park's distinction between folk spirituals and blues that was based on the rural and urban binary. Adams also discovered social songs, like those about Adolph Hitler, that revealed that the plantation Blacks were attentive to outside worldly events via newspapers and radio. But more to Alan's dismay, Adams found out that almost half of his informants enjoyed and knew popular (or radio) musicians such as Count Basie, Memphis Mimie, Rosetta Tharpe, Mary Lou Williams, and the Golden Gate Quartet. Access to the city accelerated the popularity of jazz and gospel music in Coahoma County. This appreciation for popular musicians, according to Adam, was due to the fact that 50 of his 100 families on the King and Anderson Plantation owned radios.

Alan Lomax was at pains to identify continuity over and against change. He made sure he mentioned the continuity in Coahoma County that the Fisk University sociologists ignored. Later, he occasionally noted that the Delta sharecroppers and tenant farmers maintained their African agricultural skills in the Delta region. For him, the continuity of their African cultures was further preserved due to Jim Crow segregation that prevented contact between the races. Yet his attention to the continuity was connected to his resistance to cultural dynamism and change that the Fisk University sociologists dramatized during the fieldwork. His attention to continuity reflected his own commitments and projections. For instance, he equated change in religious music (like gospel) to [white] modern imitation. Clarksdale presented a real problem for him. Where Lewis Jones documented the gospel sounds, Alan Lomax saw European imitation and bad music at the Baptist Convention. To him, gospel was a marker of urban white cosmopolitan culture. This culture was represented in the songbook, choir director, soloists, and the privileging of harmony or notation over and against sound effect. He worried about the fate of the folk spirituals with the rise of gospel and other popular music. The Baptist Convention in Clarksdale added to his disappointment. Both Fisk University sociologists and Alan Lomax were at a modern impasse in Clarksdale.

But Alan Lomax found what he had been searching for among rural Black farmers away from the commercial district. Underneath his progressive politics, he still understood folk songs as what folk-lorist B. A. Botkins noted as "vestigial" or a "fossil of culture," rather than "germinal," like "germ plasma."[52] In this sense, he was closer to his father's fossilized view of the folk than to the views of Botkins or John W. Work. Alan Lomax headed for the plantations on the outskirts of the Clarksdale. Similar to his view of the prison farms, the planta-tion space was an imaginative place that was considered a goldmine for folk song collectors. He failed to understand how Clarksdale and the surrounding plantations were intimately tied together. He also enjoyed the folk spirituals accompanied by the religious experiences on planta-tions. John W. Work joined Lomax on the field expedition to the plan-tations, where they attended church services. Work interestingly noted that the songs were performed upon request from him and Lomax.

Alan Lomax frequented Arafat Baptist Church on the King and Anderson Plantation with Lewis Jones. Arafat Church was a one-story, white wooden building with a steep bell tower. Alan Lomax used his own emotional response as the barometer for what constituted natural and authentic folk spirituals and long-meter Watts hymns. He later re-flected that he listened to the old "hallahs" with wonder and amaze-ment. Both Lewis and Alan arrived in the middle of the service, while women clad in white uniforms were restraining a woman who just "got religion." They also arrived in time to listen to Rev. Savage's "guttural" or "roaring sermon" that discussed the "pay day in heaven" in opposi-tion to the "dishonest" tenant farming system on the plantation. His sermon sent the congregants into a "frenzy." But the treat was after the service, when some of the older congregants sang the "folk" spirituals. Again, his use of the natural spirituals ignored how the recording ses-sions of the older congregants after church service were arranged. Alan marveled at "Brother Joiner," who sang first about Daniel in a "deep groaning voice" while the other members accompanied him with the refrain. Both Joiner and company "swayed" their bodies until a woman in the group took over and sang about David in the bible. The group even performed a lined Dr. Watts hymn under the direction of Rev. Savage. Subsumed under his "anti-modern modernism," Alan Lomax later described the voices, the folk spirituals, and the hymns with nature analogies—like "seaweed, waves, leafy-like, river-like, riverlike, or liquid."[53] These metaphors were intentionally designed to highlight the natural, over and against the artificialities of gospels in urban America (and Clarksdale more specifically).

Alan Lomax's fossilized view of culture was fully displayed in his observation of a Church of God in Christ (COGIC) congregation. Lomax and John Work called attention to the dancing, stomping, and clapping of the congregants. They mentioned the spiritual gifts of tongues while recording. Work jotted down that the spirituals made up the core of their service. Alan documented the predominantly female congregants, with both female and male preachers offering sermons. But Lomax neglected aspects of the COGIC that underscored the diverse musical influences. For instance, they called attention to the instruments—the guitar, tambourine, and piano—that had been popular in other musical genres and the commercial industry. Work even described the instruments as "jazzy." Work noted the "orchestra" that played songs, like the "boggie-woggie at its hottest." Other field workers observed how Black Pentecostals played renditions of the popular radio shows. Another part that Lomax missed was the fact that the COGIC composed their spirituals. What Lomax ignored was that other factors posed a challenge to his view of the so-called fossilized folk expressions. For instance, the influx of visiting preachers, gospel choirs, and college-trained composers all contributed to the COGIC spirituals and other religious expressions. Additionally, he also overlooked the simple fact that Blacks had access to Memphis that shaped the spirituals and other expressions. His brand of anti-modernism reduced the complexity of the Black Protestantism as marginal to urban cultures. These Black Protestants in the cotton South were not removed modern culture.

Conclusion

Alan Lomax's romanticism got the best of him. It blinded him from seeing that rural Blacks were already wedded to the commercial, cosmopolitan, and urban cultures that he claimed were contaminating folk religious cultures. The cultural industry was already incorporating those music cultures that he framed as its antithesis. The informants already knew about the world beyond the Mississippi plantations and participated in it, first from the Delta region and then later in the north. They knew that the experimental spirituals, chanted sermons, gospel, and jazz were at the center of the modern commercial world that Muddy Waters and other Delta farmers participated in. What was even more interesting was that Alan Lomax had altered the culture that he claimed to preserve, and facilitated its commodification in the cultural industry. He recorded, printed, photographed, and archived these songs out of their so-called local context, which later culminated in the folk revival that was so central to white baby boomers in the counterculture movement of the 1960s. Either there is no such thing as modern, or these so-called Black rural people were at the center of the modern. The nature and culture split that grounded anti-modernism was a false one. The inmate informants on the prison farms and state penitentiaries were under the impression that Lomax would grant their release should they perform the so-called natural and authentic folk religious or secular religious songs. The folk and modern dyad overlooked the networks that linked communities, farm and urban regions, religion and cultures, and technologies together. In the end, Alan Lomax had replicated the same modern logics as liberal researchers and reformers that simplified the religions and cultures of the rural Black in the Delta.

Conclusion

The Aftermath of the Religion of the Southern Folk

In the June 1986 issue of *The Atlantic Monthly*, famed journalist Nicholas Lemann published the first installment in a two-part series of articles on the "Origins of the Underclass."[1] Lemann joined an ongoing and popular debate about the Black poor that started to receive attention in American politics after the former Secretary of Labor, Daniel Patrick Moynihan, released *The Negro Family: The Case for National Action*, in 1965.[2] Lemann also deployed the concept of the black underclass to frame the debates about the Black poor in urban America. A variety of critics participated in debates about the black underclass across the conservative-liberal divide. The term "underclass" was popularized by neoconservative political scientist Charles Murray, who identified a permanent lower-level class with deviant behaviors (unemployment, crime, and broken families).[3] Sociologist William Julius also identified this lower-level class. Yet Wilson revived the liberal understanding of the underclass category of the late 1960s (à la Kenneth Clark, Lee Rainwater, and Patrick Moynihan) by attributing their deviant behaviors to the changing economy after World War II. Under Ronald Reagan's presidency, Lemann explained the origins of the category by focusing on the South Side of Chicago, with special attention to residents in the Robert Taylor Holmes housing project Similar to Wilson, Lemann mentioned that 51% of Blacks in Chicago were living below the poverty line, 24.2% were unemployed, 72% of the households were headed by women; 75% of children were born out of wedlock, and 33,000 out of 54,000 residents were on welfare.[4] During his visit, he described the South Side as teeming with illegitimacy, gang violence, and school dropouts.

To Know the Soul of a People. Jamil W. Drake, Oxford University Press. © Oxford University Press 2022.
DOI: 10.1093/oso/9780190082680.003.0007

Lemann outlined both liberal and neoconservative arguments about the origins and solutions to the underclass problem in American cities. The liberals attributed the acceleration of the underclass to unemployment. He noted that liberals explained that the "lack of jobs caused young men in the ghetto to adopt drifting, inconstant life; to turn to crime to engage in exaggeratedly macho behavior." On the other hand, neoconservatives felt that welfare programs extended in Lyndon Johnson's Great Society made the black underclass "dependent on government checks and favors." Accordingly, the state did not foster incentives to work. Both sides continued the long history of framing class in behavioral and cultural terms. These perspectives persist in America.

But Lemann argued that both liberal and neoconservative perspectives did not penetrate the root of the problem. Unemployment or welfare did not capture the power of a "distinctive culture" that was the "greatest barrier to progress." Mentioning Oscar Lewis's "culture of poverty," the journalist considered the underclass problem to be anthropological in nature. Lemann asserted that the problem "emphasiz[ed] the power over people's behaviors that culture, as opposed to economic incentives can have."[5] He highlighted the power of a "separate and self-sustaining ghetto culture" *isolated* from American mainstream values and cultures. After the civil rights legislation, he asserted that working-class Blacks had moved out of the ghettos to the suburbs and had assimilated into middle-class culture in the late 1960s and early 1970s. He argued that middle- and working-class Blacks took full advantage of the civil rights legislation and left the underclass wallowing in the deindustrialized cities.[6] According to Leman, the migration of these working-class Black families and vibrant institutions (e.g., churches and civic organizations) took certain middle-class values with them to the suburbs. In his follow-up to the first article, published a month later in July 1986, he noted that "[o]f the millions of black Americans who have risen from poverty to middle class since the mid-sixties, virtually all have done so by embracing bourgeois values and leaving the ghetto."[7]

Most interesting was where he placed the cultural origins of the urban underclass in Chicago and broader urban America. For Lemann, the origins of the urban underclass lay in the American

South. He asserted that both liberals and conservatives overlooked the "rural-South heritage." He noted that the "underclass culture in the ghettos [was] directly traceable to roots in the South." Not the South of slavery, the journalist stressed, but "of a generation ago." The Black underclass in the North was the first "nascent underclass of the sharecropper South." The journalist looked to an obvious state where many Black Chicagoans had migrated from Mississippi. He interviewed both Blacks and whites from or living in Canton, Mississippi, who exposed him to the southern roots of the urban underclass. They confirmed that the culture of dependency, illegitimacy, poor education, child pregnancy, crime, and female headed-households had beginnings in the rural and small towns in the South that had seeped into the South Side of Chicago. Lemann interviewed Mildred Nicholas, a Black woman, who migrated to Chicago in June 1955, a month after her high school graduation. Working at a nursing home, she attributed her and her family's middle-class success to her two-parent household, coupled with her father's advice on self-pride in Mississippi.[8] She described the underclass persons "who [weren't] able to deal with this society [were] the one's from the deep rural part of the South that had to drop out of school to pick cotton." She further noted that "they had no one to teach them." Nicholas and others were making a comparison between the sharecropping and welfare systems that produced pathological and deficient cultural patterns. While in Canton, Mississippi, Lemann interviewed an old white farmer who told him that he used to take care of his Black sharecroppers by giving them about $20 to $60 a month. He then complained that "they'd always want more money! They were a different class of people!" After mechanization, he had one 66-year-old year old Black sharecropper with lung disease who worked for him from "sunup to sunset and then again at four in the morning."[9] Dependency, broken families, crime, and poor education had a southern precursor to the Black underclass in urban cities in the Midwest and Northeast.

To be sure, the Black underclass had intellectual roots in the late nineteenth and early twentieth centuries. Lemann followed up his reference of W. E. B. Du Bois's 1899 *Philadelphia Negro*, on illegitimacy in the Seventh Ward, with research by E. Franklin Frazier, Gunnar Myrdal, St. Clair Drake, and Horace Clayton in the late 1930s and

1940s. Moreover, he also knew that his claim about the rural-South heritage in the urban underclass did not originate with him or his interviewees. Beyond the social sciences, he referred to the *Chicago Defender*'s pages that featured instructions about the rules and standards of dress and conduct for southern migrants after World War I. But he knew that the social scientists—Gunnar Myrdal and E. Franklin Frazier—had identified the southern origins and meanings that led to the deficient cultures of the Black underclass. For instance, he restated E. Franklin Frazier's observation that the "loosest attitudes toward marriage in turpentine camps, were lower-class Black migrant workers living in rows of cabins deep in the southern forest."[10] Additionally, he followed the Chicago School of sociology's logic of "social disorganization" that partly pinned illegitimacy, female-headed households, crime, deliberate unemployment, and other deviant behavior on the southern migrants' struggles to adjust to urban life. He was definitely influenced by Charles Johnson's early work on Chicago in 1919; and, he repeated Frazier's claim that illegitimacy and the matriarchal family were also attributed to the "persistence in the urban environment of [southern] folkways." To be sure, sociologist Charles Johnson had a separate category for the criminal urban class. But he used "folk" to capture the patterns of the Black southern culture that was fostered in social and economic isolation. The early twentieth-century social sciences contributed to the ideas about the Black poor in American life by identifying deficient southern cultural patterns in the shadows of slavery. Lemann and his interviewees continued the secular "modern" perceptions and arguments about Black southern cultures and behaviors laid out by the social scientists in their field studies in the countryside and small towns and cities in the Lower South.

To Know the Soul of a People has demonstrated the southern roots of the underclass concept that Lemann recycled in his essay. This book has added to the wealth of literature by showing that the social scientific knowledge about southern culture, otherwise known as folk culture, shaped the prevailing ideas about the Black poor in American politics. Before the discussion of an isolated black underclass, social scientists had identified a Black population that supposedly subscribed to certain patterns of behaviors that were presented as isolated from mainstream society. These early twentieth-century social scientists produced modern knowledge that identified the Black poor based on perceived cultural behaviors that were out of sync with American progress. I have demonstrated the importance of religion in the discourse about the Black poor. Moreover, the use of "folk" in the social scientific study of religion was rooted in liberal ideas of modernity that classified and defined the Black poor as outside the flow of mainstream American thoughts, values, morals, and behaviors. Focusing on study of the religion of the folk in the social sciences and liberal reform brings to light the southern and rural roots of the latter Black underclass. Additionally, it also brings into view the moral and cultural frameworks that animated discussions about race, class, and poverty in the twentieth century.

Nicholas Lemann's and his interviewees' presentation of the rural-southern heritage was nothing new under the sun. They simply replicated the folk category in the social scientific heritage of the early twentieth century. Lemann and others recycled the category by rehearsing the claim that the Black poor were constituted by their removal from the proper, good, or standard "bourgeoisie values" of the modern populations. The values were partly measured by their utility to the American economy. These early twentieth-century social scientists laid the intellectual foundations for Lemann's and other later bureaucrats' and experts' discussions about a separate, self-sustaining, isolated, and peculiar culture of the Black poor that framed public perceptions, policies, and programs. Moreover, what became known as deficient or pathological behaviors, such as dysfunctional families, illegitimate children, and ignorant individuals, emerged out of the social scientists' construction of southern folk cultures and lifeways in the "hinterlands."

The category of the folk in the early social sciences exposes the logic underneath liberal reform. This logic sought to alter the conduct of the Black lower class to American work and economic norms and standards. It was no accident that Lemann recommended policies and programs that could *discipline* the Black underclass in accordance with standard bourgeois values.[11] Lemann and the postwar liberal social scientists all recommended policy solutions that could correct the conduct of the Black poor. He noted a wealth of religious and federal organizations and programs—Catholic parochial schools, the Nation of

Islam, Project Head Start, and/or Parent-Teacher Associations—that could "help make the ghettos bloom again [by] creating a new, healthy, indigenous culture." These early social scientists' study of a distinct yet "bad" southern folk culture made it possible for policymakers, scientists, and pundits to note that "the best solution [would] be one that attacks their cultural as well as their economic problems."[12] This book demonstrates that the early twentieth-century research on folk culture of Black southerners promoted political solutions that sought to reform the Black poor through moral and cultural discipline. The folk category bolstered the idea that policies and programs should introduce and standardize them according to "mainstream culture."[13] Ideas about the Black poor show that moralizing is a constitutive part of American reform and politics.

This book historicizes the dangers of the ideas of race, class, and poverty in American thought. The dangers that have led to moralizing poverty have focused more on acculturating the Black poor into a mainstream culture than on the inequality that sits at the heart of its economy. The culture problem at the crux of earnest yet short-sighted liberal social scientists and reformers has played itself out in America's obsession with changing Black behaviors while leaving the political economy intact. Lemann showed this ugly obsession when he privileged discipline with his recommendation to create "enterprising zones" in the ghettos. This was Trinidadian-American sociologist Oliver Cox's point about liberals' tendency to moralize the race and class problem, while failing to critically examine the economy. The problem with the folk category underscored this dilemma in liberal social sciences. And this early culture dilemma showed its ugly face in the latter half of the twentieth century, from Richard Nixon's law and order policies, to Ronald Reagan's "welfare queen" trope and slash of the welfare state, Bill Clinton's Personal Responsibilities and Work Opportunities Reconciliation bill, and Paul Ryan's Expanding Opportunity in America program.

It is impossible to discuss morality and values in America without discussing religion. Religion has been a central part of the nation's attempt to flesh out its most cherished morals and values. Moreover, this book has given the intellectual roots of the creation of an immoral or amoral racial and economic population that foreshadows the devolutionary programs that caused policymakers and experts to turn to religious communities to aid governments in reforming the poor. We see how the social scientific study of religion was a central form of knowledge used to establish American morality and evaluate and govern the Black poor. These social scientists presumed that the concept of bad (or folk) and good religion was central to examining a population's moral and social development and capacities in the economy. This book claims that the modern discipline of Black religion grew out of concerns about the southern folk or the growing lower and working classes who were supposedly devoid of industrial morality. The social scientists invented categories—superstitions, emotionalism, otherworldliness, child-like, or simplistic—that helped to foreground folk religion and consequently contributed to the knowledge about the deficient Black poor. The making of folk and southern religion was used to frame the modern problem of a population. In the professional sciences, religion was a tool responsible for creating cultural difference and sanctioning hierarchy. Religion was also a modern study that contributed to solidifying behavioral standards designed to govern the conduct of populations. But more importantly, these social scientists showed how the study of religion was central to assessing the moral and social development of a population. The study also structured the moral logics informing liberal research and reform.

Folk religion emerged out of liberal researchers who had contributed to the notion of right moral and modern conduct. These moral underpinnings informed their understanding of technological, medical, and economic progress. What contemporary scholars often overlook is how these social scientists' decision to study the religion of the Black southern lower class was not only because it played a central role in their lived experiences. But this decision also underscored the privileging of morals and values within liberal reform that support social and economic growth of a population and the broader nation. Often overlooked in liberal sciences and reform is the importance they placed on moral norms that mediated their secular claims about science, medicine and health, work, and industry. Their attention to religion underscored how liberal democracy and science were just as much a focus on moral norms as truth and freedom. Essentially, their study of the folk religion was meant to demonstrate how a population was devoid of morals compatible with industrial society. What religion adds to the knowledge about the Black poor is the nature and function of morality in American democracy. Moral conduct was a central target within liberal reform. In the end, the knowledge of the poor intersected with liberal scientists' making of folk religion (and southern folk). Morality was rooted in market and economic logics.

A history of the folk religion underscored the problem of class in the field of Black religion. Oftentimes, the modern logic underneath the category is replicated when certain beliefs and practices are classed in the discipline. Why are "emotional" preaching, singing, worshipping, and other practices representatives of the Black lower class? How did this come to be? To be sure, this is not to suggest that certain people of lower economic resources did not perform these practices. But classification is not innocent. Rather, it has been loaded with prescriptive norms that fail to see how religious practices span the gamut of different classes in Black religious life. What I show is that regulating certain behaviors and practices to a class is a product of the liberal social sciences. Folk religion was the scholars' invention. The category obscured how middle-class and professional Blacks were engaged in very similar practices that were supposedly concentrated in the lower class. Moreover, my book worries that the folk category in Black religion further marginalizes the Black lower class from industrial, commercial, and scientific cultures. Like their labors, the Black lower class has always been a constitutive part of modern American religious cultures. The category overlooks the so-called aspirations, frustrations, and strivings of the Black lower class in modern life in its myriad of forms—consumptions, aesthetic taste, education, politics, and labor aspirations and pursuits. For instance, the folk category limited Black midwives who welcomed state-certified medicine that they intertwined with the community traditions. To reduce their religion to the folk category also fails to account for the communities and traditions responsible for producing various southern and lower-class people's involvement with the capitalistic enterprise, civil rights, self-help, and state governmental programs in the latter twentieth century. Folk category cannot contend with the variety of religious and political orientations of the religions of people who have to negotiate America's unjust labor markets and economy. For instance, folk religion cannot account for complexity of the religious communities responsible for a host of latter twentieth-century "southern" and "rural" religionists: Fannie Lou Hamer, Clarence Franklin, Frederick J. Eikerenkoetter, John Lewis, and others. In the end, the religion of the Black lower-class communities was never folk in the first place.

Notes

Preface: The Legacy of Hampton:
Folk, Religion, and Classifying the Cabin People

1. Alice M. Bacon, *Southern Workman*, Vol. xx, No. 12 (December 1893), p. 180.
2. Interestingly, Bacon first came to Hampton with her older sister, Rebecca, in the aftermath of the Civil War. She was 12 years old. She took classes with seniors and tutored junior students in arithmetic and spelling. She temporary left Hampton to care for her sickly mother and subsequently attend Harvard College's Radcliff College for women, where she focused on mental and moral philosophy and political economy. Alice returned to Hampton in 1883 to fulfill what she understood to be her second calling: "to be a teacher of Negroes." See: Donald J. Waters, "Introduction," in *Strange Ways and Sweet Dreams: Afro-American Folklore from Hampton*, ed. Donald J. Waters (Boston: G. K. Hall, 1983), p. 5.
3. She was a regular contributor to the updates and summaries of the Dixie Hospital and its nursing program. But due to her interests in folklore and ethnology in the emerging social sciences, she also gave cultural commentary. See: Alice Bacon, "Our Mohammedan," *Southern Workman* (February 1892), p. 31. Bacon started out, "Mention was made, in a recent article in the *Southern Workman* of a Mohammedan from Bombay, who had drifted into port at the Dixie and was there serving as cook." Bacon then wrote: "the study of his ways and character has been a constant interest now for several months to those in daily contact with him, and it seems probable that he will interest others who have not known him personally." Bacon engaged in a brand of Orientalism by first documenting his "unkempt hair and straggling beard, child-like devotion, drunkenness, religious zeal, etc. Yet, he was a devout, good, compassion worker in the hospital. Bacon ended her piece: "Cannot this simple, affectionate, honest character give to our too often Pharisaic Christianity a lesson about the despised 'masses of heathendom'?" (p. 31). To be sure, Bacon was a liberal

Protestant who understood the civilization possibilities of the nonwhite "primitive" races, like the formally enslaved populations.

4. For information on the some of the resident-staff that comprised the Hampton Folk-Lore Society, see: Ronald LaMarr Sharps, *Happy Days and Sorrow Songs: Interpretations of Negro Folk-Lore by Black Intellectuals, 1893–1928* (Dissertation, George Washington University, 1991), pp. 1–157.

5. The AFLS looked to the Hampton Society to contribute to its second division, the "Lore of the Negroes in the Southern States of the Union." See: William Newell, "On the Field and Work of Journal of American Folk-Lore," *The Journal of American Folk-Lore* (April–June, 1888), pp. 3–7. Franz Boas had a hard time with this division due to a lack of interest in black folklore. Elsie Clews was one of the society's main financial and scholarly contributors to this division after World War I. She funded and collaborated with Zora Neale Hurston and Arthur Fauset.

6. Lee D. Baker, *Anthropology and the Racial Politics of Culture* (Durham, NC: Duke University Press, 2010), p. 51.

7. Hampton Folk-Lore Society's national reputation was partly due to its affiliation with the American Folk-Lore Society.

8. Alice Bacon, *Southern Workman*, Vol. xx, No. 12, p. 180. Bacon said alums who were "teaching, preaching, practicing medicine, [and] carrying business [. . .]."

9. Bacon understood that folk expression was also constituted by the rural environment. In an address at the Ninth Annual Meeting of the American Folk-Lore Society on December 29, 1897, Alice Bacon asserted that the Hampton Folk-Lore Society needed a graphophone to record the folk spirituals, as well as the sermons, chants, prayers, in their actual religious contexts—meaning the "baptism, or revivals in log cabins, or by the riverside, or meeting-house of some little Negro settlement." She further explained, "the [religious] music cannot be studied apart from the rest of the religious service with any hope of understanding either its origin or its present status" (p. 20). Bacon, "Work and Methods of the Hampton Folk-Lore Society," *Journal of American Folk-Lore*, Vol. 11, No. 40 (January–March 1898), pp. 17–21.

10. William Thoms, a British antiquarian/folklorist, was accredited with coining the term "folklore" (although he was heavily indebted to the Grimm brothers) as a replacement for the terms "popular antiques" and "popular literature." Under a pseudonym, Ambrose Merton, he first coined the term in the *Athenaeum* in 1846. He defined folklore as the "manners, customs, observances, superstitions, ballads, and proverbs of the olden time. . . .," (361) His idea of time was shaped by his interpretations of the

forward march of industrialization or "the iron horse . . . trampling under foot all [European/British] ancient landmarks, and putting to flight all the relics of our early popular mythology. . . ." (360) See: Duncan Emrich, "Folk-Lore: William John Thoms," *California Folklore Quarterly*, Vol. 5, No. 4 (October 1946), pp. 355–374. For a history of folklore studies in America, see: Simon Bronner, *American Folklore Studies: An Intellectual History* (Lawrence: University of Kansas Press, 1986). For a history of the disciplinary conflicts and formations within American folklore studies, see: Rosemary Zumwalt, *American Folklore Scholarship* (Bloomington: Indiana University Press, 1988).

11. Ibid.
12. For a genealogy of superstition, see Jason A. Josephson-Storm, *The Myth of Disenchantment: Magic, Modernity, and the Birth of the Human Sciences* (Chicago: University of Chicago Press, 2017), pp. 46–50. According to Storm, *superstitions* evolved out of "double register" or "false double." In a theological-religious register, superstition (Lt. *superstitio*) denoted *false worship* followed by the epistemological/philosophical register's "intellectual error" beginning in the eighteenth century. Here, superstition is a product of the superstition-religion-scientific trinary. In another essay, Josephson-Storm understands this trinary as central to statecraft, see: Josephson-Storm, "The Superstition, Secularism, and Religion Trinary: Or, Re-Theorizing Secularism," *Method and Theory in the Study of Religion*, Vol. 30 (2018), pp. 1–20. But scholars of Black religion have shown how superstition has been part and parcel of the racialization process in the New World and the Americas.
13. Ibid., p. 181.
14. For more information on the hag, see: Alexis Wells-Oghoghomeh, "'She Come like a Nightmare': Hags, Witches and the Gendered Trans-Sense among the Enslaved in the Lower South," *Journal of Africana Religions*, Vol. 5, No. 2 (2017), pp. 239–274. Wells-Oghoghomeh fleshes out the West African register that scholars leave out in their discussions of the hag in the study of Black religion. Accordingly, the hag captured the "cosmological structures of the West and West Central African foreparents" that highlighted ideas about the "female-embodied, trans-sense power."
15. Ibid. Bacon also referred to hags as "vampires" as well.
16. "Folk-Lore and Ethnology: Hags and Their Ways," *Southern Workman*, vol. 23, no. 2 (February 1894), p. 26.
17. "Folk-Lore and Ethnology: Hags and Their Ways," *Southern Workman*, Vol. 23, No. 2 (February 1894), p. 26.

18. The hag, according to reports, had a weakness. Hags had to "pick up and count all small things" on her path to riding their victims. She had to collect and count these things before she could ride her victim. This is why individuals put pieces of corn, wheat, or grits on the floor to stall and prevent the hag from riding them. One woman put grains of wheat on the floor that the hag had to pick up and count. Once the hag counted the grains, she accidentally spilled them on the floor, only to have to redo her collecting and counting. The hag was still counting until dawn and was caught by the victim (dawn neutralizing their destructive powers). See: ibid., p. 27.

19. I am borrowing "applied sociology" from Sharps, *Happy Days and Sorrow Songs*. Sharps noted that Bacon taught sociological studies that included political economy for advanced seniors at the Institute.

20. Ronald Sharps argued that the Bacon and Hampton Folk-Lore Society was sociological in its orientation because Bacon was invested in the "investigation of the condition of the Negro in the South and the nation" (p. 43). Sharps discusses how Bacon's work in folklore was complemented by her decision to teach sociological studies to advanced students at Hampton. Beginning in 1895, she began to teach sociological studies that focused on political economy courses for seniors. Not only did she assign reading from Albion Small and George Vincent's *Introduction to the Study of Society*, but she also required the students to investigate and report on the social conditions of Blacks in Elizabeth County. Sharp notes, "Not surprisingly, the president of Hampton's folklore society was among the first students in Bacon's advanced class in sociology and specifically researched patterns of social groups" (p. 44). See: Sharps, *Happy Days and Sorrow Songs*. More importantly, Bacon graduated from Radcliffe College, Harvard's school for women, in 1881, where she focused on mental and moral philosophy, and political economy. For more information on Bacon, see: Donald J. Waters, "Introduction," in *Strange Ways and Sweet Dreams*, p. 5. So, Bacon was familiar with the anthropological and sociological trends in European and American thought.

21. Bacon's privileging of the mind/culture was part of the broader late-Victorian ethnology and social sciences in Western thought. In 1880, Bacon passed the preliminary exams for women at Harvard's Radcliffe College and subsequently, in 1881, advanced exams in mental and moral philosophy (p. 5). She would have been familiar to prevailing evolutionary theories of culture and mind used to map human and racial difference and social status/problems, like Herbert Spencer and E. B. Tylor. See: Waters, "Introduction," in *Strange Ways and Sweet Dreams*, p. 5. In a similar fashion to Tylor, Bacon's view of culture (or civilization) was essentially

about mental development, presumably grounded on the "physic unity of the races." Without question, Bacon's study of folk beliefs and customs was rooted in her intellectualist model of culture.

22. "Folk-Lore Meeting," *Southern Workman* vol. 23, no. 1 (Jan., 1894), 15.

23. For more on the Bureau of Ethnology (BEA) and its folklore research of Native Americans to provide knowledge about their racial development for the US government, especially reservation policies, see: Curtis M. Hinsley, Jr., *Savages and Scientists: The Smithsonian Institute and the Development of American Anthropology, 1846–1910* (Washington, DC: Smithsonian Institute Press, 1981), chapter 5. For instance, BEA's director, John W. Powell, felt that the government needed to acknowledge the stages of human and cultural development/evolution when organizing reservations for Native populations. For Powell's argument regarding knowledge about cultural evolutionism in reservation policies, see: John W. Powell: "From Savagery to Barbarism: Annual Address of the Present," *Transactions of the Anthropological Society of Washington*, Vol. 3 (November 6, 1883–May 19, 1885), p. 173.

24. See: Georgiana Simpson, *Herder and The Concept of the Volk* (Dissertation, University of Chicago, 1921), p. 1. Simpson was a prominent African American philologist in the German Department at the University of Chicago. She was the first African American woman to receive her doctoral degree in the United States.

25. Simpson noted that Johann Gottfried Herder used the concept in multiple ways. According to Simpson, Herder was ambivalent about the class and social position of the *volk*. On one hand, the *volk* was not the lower rabble rouser or the noble class. Yet, they represented a "primitive class." But he also used the term to identify a "nation of people." British and American antiquarians, such as William Thomas and John Fanning, sought to identify the Old European lore amid the onslaught of industrialization. For more on antiquarians, see: Simon J. Bonner, *American Folklore Studies: An Intellectual History* (Lawrence: University of Kansas, 1986), pp. 1–14. But by the nineteenth century, with the rise of the "new sciences," such as anthropology, the folk concept was reserved for the "backward races." Folk underscored the entanglement of ideas about both race and class in social thought. The examples I gave of the "backward races," comes from the nineteenth-century American folklore chronicler Lee J. Vance, "The Study of Folk-Lore," *Forum* (October 1896), p. 249. Lee chronicled the classification of the backward races within the rise of the "new science" of culture or anthropology.

26. Yvonne Chireau, *Black Magic: Religion and the African American Conjuring Tradition* (Berkeley: University of California, 2006), pp. 130–131.

27. Armstrong did not ascribe to the view that race traits hindered the intellectual and moral capacity of Black people. Armstrong's views were a response to Nathaniel Shaler; see: *Strange Ways and Sweet Dreams: Afro-American Folklore from Hampton Institute*, ed. Donald J. Waters (Boston: G. K. Hill, 1983), pp. 14–17. Waters still notes that despite Armstrong's belief in racial reform and uplift, he nevertheless deemed the former enslaved populations and their descendants as an inferior race. This contradiction, according to Khalil Gibran Muhammad, was at the heart of a nineteenth- and early twentieth-century racial liberal theory, like that of geologist Nathaniel Shaler. According to Muhammad, racial liberals "believed in an activist education program to uplift black people while simultaneously believing in black inferiority." See: Muhammad, *The Condemnation of Blackness: Race, Crime, and the Making of Modern Urban America* (Cambridge, MA: Harvard University Press, 2010), p. 295.

28. Alice Mabel Bacon, "Work and Methods of the Hampton Folk-Lore Society," *Journal of American Folk-Lore Society*, Vol. 11, No. 40 (January–March 1898), pp. 17–21.

29. Ibid. Bacon noted that the education (e.g., common schools) was the greatest enemy to folklore. There are numerous studies on the Hampton Folk-Lore Society. In my opinion, the best treatment of the society is presented by Ronald Sharps, *Happy Days and Sorrow Songs: Interpretations of Negro Folklore by Black Intellectuals, 1893–1928*, chapter 2.

30. Bacon helped to found Dixie Hospital in 1891. The hospital was named after her horse, Dixie. Additionally, she also helped to found the hospital's training school for nurses on Hampton's campus. Virginia's General Assembly passed the 1892 act that granted Dixie Hospital the right to add a training school for nurses. The nursing school was on Hampton's campus, but had separate funding from the Institute. And graduates from the Institute attended the nursing school, like Anna De Costa Banks, one of its first students. For the announcement regarding the nurse training school, see: *Southern Workman*, Vol. xxii, No. 3 (March 1893), p. 50.

31. Alice Bacon, "The Dixie Work—Is It Worth Continuing," *Southern Workman*, Vol. xxii, No. 2 (1893), p. 27.

32. *Southern Workman* (October 1894), Vol. xxiii, No. 10, p. 176.

33. Harriet M. Lewis, *Southern Workman*, Vol. xxi, No. 6 (June 1892), p. 109.

34. Bacon, "The Dixie Work—Is It Worth Continuing," p. 27.

35. Ibid.

36. Ibid.

37. At the age of 11, her family in New Haven hosted the future Princess of Oyama, Sutematz Yamakawa, while she attended Vassar College in 1882. Bacon and Yamakawa established an extremely close relationship, which prompted Alice Bacon to embark on her first trip to Japan where she helped to "westernize" the schools for elite Japanese women from 1887–1888. For Bacon's experiences in Japan, see: Peter Hamilton, "An American Family's Mission in East Asia, 1838 to 1936: A Commitment to God, Academia, and Empire," *Journal of the Royal Asiatic Society Hong Kong Branch*, Vol. 49 (2009), pp. 229–265.

38. I am indebted to Webb Keane's secularism as a moral narrative of modernity. Keane discusses "secularism as a moral narrative of modernity" that "projects onto chronological time of a view of human moral and pragmatic transformation." He further notes, "[t]his moralization of history can (but doesn't necessarily) produce a largely tacit set of expectations about what a modern, progressive person, subject, and citizen, should be" (p. 160). See Keane, "Secularism as a Moral Narrative of Modernity," *Transit: Europaische Revue* 43 (2013), pp. 159–170.

Introduction

1. Elizabeth Hinton, *From War on Poverty to the War on Drugs to the War on Crime: The Making of Mass Incarceration in America* (Cambridge, MA: Harvard University Press, 2016). Hinton brilliantly demonstrates how the Kennedy administration's Juvenile Delinquency program for urban Blacks was extended by the Johnson administration into the crimes law, which neoconservative adopted and extended in the twentieth century.

2. Alice O'Connor, *Poverty-Knowledge: Social Science, Social Policy, and the Poor in Twentieth-Century U.S. History* (Princeton, NJ: Princeton University Press, 2001).

3. For more information on postwar liberalism, see: Daniel Geary, *Beyond Civil Rights: The Moynihan Report and Its Legacy* (Philadelphia: University of Pennsylvania Press, 2015); Robin Marie Averbeck, *Liberalism Is Not Enough: Race and Poverty in Postwar Political Thought* (Chapel Hill: University of North Carolina Press, 2018).

4. For a connection of the underclass and the "undeserving poor," see: Michael Katz, *The Undeserving Poor: From the War on Poverty to the War on Welfare* (New York: Pantheon Books, 1989); *The Underclass Debate: Views from History*, ed. Michael B. Katz (Princeton, NJ: Princeton University Press, 1993), pp. 1–23.

5. Robert Park "Introduction," in Charles S. Johnson, *In Shadow of the Plantation* (Chicago: University of Chicago Press, 1934), p. xiii. Additionally, I will use "folk" as an adjective (folk religion) and noun (the folk) throughout this book.

6. These liberal scholars recycled European terms, such as *feudal, peasants,* and *folk,* in their analyses of both Black and white workers in the 1930s.

7. For more on southern diaspora in mainstream poverty, see: Jacqueline Jones, *The Dispossessed: America's Underclasses from the Civil War to the Present* (New York: Basic Books, 1992). Jones's story is a "continuity narrative" that discloses the relationship between the structures of racial prejudice and exploitation in the postbellum South and the postindustrial North. The "plantation South," as migrants knew, was very much in the mainstream northern ghettoes and other regions in the United States. I am indebted to Jones's argument, which has helped me discuss the "southern" antecedents of the culture of poverty idea that she has so carefully criticized.

8. J. Z. Smith, "Religion, Religious, and Religions," in *Critical Terms for Religious Studies*, ed. Mark C. Taylor (Chicago: University of Chicago Press, 1998), p. 296. My reading of folk religion is indebted to Smith's perspective that religion operates as a taxonomy responsible for the production of human differences within "arrangements of power." Additionally, I take the view that folk religion is (partly) a term "created by scholars for their intellectual [and, I add, political] purposes and therefore is theirs to define" (p. 281).

9. This is not a book within the scope of secular studies. However, I often use secular-modern ideas or narratives to discuss how these liberal social scientists used "folk" in their classifications of Black southern and poor religion as un- or not modern (folk). My understanding of the secular-modern (or, more appropriately, secularization thesis in social thought) focuses on the ideas and framework that present historical and social processes (industrialization) in a teleological or triumphal scheme. This secular telos has functioned as a modern project that classifies and manages human and racial/religious differences. This view of the modern-secular is inspired by Josef Sorett in *Race and Secularism* (New York: Columbia University Press, 2016), pp. 43–73. I am also indebted to secular studies, particularly as it pertains to religion as a mode of state governance. Charles McCrary and Jeffrey Wheatley, "The Protestant Secular in the Study of America: Reappraisal and Suggestions," *Religion*, Vol. 47 (2017), pp. 257–276; and Jason Ananda Josephson-Storm, "The Superstition, Secularism, and Religion Trinary: Or, Re-Theorizing Secularism," *Method & Theory in the Study of Religion*, Vol. 31 (2019), pp. 1–20.

10. For important works on "Black folk religion" and the Great Migration, see: Milton Sernett, *Bound for the Promised Land: African American Religion and the Great Migration* (Durham, NC: Duke University Press, 1997); Wallace Best, *Passionate Human, No Less Divine: Religion and Culture in Black Chicago, 1915–1952* (Princeton, NJ: Princeton University, 2007); Lerone Martin, *Preaching on Wax: The Phonograph and the Shaping of Modern African American Religion* (New York: New York University Press). Sernett distinguishes between rural and urban religion on the basis that the former was more "folk" or expressive in its religious orientation, as opposed to the latter's social instrumentalism. My research seeks to challenge and disrupt ways in which "folk" is a familiar term to identify Black southern religion. Both Best and Martin's histories challenge the folk/modern divide in their important works on southern migrants.

11. John Hayes, *Hard, Hard Religion: Interracial Faith in the Poor South* (Chapel Hill: University of North Carolina Press, 2017). Religious scholar Robert Orsi makes a distinction between popular and lived religion, especially with the former's strict contrast between elite and popular forms of religion.

12. I'm indebted to Leonard Norman Primiano for his discussion of the two-tiered model implicit in the categories of folk and popular religion. This two-tiered model underscores that folk religion "residualizes certain beliefs and practices, . . . dichotomizing official and unofficial religiosity." See: Leonard Norman Primiano, "Vernacular Religion and the Search for Method in Religious Folklife," *Western Folklore*, Vol. 54, No. 1 (Jan. 1995), pp. 37–56.

13. Robin Kelley, "Notes on Deconstructing the Folk," *The American Historical Review*, Vol. 97, No. 5 (Dec. 1992), pp. 1400–1408.

14. Odum's student George L. Simpson said that "many souths" was his teacher's favorite phrase. George L. Simpson Jr., "Howard W. Odum and American Regionalism," *Social Forces*, Vol. 34, No. 2 (December 1955), p. 104. See: Howard Odum, *Southern Regions of United States* (Chapel Hill: University of North Carolina, 1936).

15. For works on racial liberalism in the twentieth century, see: Walter A. Jackson, *Gunnar Myrdal and America's Conscience: Social Engineering and Racial Liberalism, 1938–1987* (Chapel Hill: University of North Carolina Press, 1990); Daryl Michael Scott, *Contempt and Pity: Social Policy and the Image of the Damaged Black Psyche, 1880–1996* (Chapel Hill: University of North Carolina Press, 1997); Mark Ellis, *Race Harmony and Black Progress: Jack Woofter and the Interracial Cooperation Movement*; Mark Anderson, *From Boas to Black Power: Racism, Liberalism and American Anthropology* (Berkeley: University of California, 2019).

16. For more on the separate regional southern economy before World War II, see: Gavin Wright, *Old South and New South: Revolutions in the Southern Economy since the Civil War* (Baton Rouge: Louisiana State University Press, 1986).

17. Charles Johnson, "Rise of Liberalism in the South," *World Outlook XXVII*, No. 9 (Sept., 1938), p. 27.

18. Charles S. Johnson, "The Present Status of Race Relations, with Particular Reference to the Negro," *Journal of Negro Education*, vol. 8, no. 3 (July 1939), p. 326. This article is significant because he accredits the Depression as contributing to a shift in thinking about race relations, and particularly about Black people. "Ten years of a widespread economic depression have brought about a mood at least for questioning some of these sacred racial institutions and traditions. . . . What is, perhaps, most significant about the recent change in the status of race relations is the shift of focus from the Negro as the South's economic problem number one, to a recognition of the complex of economic problems themselves as the South's major ill" (ibid.). However, Johnson had a broad view of liberal thought.

19. Jerrold Roll and Erik Gellman, *The Gospel on the Working-Class: Labor's Southern Prophets in the New Deal America* (Champagne: University of Illinois Press, 2011); John Hayes, *Hard, Hard Religion*.

Chapter 1

1. Edward L. Ayers, *The Promise of the New South: Life after Reconstruction* (New York: Oxford University Press, 2007), pp. 422–423.

2. Howard Odum, "Religious Folk-Songs of the Southern Negroes," *The American Journal of Religious Psychology and Education*, Vol. 3, No. 3 (July 1909), p. 266.

3. Oxford was the county seat of Layfayette County. The county had a total population of 22,110 in 1900 and 21,883 in 1910. Covington was the county seat of Newton County. Similarly, the county had a population of 21,883 and 18,499 in 1910.

4. Odum pretty much had his mind set on his research before he arrived at Clark University. He spent time with his former professor, Thomas Bailey, working with folk songs to understand the "character-traits" of Black southerners in Oxford, Mississippi. Bailey graduated from Clark University and helped his protégé get into the school when he was rejected from Columbia University. It is plausible that Bailey communicated to

G. Stanley Hall about his student and his research interests. In a letter on June 15, 1908, Hall already knew about Odum's research interests in Black folk songs. Hall recommended that Odum consult Clark University anthropologist Alexander Chamberlain for his research interests on race and Black people in particular. "G. Stanley Hall to Howard Odum," June 15, 1908, Clark University, Robert H. Goddard Library, Archives and Special Collections. Special thanks to Fordyce Williams for showing me the letter and overall assistance with information on G. Stanley Hall and the history of the psychology department at Clark University.

5. Odum, "Religious Folk-Songs of the Southern Negroes," p. 269.

6. His first dissertation was titled, *Negro Folksongs and Character-Traits*. The whole dissertation was lost. The only surviving chapters were 1 and 2, which covered the "Religious Folk-Songs of the Southern Negroes," printed in *The American Journal of Religious Psychology and Education*, Vol. 3, No. 3 (July 1909), pp. 265–365.

7. Howard Odum is remembered in the American social sciences for his focus on folk southern regionalism that he institutionalized at the University of North Carolina, particularly its Institute for Research in the Social Sciences (IRSS). I will engage the IRSS in Chapter 2.

8. Odum was born in Bethlehem, Georgia. His great grandfather, Elisha, had left North Carolina to settle in Bethlehem in Walton County, presumably either in 1820 or 1821, during the land lottery, after the Creek Nation had been defeated and had "ceded" land in 1818. But Walton, like Jasper and Henry counties, became Newton County in 1821. See: Newton County Historical Society, *History of Newton County Georgia* (Covington, 1988), pp. 3–29.

    But Odum's family moved to a farm in the county seat of Newton around 1897 (according to biographer Wayne D. Brazil): Covington. The farm was on what today is Odum Street in Covington, Georgia. In his *Howard W. Odum: The Building Years, 1884–1930*, Brazil noted that the family chose to move to Covington because it was near the Methodist college, Emory. He grew up southern Methodist. Given his mother's former aristocratic lifestyle, I am sure she was responsible for the move. Also, there were probably real economic benefits to living in the county seat. See: Brazil, *Howard W. Odum: The Building Years, 1884–1930* (New York: Garland, 1988), chapter 1.

9. "Watson and Cobb in Covington, Ga.: Populist[s] Hear Two Orators Speak in Newton County," August 23, 1896, *Atlanta Journal Constitution*, p. 12.

10. Howard Odum's writing is full of contradictions, coupled with incoherent and unfinished thoughts. While he wanted to show the value of the folk

songs to the debates around race during his day, he also noted that the songs needed to be quickly gathered because they were vanishing due to "changing environment." Odum, "Religious Folk-Songs of the Southern Negroes," p. 266.

11. Odum, "Religious Folk-Songs of the Southern Negroes," p. 266.

12. Odum went to Emory College, approximately five minutes from his family's farm. By "hub of southern Methodism," I am referring to how Emory College bishops were at the center of the controversy over slavery that led to the regional denominational split in 1844. The story revolved around Kitty Andrew Shell, an enslaved woman. The 12-year-old Shell was "bequeathed" to the Bishop James Andrews of Emory College from a "Mrs. Powers of Augusta, Ga." Mrs. Powers's will stated that at the age of 19, Kitty should be freed by the family and sent to Liberia. Under Georgia law, the family could only grant Kitty freedom if she left for Liberia. The story goes that Kitty did not want to leave. James Andrews built her a cottage in his backyard and told her that "you are free as I am." Kitty later married Nathan Shell and left the cottage. I'm thankful to my mother, Regina Drake, for finding this material in the archives at Emory-Oxford College.

13. For more information on religion and new psychology, see: Christopher White, *Unsettled Minds: Psychology and the American Search for Spiritual Assurance, 1830–1940* (Berkeley: University of California Press, 2009), chapter 1.

14. For more on the construction of Black religion as a "foil" of, or anathema to, secular modern, or in this case, modern civilization, see: Josef Sorett, "Secular Compared to What?: Toward a History of the Trope of Black Sacred/Secular Fluidity," in *Race and Secularism in America*, eds. Vincent W. Lloyd and Jonathan S. Kahn (New York: Columbia University Press, 2016), pp. 43–74.

15. My understanding of the emergence of the social sciences in America is indebted to Dorothy Ross, *The Origin of the American Social Sciences* (Cambridge: Cambridge University Press, 1991), chapter 3. Ross noted that the American social sciences evolved out of a northeastern, cosmopolitan, educated, and liberal gentry class in the late nineteenth century. Ross notes that the American social sciences emerged due to the crises in the authority of knowledge and society. There was a crisis in intellectual authority where the natural sciences discredited notions of divine providence. The social crisis revolved around the political challenges of rapid industrialization, especially labor and wealth.

16. Such social scientists were Carroll Wright of the US Bureau of Labor Statistics and John Wesley Powell of the Bureau of Ethnology. W. E. B. Du Bois also studied Black communities in Georgia and Virginia on behalf

of Bureau of Labor Statistics: "The Negro of Farmville, Virginia: A Social Study" (1898), "The Negro in the Black Belt: Some Social Sketches" (1899), and "The Negro Landholder in Georgia" (1901). Du Bois and his students at Atlanta University studied Black communities in Odum's hometown, Covington, the county seat of Newton County, in "The Negro in the Black Belt," in 1899.

17. Nathaniel S. Shaler, "Science and the African Problem," *Atlantic Monthly* (July 1890).

18. Ibid.

19. For more information on Shaler and Alice Bacon, see: Donald Waters, ed., *Strange Ways and Sweet Dreams: Afro-American Folklore from the Hampton Institute* (Boston: G. K. Hall & Co., 1983), p. 9.

20. G. Stanley Hall, "Proceedings of the Massachusetts Historical Society," February 2, 1905, p. 98.

21. Ibid. What's interesting was that in the same address, he said he regretted his former stance on abolitionism. Hall noted, "For myself, an abolitionist both by conviction and descent, I wish to confess my error of opinion in those days . . ."(p. 104). He perpetuated racial polygenetic thought by implicitly affirming Samuel Cartwright (the "southern physician") and the southern school of racial thought and practice.

22. It appears from the sources that Hall was president of the Congo Society, 1907–1908(?). The *Journal of Race Development* was founded in 1910. He used this journal to criticize both colonialism and Christian missions for not allowing non-white races to practice their unique cultures and govern themselves. For Hall, these practices were attributed to their distinct and natural racial composition.

23. For more on racial polygenesis or the belief that the races had different origins (and constituted a different species), see: Stephen J. Gould, *The Mismeasure of Man* (New York: W. W. Norton, 1991), chapter 2. Despite postbellum progressive scientists ascribing to racial monogenesis (beliefs that races have the same origins) over and against their predecessors, their analysis of race, and Black people more specifically, fell prey to polygenetic thought, way into the first half of the twentieth century. For more on this argument, see: George Stocking, Jr., "The Persistence of Polygenist Thought in Post-Darwinian Anthropology," in his *Race, Culture, and Evolution: Essays in the History of Anthropology* (Chicago: University of Chicago, 1982), pp. 42–68.

24. Shaler, "The Negro Problem," *Atlantic Monthly* (November 1884). https://www.theatlantic.com/magazine/archive/1884/11/the-negro-problem/531366/

25. W. E. B. Du Bois, "The Study of the Negro Problems," reprinted in *W. E. B. Du Bois: The Problem of the Color Line at the Turn of the Twentieth Century* (New York: Fordham University Press, 2015), p. 78. This essay was originally printed in 1897.

26. Du Bois, "The Study of the Negro Problems," p. 83.

27. Robert E. Park, "An Autobiographical Note," reprinted in *The Collected Papers of Robert Ezra Park* (New York: Arno Press, 1974), p. xii. Park was Washington's publicist before he joined the faculty at the University of Chicago.

28. Ibid.

29. Howard Odum, *Social and Mental Traits of the Negro: Research into the Conditions of the Negro Race in Southern Towns* (New York: AMS Press, 1910), p. 276.

30. James Vaardman was a white racist populist candidate, like Ben Pitchfork Tilman of South Carolina, who openly endorsed lynching and mob violence as a constitutive part of southern governance (along with other restrictions, like exclusion from education). He also championed policies that regulated large corporations, against the convict lease system, supported child labor laws, and public education for poor whites. There were lynchings in Oxford during Odum's tenure. https://teachingamer icanhistory.org/library/document/a-governor-bitterly-opposes-negro-education/. In this speech, he ultimately endorsed Black industrial and moral education due to their cultivation of efficient laborers. He ultimately championed Black servitude. He used both Walter Willcox, George Winston, and J. R. Stratton to note that "negroes who can read and write [were] more criminal than the illiterate, which [was] true of no other element of our population." He was in opposition to the "more than $250,000,000 has been spent since the years 1861–1865 by the white [philanthropists] of the North and the South in a foolish endeavor to make more of the nigger than God Almighty every [*sic*] intended." The speech was given February 4, 1904.

31. After his tenure in Oxford, Mississippi, Odum enrolled in the psychology program at Clark University. According to his biographer, he initially wanted to go to Columbia where he would study with Franklin Gidding, but was denied entrance. Of course, he would get his opportunity in 1909. Like first-generation sociologists, Odum was inclined toward studies of human behaviors. So it was not a difficult transition from psychology to sociology since he was primarily working on the group mind (or cultural anthropology) at Clark University. In a letter to G. Stanley Hall, Odum had expressed his ambitions in the professional of sociology. Hall replied, "I

think sociology and psychology immensely strengthen each other." "G. Stanley Hall to Howard Odum," June, 15, 1908.

32. I borrowed this quote from Scott L. Matthews, *Capturing the South: Imaging America's Most Documented Region* (Chapel Hill: University of North Carolina, 2018), p. 24.

33. Bailey was a Victorian who understood the scientific endeavor in very moralistic and vocational ways. For more on this approach to science, see: David Hollinger, "Inquiry and Uplift: Late Nineteenth Century American Academics and the Moral Efficacy of Scientific Practice," in Thomas Haskell, ed., *The Authority of Experts: Studies in History and Theory* (Bloomington: Indiana University Press, 1984), pp. 142–156. In an essay that Bailey wrote (which Odum put in the appendix to his second dissertation), he also called for more science and less mob violence in the "Negro Question." Bailey noted, "It is science, and science alone, star-eyed science, truth-loving science, spiritually intellectual science—it is the Twentieth Century's greatest power, the scientific research of today, that can prepare us for the doing of this Nation's greatest duty—the solution of this [Negro] problem, so as to free two unallied people and make the states of this union United States indeed and in truth!" Bailey, "Children Differ in Environment," in Odum, *Social and Mental Traits of the Negro*, p. 302.

Also, as depicted in Bailey's first dissertation and later works, he did not shy away from using Jesus as a moral exemplar, to cultivate the psychological control and moral habits of the child in the classroom. See: Bailey, *The Development of Character* (Columbia: Presbyterian, 1891), p. 21. He noted, "There is but one Ethical Ideal that all can strive to exemplify each one in himself. It is Jesus of Nazareth. The Ethics of the school-room must have Him in mind. Is not the time at hand, or almost at hand when That Character can be held up to all, old and young, without metaphysical or dogmatic comment?" *Development of Character* was his first dissertation at the University of South Carolina.

34. Thomas Bailey, *Race Orthodoxy in the South, and Other Aspects of the Negro Question* (New York: Neale, 1914), p. 361.

35. Ibid.

36. My understanding of neo-Lamarckian is influenced by George Stocking, Jr. Lamarckian evolutionary thought posited that organisms adapted to their environment (through acts that become habits) to fulfill certain needs. This adaptation altered the organisms' structure and were transmitted by heredity to their offspring. According to George Stocking, neo-Lamarckian, a "behavioral theory of biological evolution," was central to late nineteenth- and early twentieth-century social scientists, especially in

their discussion of "race formation" in the Negro Problem. Stocking noted, "The central concept of the Lamarckian view of race formation was adaptation: changes in organic behavior or structure which were caused either by direct environmental influences or were transmitted by hereditary from parent to child . . . the adaptations of each individual are transmitted to its offspring and by this process mankind was molded into races and varieties" (p. 243). More importantly, social reformers used Lamarckianism to note that environmental changes could alter the behavioral and hereditary structure of Black folk. But racial biological determinists also used Lamarckianism. See: Stocking, "Lamarckianism in American Social Science," in his *Race, Culture, and Evolution: Essays in the History of Anthropology*, pp. 134–269.

37. George Stocking Jr. is right to claim that many evolutionary psychologists and broader social scientists confused "social and physical hereditary, and. . . assume[d] the physical inheritance of complex cultural characteristics" (p. 251). Stocking, "Lamarckianism in American Social Science."

38. Thomas Bailey mentioned that he and Odum worked together on black folklore at the University of Mississippi. Ibid.

39. See: W. I. Thomas, "The Scope and Method of Folk-Psychology," *American Journal of Sociology*, Vol. 4 (Jan., 1896), pp. 434–445. Wundt understood folk psychology as the study of the laws of mental development from primitive to civilized peoples and societies. For more on the history of folk psychology (Volkpsychologie) in Germany, see: Egbert Klautke, *The Mind of the Nation: Volkerpsychologie in Germany, 1851–1955* (New York: Berghahn, 2010), chapter 2.

40. See: Emily D. Cahan and Sheldon H. White, "Proposals for a Second Psychology," *American Psychologist*, Vol. 47, No. 2 (February 1992), pp. 224–235.

41. Dorothy A. Ross, *G. Stanley Hall: The Psychology as Prophet* (Chicago: University of Chicago Press, 1972), pp. 186–204.

42. "Register and Twentieth Official Announcement," *Clark University in the City of Worcester Massachusetts*, 1908, 72. Special thanks to Fordyce Williams, Coordinator of Archives and Special Collections at Clark University, for materials on the psychology department and G. Stanley Hall.

43. Lee J. Vance, "On the Nature and Value of Folk-Lore," *The Chautauquan* (Sept. 1890), Vol. 11, No. 6, p. 686.

44. T. J. Jackson Lears, *No Place of Grace: Antimodernism and the Transformation of American Culture, 1880–1920* (Chicago: University of Chicago Press, 1981), p. 147.

45. Vance, "On the Nature and Value of Folk-Lore," p. 686.

46. G. Stanley Hall, "The Moral and Religious Training of Children and Adolescents," *The Pedagogical Seminary*, Vol. 1, Issue 2 (1891), p. 196.

47. G. Stanley Hall and J. E. W. Wallin, "How Children and Youth Think and Feel about Clouds," *The Pedagogical Seminary*, Vol. 9, Issue 4 (1904), p. 503. They noted that "both myth and folk lore testify to the prevalence of this same tropism among primitive peoples and to its powerful influence upon their moral, religious, and aesthetic development" (p. 505).

48. Hall, "The Study of the Negro in America," *Proceedings of the Massachusetts Historical Society*, Second Series, Vol. 19 (1905), p. 97.

49. See: Ross, *G. Stanley Hall: The Psychologist as Prophet*, p. 51.

50. I'm thinking of one of the first complied songbook on the black spirituals published in 1867 in the United States, *Slave Songs of the United States*, by William Francis Allen, Lucy McKim Garrison, and Charles Pickard Ware.

51. For discussion on the religious aspect of the romantic racialist, see: Curtis Evans, *The Burden of Black Religion* (New York: Oxford University Press, 2008), chapter 1. For another account of romantic racialist, see: George M. Frerickson, *The Black Image in the White Mind: The Debate on Afro-American Character and Destiny, 1817–1914* (New York: Harper & Row, 1971), chapter 4.

52. Thomas Wentworth Higginson, "Negro Spirituals," https://www.theatlantic.com/magazine/archive/1867/06/negro-spirituals/534858/

53. Thomas Wentworth Higginson, "Leaves from an Officer's Journal," https://www.theatlantic.com/magazine/archive/1865/01/leaves-from-an-officers-journal/308757/

54. Odum, "Religious Folk-Songs of the Southern Negroes," p. 273.

55. W.E.B. Du Bois, *The Souls of Black Folk* (New York: Bantam Dell, 2005), pp. 188.

56. Odum, "The Religious Folk-Songs of the Southern Negroes," p. 272.

57. Dorothy Ross argues that the American Social Sciences preferred the natural sciences to shape their understanding of American history. This was to project American exceptionalism, as represented in republican government and market capitalism. See: Ross, *Origins of the American Social Sciences*.

58. Odum, "The Religious Folk-Songs of the Southern Negroes," p. 273.

59. Ibid., p. 266.

60. But he rehashed the recapitulation theory within the natural history of Black people—that the "folk songs enhance the knowledge of the phyletic and genetic concept of a people." Ibid.

61. See: Stocking, "The Persistence of Polygenetic Thought in Post-Darwinian Anthropology," in his *Race, Culture, and Evolution: Essays in the History of Anthropology*, pp. 42–68.

62. Odum, "The Religious Folk-Songs of the Southern Negro," p. 266.

63. Ibid., p. 276.

64. Ibid.

65. For more on the effects of the social scientific disciplines of Black religion, especially new psychology, see: Evans, *The Burden of Back Religion*, chap. 3.

66. Odum, "The Religious Folk-Songs of the Southern Negroes," p. 298.

67. Ibid., p. 334.

68. Ibid., p. 287.

69. Odum, *Social and Mental Traits of the Negro*, pp. 575, 271.

70. Ibid., pp. 240–241.

71. Ibid., p. 239.

72. "Columbia University Bulletin Information: Faculties of Political Science, Philosophy, and Pure Science," Eightieth Series, No. 10 (March 21, 1908), p. 19. Howard Odum's registration information said that he took American History 267 and 268 under William Dunnings. "Howard Odum, Political Registrar." I am thankful to Joana Rios of the Columbia University Archives and Special Collections.

73. "Political Science," Howard Odum's transcript. His primary focus was sociology, where he took courses with Giddings and Tenney. Additionally, he took courses in Seligman's Economics 107, Fiscal and Industrial History of the United States. He also took Clark's Economic Theory I and II.

74. Covington, Georgia, was located about 20 miles east of Atlanta in Newton County (today Rockdale Co.). More importantly, Covington was located about 5 miles from the hub of southern Methodism, Oxford, where Emory College was located. Both Howard Odum's grandfather, William Pleasants, and father-in-law fought in the Civil War. Odum celebrated the fact that his father came from hardworking and slaveless lineage.

75. Faculties of Political Science, Philosophy, and Pure Science: Instruction for Candidates for the Degrees of Master of Arts and Doctor of Philosophy, 1908–1910, *Columbia University Bulletin of Information: Eighth Series, No. 10* (New York: Columbia University, 1908).

76. Bracey Harris, "Where Two or Three Gather In My Name: A History of the Burns-Belfry Restoration and Racial Reconciliation Between Churches in Oxford, Mississippi" (Undergraduate thesis: University of Mississippi, 2013), 6.

77. Odum, *Social and Mental Traits of the Negro*, p. 88.

78. Odum, "The Religious Folk-Songs of the Southern Negroes," p. 275.

79. Evans, *The Burden of Black Religion*, p. 105.

80. Frederick Davenport, *Primitive Traits in Religious Revivals* (New York: Macmillan, 1905), p. 54.

81. Ibid.

82. W. E. B. Du Bois, *Dusk of Dawn: An Essay Toward an Autobiography of a Race Concept* (New Brunswick, NJ: Transaction, 1997), p. 51. This book was originally published in 1940. Du Bois was jutxposing his more historically situated sociology that he learned in Germany from American thinkers who were following Herbert Spencer's Synthetic Philosophy by describing social laws that were analogous to physical laws. This more speculative and ahistorical approach to society was exemplified in "phrase[s] like consciousness of kind" (p. 51). This was a direct reference to Franklin Giddings.

83. Odum, *Social and Mental Traits of the Negro*, p.92.

84. Ibid., p. 84.

85. Davenport, *Primitive Traits in Religious Revivals*, p. 45.

86. Ibid., p. 58.

87. Davenport cited the Englishman Benjamin Jowett's claim of an age before morality when human beings did not consider their relationality to each other. Black southerners removed from civilizing missions of the industrial schools were suspended in the primitive stage prior to morality and ethics.

88. Odum, *Social and Mental Traits of the Negro*, p. 278.

89. Odum, *Social and Mental Traits of the Negro*, p. 83.

90. See: ibid., pp. 277–278.

91. See: Howard Odum, *An American Epoch* (New York: Henry Holt, 1930). He was working on an autobiography before his sudden death in 1954. Drafts of the "White Sands of Bethlehem," that sought to partly show the "middle group of white folk" who confronted "harsh realities" from the changing markets, but who maintained the higher ideals of the Protestant work ethic on the lands, that served the backbone of the South and broader America. I am thankful to Matthew Turi of the University of North Carolina–Chapel Hill's Louis Round Wilson Special Collection for sending me drafts of Odum's unfinished autobiography.

92. See: Robert Park, "Education by Cultural Groups," in the *Robert Ezra Park Collection, 1882–1979*, Hanna Holborn Grey Special Collections, University of Chicago, p. 5.

93. Ibid.

94. See the discussion on Black farmers who "paid out their debt" to white planters, purchasing land, and/or grocery store owner Thomas Moss of Memphis (his murder was noted in Ida B. Wells's *Crusade for Justice*) in Leon F. Litwack, *Trouble in Mind: Black Southerners in the Age of Jim Crow* (New York: Vintage Books, 199), pp. 152–157.

95. What is interesting is that the songs were from Newton County, Georgia, and were recorded and transcribed by Howard Odum. It was placed in his co-authored text, *The Negro Workaday Songs* (Chapel Hill: North Carolina, 1926), p. 115. I explain in Chapter 2 what prompted Odum's change in tone. It was largely accredited to Guy Johnson, his student. Lynn Moss Sanders makes this claim in her *Howard W. Odum's Folklore Odyssey: Transformation to Tolerance through African American Folk Studies* (Athens: University of Georgia Press, 2003), chapter 2 . Several scholars have documented Odum's shift in racial thinking from his graduate dissertation. He renounced his second dissertation. Yet, I argue that he never departed from his view of unique racial traits and environments that he just simply romanticized in the 1920s. This primitive romanticism was most evident in his fictional trilogy on the folk hero, Black Ulysses.

96. I do not want to mistake Washington for holding the same beliefs as Odum. Washington believed in equality, whereas Odum did not. What united them was their shared belief in the salvation of character and work. This belief united many late Victorians across the diverse political ideological landscape.

97. Odum, *Social and Mental Traits of the Negro*, p. 283.

98. For discussion on Max Weber and the Tuskegee Institute, see Andrew Zimmerman's excellent book, *Alabama in Africa: Booker T. Washington, the German Empire, and the Globalization of the New South* (Princeton, NJ: Princeton University Press, 2010), chapters 2 and 5.

99. W. E. B. Du Bois, "The Negro in the Black Belt: Some Sketches," *Bulletin of the Department of Labor*, No. 22 (May 1899), 408. The study looked at 50 families of the best class with an eye to the general conditions of Blacks. They did discuss the unemployed and criminal class of Blacks in Covington.

100. Ibid., 465.

101. The demonstrators probably had to navigate Jim Crow governance by not detesting tenant farming and sharecroppers in Newton County. The organizers invited G. F. Hunnicuts who extolled the Black farmers that they should rent a couple of years, and not one. He noted that with good and honest work, there will be plenty of white owners who will gladly comply with the working arrangements. This statement overlooked how the modern New South was founded on Black dependency, debt, and tenant farming and sharecropping. He also told Black farmers to stop planting all the cotton. But again, he failed to understand that the New South economy was built on the store credit system.

102. Odum, *Social and Mental Traits of the Negro*, pp. 289–290.

Chapter 2

1. Guy B. Johnson, "Memorandum on Church Service at Scottsville Baptist Church," unpublished. Guy Benton Johnson Papers, 1830–1882, 1901–1987, *The Southern Historical Collection*, University of North Carolina–Chapel Hill. The others in attendance were involved in the St. Helena Study, too. A UNC–Chapel Hill social historian, Guion Johnson, who was pregnant at the time, was working on a portion of the study that covered the history of St. Helena. Woofter, a sociologist at the Institute for Research in the Social Sciences (IRSS), was the director of the community study. Woofter's wife was in attendance, too. In her own right, Ethel Ophelia Woofter was a director of the New York Mutual Life Insurance Company in the Atlanta office. Her promotion was the result of her success over "$300,000 worth of life insurance annually." For information on Ethel Woofter, see Mark Ellis, *Race Harmony and Black Progress: Jack Woofter and the Interracial Cooperation Movement* (Bloomington: Indiana University, 2013), p. 198. Although not a part of the IRSS, Columbia University's sociologist Frank A. Ross, a sociologist, and his wife were also in attendance.

2. In contrast to their white counterparts, Johnson noted that Black Protestants characteristically lined hymns were very long. He explained that the lined hymns were performed the same way in the antebellum days. He explained that the songs were lined when "[e]ach syllable, each tone is prolonged to the breaking point, and when four or five words in succession fall on the same pitch, the effect is maddening to the uninitiated." His reference to maddening was that he noted that "where it would take the ordinary church singer about fifteen seconds to sing lines,

   > Jesus, lover of my soul
   > Let me to thy bossom fly,

   it takes these people forty or more" (p. 64). See Johnson, *Folk Culture on St. Helena Island, South Carolina* (Chapel Hill: University of North Carolina, 1930), p. 64.

3. It is plausible that Guy Johnson was referring to William Branswell. Branswell was a teacher at Penn School.

4. Before Franklin D. Roosevelt repealed Prohibition, both Cooley and House led a crusade to stop the making, selling, and distribution of liquor on the Island. Students and others affiliated with the Penn School had to sign a pledge that they Cooley wrote a letter to the Federal Prohibition Agent of Charleston to "send a [sic] agent to this island to investigate conditions on Horse Island which is a small island off our coast of Frogmore Plantation." She reported the alleged bootlegger, Mordecaiah Warren, for

his involvement in "distilling liquor," particularly to young girls and boys 14 to 16 years old. "Rossa Cooley to Federal Prohibition Agent," October 1, 1926, Penn School Papers, 1862–2005, *Southern Historical Collection*, Louis Round Wilson Special Collection Library, University of North Carolina–Chapel Hill.

5. Johnson said that House had Washington preach over Scottsville's pastor, Issac Brisbane. He noted that "I judged that it is felt that Rev. Brisbane is a very poor type of preacher and Miss House was probably responsible for getting Rev. Washington to preach" (p. 2). Johnson, "Memorandum on Church Service At Scottsville Baptist Church," Guy Benton Johnson Papers, p. 3.

6. During the antebellum period, the enslaved populations established "praise houses" to practice a distinct religious culture separate from "slave-owning Christianity." Praise houses were usually small wooden houses on plantation.

7. "Praise House," Guy Benton Johnson Papers.

8. Ibid.

9. "Samuel E. Veaux (?): Bad Luck Signs and Superstitions," March 21, 1928, Guy Benton Johnson Papers.

10. These small plots of land were former plantations that the federal government divided and resold to a few of the formerly enslaved populations during the Civil War and Reconstruction.

11. Woofter divided the $420 in two ways. He noted that $275 was in actual wages and $145 was in farm produce. See Woofter, *Black Yeomanry: Life on St. Helena Island* (New York: Henry Holt, 1930), p. 118.

12. Guion Johnson and Guy Johnson, *Research in Service to Society: The First Fifty Years of the Institute for Research in Social Science at the University of North Carolina* (Chapel Hill: University of North Carolina Press, 1980), p. 27.

13. University of California anthropologist Carl Sauer praised Odum and the sociologists in IRSS for their regional studies that emphasized "folk-soil-study." Sauer noted, "We geographers and anthropologists have been talking about the concept of culture and the fact that culture is a spatial manifestation, but your [Odum's] is about the only one that has done anything about it." Johnson and Johnson, *Research in Service to Society*, p. 161.

14. Howard Odum, Guy Johnson, and other white southerners of the IRSS were considered "gradualist" on the issue of race in the South. In fact, they acknowledged that certain racial folkways (or "[white] southern way of life") made racial change slow and gradual. Their gradualism was

a conservative strategy of bureaucratic and state planning, and an outright rejection of direct protest movements that called for an end to Jim Crow governance. The "southern" in white southern liberalism was partly in support of racial equality without directly confronting Jim Crow. For more on the limits of the white southern liberalism of the "Chapel Hill" amid emerging progressive and leftist organizations ("southern popular front"), see: Glenda Gilmore, *Defying Dixie: The Radical Roots of Civil Rights, 1919–1950* (New York: W. W. Norton, 2008), pp. 201–246.

15. T. J. Woofter actually used the phrase "white paternalism" in his discussion about the benefits of the Penn School on rural Blacks.

16. See: Guy Johnson's "Love Affair with Music with Other Personal Reflections," jointly published by Guy Johnson and the Institute of Research in the Social Sciences and the Department of Sociology, 1986, pp. 1–15. Guy Johnson Papers, 1862–1889, 1901–1987. This is a short autobiography.

17. Johnson recalled that his father took him to Dallas where he attended "matinee performance" of popular artists, such as John Thomas, Mary Garden, and possibly, Caruso. Ibid., 3.

18. Johnson came into Baylor with a focus on the pre-ministerial program. But he was turned off by his Bible professor, who humiliated "non-ministerial" students for asking a question that cut against his biblical literalism. This led him to take courses in the new Sociology Department, where he found his mentor and teacher, G. S. Dow. Dow helped Johnson get into the University of Chicago. Dow was later forced to resign from his job at Baylor. Baptist fundamentalist J. Frank Norris and other Baptist fundamentalists protested his teaching of evolution at the University. This event turned Johnson away from the Southern Baptist tradition. See Johnson, "Love Affair with Music with Other Personal Reflections," p. 20.

19. Guy Johnson and Guion Johnson, *Research in Service Society: The First Fifty Years of the Institute for Research in Social Science at the University of North Carolina* (Chapel Hill: University of North Carolina Press, 1980), p. 134.

20. I borrowed this Johnson quote from Lynn Moss Sanders, *Howard W. Odum's Folklore Odyssey: Transformation to Tolerance through African American Folk Studies* (Athens: University of Georgia Press, 2003).

21. Odum's interviews with John Wesley on his adventures as a migrant laborer led to the former's fictional trilogy on a folk hero, "Black Ulysess, a musician physicianer and migrant worker": *Rainbow Round My Shoulders* (Indianapolis: Bobbs-Merrill, 1928), *Wings on My Feet* (Indianapolis:

Bobbs-Merrill, 1929), *and Cold Blue Moon* (Indianapolis: Bobbs-Merrill, 1931).

22. They were also attentive to regional and age variation.

23. Howard Odum and Guy Johnson, *Negro Workaday Songs* (Chapel Hill: University of North Carolina Press, 1926), pp. 8–9.

24. This chapter became *John Henry: Tracking Down a Negro Legend* (Chapel Hill: University of North Carolina Press, 1929). This is his best book on folklore that provides a functional analysis of the story import for Blacks working on the Big Bend Tunnel. For Johnson's chapter on John Henry, see: Odum and Johnson, *Negro Workaday Songs*, chapter 13.

25. UNC sociologists understood that black folk culture was both rural and urban, especially with migration. But University of Chicago sociologist Robert Park argued that black folk culture was a rural phenomenon, not urban. For instance, Park said that the spirituals were rural, while the blues were urban. The rural-urban split is a bit reductive.

26. See Guy Johnson, *A Study of the Musical Talent of the American Negro* (dissertation, University of North Carolina, 1924).Guy Benton Johnson Papers.

27. Odum and Johnson, *Negro Workaday Songs*, p. 264.

28. These new hires were made possible by a $240,000 grant from the Laura Spelman Rockefeller Memorial Fund (LRSM). In addition to Guy Johnson and his wife, social historian Guion Johnson, sociologist T. J. Woofter, economist Clearance Herr, and social psychologist Ernest Grooves were all hired as well.

29. For an intellectual biography on Woofter, see: Mark Ellis, *Race Harmony and Black Progress: Jack Woofter and the Interracial Cooperation Movement* (Bloomington: Indiana University Press, 2013).

30. Woofter, "Saint Helena Island: A Study of Negro Culture and Social Development," p. 1 (1927). This was a typed manuscript.

31. Johnson later noted that paved highways, cars, commercial trucking farming, education, radio, television, white capital (purchasing of homes and resorts on seashore park) have contributed to the breakdown of the obsolete culture. Yet, I would also bet that tourists were still coming to the islands to observe "folk" practices that he saw when the islands were supposedly isolated from the larger commercial and industrial world. See: Guy Johnson, "The Gullah Dialect Revisited: A Note on Linguistic Acculturation," *Journal of Black Studies*, Vol. 10, No. 4 (June 1980), p. 423.

32. Ernest R. Groves was a social psychologist. Prior to his tenure at UNC, he was head of the Department of Sociology at Boston University, 1920–1927. Born in 1877 in Framingham, Massachusetts, Groves aspired to the

Christian ministry and attended Yale Divinity School. He made a name for himself in the profession with his studies of family and marriage.

33. By the "new choir songs," he meant songs performed by a choir with a choir leader/director. Choirs performed the songs with purchased song books of a more "modern type." He described that the songs were performed in "ordinary tempo" and "fair harmonization." What is interesting here is that Johnson's argument about the perceived cultural isolation of the rural residents does not hold up with his brief and very short description of these modern songbooks that were purchased on the market. This presence of these books problematizes the isolation trope. Also, it begs the question of what other cultural expressions were ignored in order to make these people and their religious songs "folk." Lastly, he also noted that the "secular songs" were noticeably "conspicuous" among the residents.

The only secular songs he heard were a few minstrel, vaundeville songs, and other "insignificant songs" introduced by returning World War I soldiers. Also, the phonograph songs and children's game songs. His observation could have been due to the informants' decision not to sing "secular songs" for a variety of reasons. Johnson does not consider this. Lastly, he again doesn't call attention to the impact of traveling residents on the cultures there. His emphases on folk spirituals obscured other elements that might have exposed the limits of his claim that they were an isolated people with a folk culture.

34. Johnson, *Folk Culture on St. Helena Island*, p. 65.

35. In his study, Johnson acknowledged two distinct heritages of "white hymnology:" (1) the formal, dignified, and poetic hymns of Watts, Wesley, Newton, Cowper, and others; (2) the great revival and camp-meeting movement in the antebellum period. Johnson, *Folk Culture on St. Helena Island*, p. 75.

36. I borrowed this quote from Nathaniel Hatch, *Democratization of American Religion* (New Haven, CT: Yale University Press, 1989), p. 146.

37. Johnson, *Folk Culture on St. Helena Island*, p. 91.

38. Guy Johnson, "Supplementing Memorandum on Research on Cultural Isolates," *Committee on University Social Science Research Organizations: Conference on Research on Isolated Culture Groups (Cultural Islands)*, University of Chicago, January 21–22, 1939, p. 9 The Guy Johnson Papers.

39. Johnson did say that the one trait that was dominant in St. Helena and Black music and not in Euro-white music was the former's syncopation. He argues that this one trait could have been "traceable" to Africa. Ibid., p. 115. He even noted that his argument does not translate into the claim

that Blacks contributed nothing unique to the spirituals. He said there were a "few" white songs of Negro origin and that they were potentially traced to Africa. But he does not list them in his study.

40. White made the white derivative argument in his study of the Black spirituals in his *American Negro Folk-Songs* (Cambridge, MA: Harvard University Press,1926). George Pullen Jackson made the same claim in *White Spirituals in the Southern Upland* (Chapel Hill: University of North Carolina Press, 1933).

41. This derivative camp was tagged by Lawrence Levine, *Black Culture and Black Consciousness.*

42. Johnson gradually gets more confident in his argument over the years after the publication of his *Folk Culture on St. Helena Island* in 1930.

43. Guy Johnson, "The Negro Spiritual: A Problem in Anthropology," *American Anthropologist*, Vol. 33, No. 2 (April–June 1931), p. 170.

44. Some scholars argue that "Scots-Irish" as a term did not come into existence until the 1600s with the "Irish Plantation of Ulster (1609)"—where James I encouraged both poor Scots and English to migrate to northern Ireland (especially Ulster) for colonization. These Scots (and English) living in Ireland embraced the Protestantism/Presbyterianism over and against the Church of England. Religious and economic factors led to their migration to the American colonies before and during the fight for independence.

45. Guy Johnson, Folk Culture on St. Helena Island (Chapel Hill: University of North Carolina Press, 1930), pp. 101.

46. Ibid., p. 11.

47. Ibid., p. 62.

48. Guion Johnson, *The Social History of the Sea Islands* (Chapel Hill: University of North Carolina Press, 1930), p. 215.

49. Guy Johnson, "Some Factors in the Development of Negro Social Institutions in the United States," *American Journal of Sociology,* vol. 40, no. 3 (Nov., 1934), p. 334.

50. "George F. Peabody to Guy Johnson," May 28, 1931. Guy Benton Johnson Papers.

51. Contemporary musicologist Dena Epstein continued Krehbiel's argument: "any theory about folk music that ignores the sound of music and how it is performed cannot be valid." See: Epstein, "White Origin for the Black Spiritual? An Invalid Theory and How It Grew," *American Music*, Vol. 1, No. 2 (Summer 1983), pp. 57–58.

52. I borrow this quote from Sarah Caroline Thussen, "Taking the Vows of Southern Liberalism: Guion and Guy Johnson and the Evolution of

an Intellectual Partnership," *The North Carolina Historical Review*, Vol. LXXIV, No. 3 (July 1993), p. 304.

53. Johnson, "Some Factors in the Development of Negro Social Institutions in the United States," p. 332.

54. He does not consider West Central Africa.

55. Guy Johnson, "Conversion or Seeking," unpublished, 2–3. He scribbled Robinson's vision on a notecard. Guy Johnson Papers.

56. "Guy Johnson to William R. Laidlow," February 12, 1929. He did say that he should go to Louisiana for voodoo. Guy Benton Johnson Papers.

57. He made this argument in his research with the Gunnar Myrdal-Carnegie Study. I discuss this claim more in Chapter 4.

58. Johnson, *Folk Culture on St. Helena Island*, p. 78.

59. Callie S. to Guy Johnson [1928?]. The Guy Johnson Papers.

60. Woofter, *Black Yeomanry*, p. 251.

61. Ibid., p. 252.

62. Ibid., p. 149.

63. Woofter, *Black Yeomanry*, p. 247.

64. With regard to the Cooperative Association, Woofter described it as of "great value to the island farmer in advocating better methods of breeding and standardization of products." Other cooperative organizations included Farmer's Fair Committee, Trucker's Club, Poultry Club, Tomato Club, Junior Club, and Rosenwald School Committee (ibid., p. 153).

65. Ibid.

66. Ibid., p. 24.

67. See: Eric Sean Crawford, "The Penn School's Educational Curriculum: Its Effects on the St. Helena Songs," *Journal of African American Studies*, Vol. 17, No. 3 (September 2013), pp. 347–369.

68. Woofter noted that the praise houses keep crime at a minimum in the township. He further explained that "this trait of the community will doubtless surprise those who consider that the Negro has inherent criminal tendencies" (*Black Yeomanry*, p. 233).

69. Woofter, *Black Yeomanry*, p. 238.

70. He attributed the law and order environment to landowners, lack of economic and class divisions, and less racial friction. See: ibid., p. 238.

71. T. J. Woofter, "Saint Helena Island: A Study of Negro Culture and Social Development," (1927), 2 unpublished.

72. Guy Johnson, "The Gullah Dialect Revisited: A Note on Linguistic Acculturation," *Journal of Black Studies*, Vol. 10, No. 4 (January 1980), p. 423.

Chapter 3

1. "Emma Morris," Mass Venereal Disease Control Program, The Julius Rosenwald Fund Archive. Fisk University Special Collections and Archives.

2. The researcher interviewed Morris's daughter, Adair Smith, in Smith's home. Smith had children and also worked the same land as her mother. The researcher gathered from Smith that she and her mother worked part-time on Glen's farm. Smith's two youngest children worked when school was out. Smith, according to the researcher, stated that the family worked 12 weeks, four weeks each from her, the daughter, and son. She did not receive her daily rates of 50 cents. Instead, she usually received food and seeds. Last year, she raised 40 pounds of cotton for $1.00. "Adair Smith," Mass Venereal Disease Control Program.

3. The reference to her scaly feet was probably a suggestion that she had pellagra.

4. By family, I'm assuming that Morris meant her son, daughter, and two grandchildren.

5. At the end of his instruction to the patients, Eugene S. Miller, county health officer, told them that they "must continue treatment for twelve months if you hope to get your blood pure." "Instruction to Patients," Eugene S. Miller, Mass Venereal Disease Control Program, Julius Rosenwald Fund Papers.

6. Michael Davis to Charles Johnson, December 1, 1933. Davis was informing him about the cost, negotiations, and marketing aspects of the *Shadow of the Plantation*, with the University of Chicago Press. The fund actually paid the University of Chicago Press to publish the survey. Davis recommended that the book, with its pictures and testimonies, and scientific value, should be marketed in a magazine article that would highlight its relevance to the New Deal welfare state. He also recommended that Johnson's Fisk colleague, James Weldon Johnson, write an article in a magazine to further publicize the book.

7. For more on this transition, see: Alison Greene, *No Depression in Heaven: The Great Depression, the New Deal, and the Transformation of Religion in the Delta* (New York: Oxford University Press, 2016).

8. Ibid., p. 117. NRA codes "prevented direct discrimination by race in wages." Yet, the South would not adhere to these federal codes around race. Southern industrialists still found ways to discriminate against black workers through hiring schemes, such as downgrading their jobs to pay

them less than their white counterparts. Greene shows … Alison Greene, *No Depression in Heaven*, 117.

9. Michael Davis to Charles Johnson, December 1, 1933. Venereal Disease Control Program. After discussing the negotiations with the University of Chicago Press about the cost of publication, Davis informed Johnson that he had a discussion with Edwin Embree about how the book had both a "human interest as well as scientific value." Both the human interest and scientific value would be timely for the National Recovery Program that was largely affecting the South. This attempt was to partly address the shortcomings of the Agricultural Adjustment Act that excluded the predominantly Black (and white) tenant farmers and other landless workers. Johnson, Edwin Embree, and Will Alexander cowrote *The Collapse of Cotton Tenancy* and criticized the Agricultural Adjustment Act for "assum[ing] many of the risks of the landowners, and throwing them on the tenant (50). Charles Johnson, Edwin Embree, and Will Alexander, *The Collapse of Cotton Tenancy* (Chapel Hill: University of North Carolina Press, 1935), 50.

10. Charles Johnson, *Shadow of the Plantation* (Chicago: University of Chicago Press, 1934), p. 6.

11. Ibid.

12. In Johnson's report on his visit to Macon County, he noted that included the prevalence of other illnesses alongside syphilis were malaria, tuberculosis, pellagra, and infant death.

13. Johnson wrote about his personal experiences when his town finally implemented the separate but equal edict when he was seven years old. He recalled that the de jure segregation virtually remained abstract when it was first handed down by the Supreme Court. Then, he said "one Saturday afternoon," he went with his mother to the local drug store for an ice cream soda. They were regular customers of the drug store and had a friendly acquaintance with its white owner. But on this day, they went to the check-out line, the clerk hesitated, and went to go get the owner. He told Johnson's mother that "something had happened, it seemed, and that he could not serve [them] any more at the counter." He then narrated that the owner "became extravagant in his experiences of respect for the family, of my father's profession and character, and the virtuous qualities of a long string of Negroes whom he knew and who were in about the same relationship as we were to his business" (pp. 6–7). Blacks were confused as local businesses and trolleys began to enforce segregation while a "new self-consciousness burned within them." Johnson, "My Spiritual Autobiography,"

unpublished, Charles Johnson Papers. Fisk University, John Hope and Aurelia E. Franklin Library, Special Collections.

14. Alyssa Oursler, "Charles S. Johnson's Father Put Lee Street Baptist on the Map," *Bristol Herald Courier* (December 17, 2017).

15. Charles S. Johnson, "My Spiritual Autobiography," p. 2, undated, Charles S. Johnson Papers, 1866–1956, John Hope and Aurelia E. Franklin Library, Fisk University.

16. Charles S. Johnson, "My Spiritual Autobiography," p. 1.

17. Ibid., p. 8.

18. Charles S. Johnson, "A Layman's View on Religion: Real Courage Required To Apply Religion Without Comprise," *The Nashville Tennessean* (February 14, 1951), Charles S. Johnson Papers.

19. Charles Johnson, "A Sociologist amongst the Theologians," *Advance* (September, 1948), pp. 1–2. I have the typed draft of this article in my possession. Johnson affirmed the Amsterdam Conference's mandate for the churches to assume social responsibility amid the Cold War. He noted, "It is not sufficient to rest the case of Divine Witness with personal salvation. There are problems in society and, even more menacing, problems in international relations, that claim the attention of Christians and which require the adoption of a definite attitude and Christian action now, as responsible members of society [2]." The World Council of Churches founded a fellowship of churches to work towards tolerance and understanding that resulted in the first conference in 1948.

20. For the gender division of science and social work, and the tension between University of Chicago men and Hull House women, see: Mary J. Deegan, *Jane Addams and the Men of the Chicago School, 1892–1918* (New York: Routledge, 1990).

21. The Black Commissioners were Robert A. Abbott (*Chicago Defender* editor), George Cleveland Hall (physician), George Jackson (real estate), Edward Morris (lawyer), Adelbert Roberts (lawyer), and Lacey K. Williams (minister). The white Commissioners were Edgar A. Bancroft (lawyer), William S. Bond (real estate dealer), Edward Osgood Brown (lawyer), Harry Eugene Kelly (lawyer), Victor F. Lawson (editor), and Julius Rosenwald (business merchant). Francis Shpeardson of the State Department of Registration and Education later replaced Bancroft due to illness.

22. See: https://tamaratabel.com/2020/09/24/part-1-the-negro-in-chicago-a-study-of-race-relations-and-a-race-riot/.

23. See Robert E. Park, "Racial Assimilation in Secondary Groups," reprinted in *The Collected Papers of Robert Ezra Park, vols. 1, 2, 3* (New York: Arno Press, 1974), pp. 204–220. This essay was originally published in *The American Sociological Survey*, VIII (1913).

24. Toure Reed, *Not Alms but Opportunity: The Urban League and the Politics of Racial Uplift, 1910–1950* (Chapel Hill: University of North Carolina Press, 2008), p. 100.

25. Robert Park, "Introduction," in Johnson, *Shadow of the Plantation*, x. Park's rural/urban binary was indebted to Ferdinand Tonnies's *Gemeninschaft und Gessellschaft*. He was partly found of Tonnies's sacred and secular societies. The former "is typically a small, isolated community and more particularly the primary group—i.e. the family, the clan, or the religious sect,—a society, in short, where everything is known and everyone is bound to everyone else by obligation[s] that are at once personal and sacred. The secular society is given by mobility that accents the market place, "where people come together, not because they are alike, but because they are different, not for collective action, but for trade; for exchange of goods, of services, and of ideas. Nothing is sacred in secular society." See: Park, "The Problem of Cultural Differences," in *The Collected Papers of Robert Ezra Park*, p. 13.

26. Yvonne Chireau, *Black Magic: Religion and the African American Conjuring Tradition* (Berkeley: University of California Press, 2003).

27. Charles S. Johnson, "Review of Folk Beliefs of the Southern Negro," *Opportunity: Journal of Negro Life* (October 1926), p. 324.

28. W. I. Thomas, "Race Psychology: Standpoint and Questionnaire, with particular reference to the Immigrant and the Negro," *American Journal of Sociology*, Vol. 17, No. 6 (May 1912), p. 744.

29. See: Jason Ananda Josephson-Storm, "The Superstition, Secularism, and Religion Trinary: Or, Re-theorizing Secularism," *Method and Theory in the Study of Religion*, Vol. 30 (2018), pp. 1–20.

30. Charles Johnson, "Superstition and Health," *Opportunity: Journal of Negro Life* (July 1926), p. 207.

31. Puckett argued that a purely literary-based educational curriculum will not "do away with superstition." But he prioritized educating women (essentially future mothers who would hand down knowledge to their offspring) in the natural sciences as a way to "do away with superstition." See: Puckett, *Folk Beliefs of the Negro* (Chapel Hill: University of North Carolina Press, 1926), p. 580.

32. E. Franklin Frazier joined the department as faculty from 1929 to 1934, before moving to Howard University. For more on the hiring process involving Johnson and Frazier, see: Jonathan Holloway, *Confronting the Veil: Abram Harris, Jr., E. Franklin Frazier, and Ralph Bunche, 1919–1941* (Chapel Hill: University of North Carolina Press, pp. 141–143.

33. Floyd Calvin, "Charles S. Johnson Foresakes Harlem for Sunny South," *The Pittsburgh Courier,* July 28, 1928.

34. Ibid., p. 143. Also, interesting, Robert Park became an emeritus at the University of Chicago in 1933 and headed to Nashville, Tennessee in 1935 to join his mentee, Johnson, in the Social Science Department at the Fisk University in until his death in 1944.

35. For more work on the history of syphilis and policy, see: Alan Brandt, *No Magic Bullet: A Social History of Venereal Disease in the United States since 1880* (New York: Oxford University Press, 1987). Brandt documented the tension between moral reformers and medical practitioners on the best solutions to combat syphilis and other venereal diseases from the Progressive era to the New Deal. One of the Progressive organizations to identify and combat "white slave traffic," or prostitution, was the American Vigilance Association. See: "Vigilance Association," *Journal of the American Institute of Criminal Law and Criminology*, Vol. 13, No. 5 (January 1913), pp. 806–809.

36. On history of PHS in matters pertaining to syphilis, see: Susan M. Reverby: *Examining Tuskegee: The Infamous Syphilis Study and Its Legacy* (Chapel Hill: University of North Carolina Press, 2009), pp. 1–28. Brandt, *No Magic Bullet.*

37. I borrowed this information and quote from James H. Jones, *Bad Blood: The Tuskegee Syphilis Experiment*: New and Expanded Version (New York: Free Press, reprinted 1993), pp. 51–54.

38. Wenger to Davis, August 8, 1929. Venereal Disease Control Program. Wenger stated that after World War I, the federal government was interested in a venereal disease campaign and that Mississippi organized a Venereal Disease Division (p. 2).

39. Allan M. Brandt, "Racism and Research: The Case of the Tuskegee Syphilis Study," in *Sickness and Health in America: Readings in the History of Medicine and Public Health*, eds. Judith Walzer Levitt and Ronald Numbers (Madison: University of Wisconsin Press, 1997), p. 394. The US PHS continued to continue the study after the Rosenwald Fund pulled out because the state agencies could not hold up their share of the bargain in funding a wider comprehensive health program and social welfare plan due to the Great Depression in 1931. After Rosenwald pulled out of Macon County, officials like Clark, Wenger, and others stayed with the demonstration,

although changing its emphasis to an experiment on the latent and untreated effects of syphilis on Black men.

40. Counties for the venereal control demonstrations were Bolivar County, Mississippi; Macon County Alabama; Glynn County, Georgia; Pitt County, North Carolina; Tipton County, Tennessee; and Albemarle County, Virginia. Michael Davis to Charles S. Johnson, March 3, 1931. Venereal Disease Control Program. It is also important to note that philanthropies played a huge part in the administration of social welfare due to the dire situation of state and local agencies due to the Depression.

41. This estimate was given in by Jones in *Bad Blood*. In a letter to Michael Davis, Wenger asserted that the he had "approximately 1,000 cases of syphilis under treatment or observation in Macon County."

42. See: Edwin R. Embree and Julia Waxman, *Investment in People: The Story of Julius Rosenwald Fund* (New York: Harper & Brothers, 1988), pp. 28–36, 107–131.

43. Ibid., p. 33.

44. O. C. Wenger to Michael Davis, August 8, 1929, The Venereal Disease Control Program.

45. Michael Davis to Charles Johnson, March 3, 1931. The Venereal Disease Control Study. Davis' directions to Johnson about his "a social and economic study of the Negro population," was restated by Carl Buck in a letter on April 18, 1931. See: Carl Buck to Thomas Parran, April 18, 1931, Venereal Disease Control Program, Julius Rosenwald Fund Archives, John Hope and Aurelia E. Franklin Library, Fisk University.

46. Michael M. Davis, "Wanted: Research in the Economic and Social Aspects of Medicine," *Milbank Memorial Fund Quarterly*, Vol. 13, No. 4 (October 1935), p. 346.

47. Michael Davis to Charles Johnson, March 3, 1931. The Venereal Disease Control Study.

48. Davis to Julius Rosenwald Fund, "Differential Mortality in Central Tennessee," June 30, 1930. University of Chicago Special Collections.

49. Charles Johnson, "Health: Mortality Trends and the Transition from Folk Medium to Scientific Medium" (undated), Charles S. Johnson Papers Collection, Fisk University Archives and Special Collections, p. 1.

50. Charles Johnson, "Social Problems of Communities as Related to Public Health," Address on March 17, 1952, at the Institute of Public Health at Tuskegee Institute. Charles S. Johnson Papers Collections.

51. Paul Lombardo and Gregory Dorr, "Tuskegee Syphilis Experiment," *Bulletin of the History of Medicine*, Vol. 80, No. 2 (Summer 2006), p. 299.

52. Fredrick Hoffman, *Race Traits and Tendencies of the American Negro* (New York: Macmillan, 1896), p. 95.

53. For more information on eugenics and the Tuskegee Experiment, see: Paul Lombardo and Gregory M. Dorr, "Eugenics, Medical Education, and the Public Health Service: Another Perspective on the Tuskegee Syphilis Experiment," *Bulletin of the History of Medicine* (Summer 2006), pp. 291–316.

54. For discussion of eugenics in the South, see: Edward J. Larson, *Sex, Race, and Science: Eugenics in the Deep South* (Baltimore, MD: Johns Hopkins University Press, 1996).

55. For an excellent essay on the specific eugenics in syphilis studies, see Christopher Crenner, "The Tuskegee Syphilis Study and the Scientific Concept of Racial Nervous Resistance," *Journal of the History of Medicine and Allied Sciences*, Vol. 67, No. 2 (April 2012), pp. 244–280.

56. During 1891–1910, Normady Ceasur Boeck tested 2,000 white patients with latent syphilis to prove that they had self-defensive mechanisms that could better combat disease over anti-syphilis treatment.

57. Yet, Charles Johnson was a proponent of what he called "eugenic discrimination," particularly regarding birth control. He framed birth control for Black populations as a right, as for white people. He noted that the racist underpinnings have obscured the uses of eugenics for Black people. Johnson was a member of Margaret Sanger's Division of Negro Service of the Birth Control Federation (which eventually became the Planned Parenthood Federation of America). See: Charles S. Johnson, "A Question of Negro Health," *Birth Control Review*, Vol. 16, No. 6 (June, 1932), 167–169.

58. Human documents relied on "allowing subjects to [share] their outlook on life." For more discussion on human documents, see Patrick Gilpin and Marybeth Gasmen, *Charles S. Johnson: Leadership under the Veil* (Albany: State University of New York, 2003).

59. Johnson, "Supplementary Study of Macon County V.D. Demonstration" (November 1931), Venereal Disease Control Study.

60. Charles Johnson, "Health: Mortality Trends and the Transition from Folk Medium to Scientific Medium," p. 1. Charles S. Johnson Papers.

61. Johnson, *Shadow of the Plantation*, p. 6.

62. For more on modern agricultural, see: Jack Temple Kirby, *Rural Worlds Lost: The American South, 1920–1960* (Baton Rouge: Louisiana University Press, 1987), pp. 1–22.

63. Charles S. Johnson, "The Rise of Liberalism in the South," *World Outlook* XXVIII, No. 9 (September 1938), p. 27.

64. As Susan Reverby notes, the venereal control demonstration also took place amid many protests by Black farmers and the Communist Party in

Alabama. During the Macon County demonstration, "sharecroppers and industrial workers were organizing." The tension between sharecroppers and the police force was pervasive in Alabama during the study: in 1931, in Talladega County, a sharecroppers' protest led to a shootout with local sheriffs. "In December of 1932, in Reelstown in Tallapossa County on the Macon Border, another shootout over land foreclosure put the Sharecroppers' Union organizer in jail for 13 years" (p. 30). This study was also during the conflict stemming from the Scottsboro Boys controversy. See: Susan Reverby, *Examining Tuskegee: The Infamous Syphilis Study and Its Legacy* (Chapel Hill: University of North Carolina, 2009), pp. 31–33. For extensive treatment on Black sharecroppers and the Communist Party in Alabama, see Robin Kelley, *Hammer and Hoe: Alabama Communists during the Great Depression* (Chapel Hill: University of North Carolina, 1990).

65. Johnson, "Concept of the Folk," lecture (undated), p. 4.

66. Charles S. Johnson, "The Concept of the Folk Negro," lecture, p. 2. Unpublished. Charles S. Johnson Papers.

67. Charles S. Johnson, *Growing Up in the Black Belt: Negro Youth in the Rural South* (District of Columbia: American Council on Education, 1941), 75.

68. Alice O' Connor, *Poverty-Knowledge: Social Science, Social Policy, and the Poor in Twentieth-Century U.S. History* (Princeton, NJ: Princeton University Press, 2001), p. 55.

69. Johnson, *Shadow of the Plantation*, p. 6.

70. Charles S. Johnson, "Negro Health: From Folk Medium to Scientific Medium," lecture, Charles S. Johnson Collection, p. 1.

71. "Mental antiques" or "heirlooms" were terms used by folk sociologist Niles Newbell Puckett in *Folk Beliefs of the Southern Negro*. In his introduction, he said that southern Blacks were custodians of an American past, especially in thought. Johnson was definitely influenced by Puckett. Puckett received his Ph.D. at Yale University under A. G. Keller, who was in turn trained by William Graham Sumner.

72. Johnson, *Shadow of the Plantation*, p. 195.

73. Ibid., p. 193. The daughter died from tuberculosis.

74. Ibid., 195.

75. Ibid., p. 199.

76. "Interviews Concerning Health," Fisk University, Department of Social Science: Fisk University Archives and Special Collections.

77. Johnson, *Shadow of the Plantation*, p. 27.

78. Ibid., p. 151.

79. Ibid., p. 159.

80. Charles S. Johnson, "Health: Mortality Trends and the Transition from Folk Medium to Scientific Medium," 30. Charles S. Johnson Papers.

81. Nancy Tomes, *The Gospel of Germs: Men, Women, and the Microbe in American Life* (Cambridge, MA: Harvard University Press, 1998), p. 27.

82. Ibid., p. 47. According to Tomes, the new germ theory of disease "neatly harmonized" with the "sanitary science" that had already been in existence.

83. O. C. Wenger, "Macon County Alabama Demonstration for the Control of Syphilis among the Rural Negro Population, April 16–May 24, 1930," p. 2. Venereal Disease Control Program.

84. Johnson, *The Shadow of the Plantation*, p. 14.

85. Ibid, p. 153.

86. Ibid., p. 153.

87. Ibid., p. 151.

88. Charles Johnson, "Report on Visit to the Macon County Demonstration for the Control of Syphilis," p. 4. Venereal Disease Control Program. Johnson also included that the Rosenwald schools and special meetings had purchase among Macon County residents. The Rosenwald name resonated with the residents due to the school building programs in the area. He said in his report that the residence had an automatic deference to "official authority." Johnson stated, "The Negro population is considerably subdued, and gives the impression of accepting or following without much question the dictum of the local government" (p. 5).

89. Johnson, "Memorandum to Dr. Michael Davis: Supplementary Study of Macon County V.D. Demonstration." Venereal Disease Control Program (November 1931), p. 4.

90. O. C. Wenger to Michael Davis, August 8, 1929. Venereal Disease Control Program.

91. Embree and Waxman, *Investment in People: The Story of Julius Rosenwald Fund*, p. 33.

92. See: Michael M. Davis, "How Medical Care Should Fit into an Emergency Relief Program, *Social Service Review*, Vol. 7, No. 3 (September 1933), pp. 481–484. The Research in the Social and Economic Aspect of Medicine also contributed to President Harry Truman's National Health Insurance Bill in 1945 that was cut down in 1946 by a Republican-led Congress.

93. Johnson, "Report on Visit to the Macon County Demonstration for Control of Syphilis," [undated], p. 3. Venereal Disease Control Program.

94. Edward H. Beardsley, *A History of Neglect: Health Care for Blacks and Mill Workers in the Twentieth-Century South* (Knoxville: University of Tennessee Press, 1987), p. 28.

Chapter 4

1. The Negro in America: Research Memorandum for Use in the Preparation of Dr. Gunnar Myrdal's *An American Dilemma*, microfilm, p. 3.

2. Guy Johnson, "Notes on Behavior at Religious Service at the Father Divine Peace Mission," unpublished, Guy Benton Johnson Papers, Southern Historical Collection, Louis Wilson Library Special Collection, University of North Carolina, pp. 3–4.

3. Johnson stated that Edward Nelson Palmer had visited the banquet before. In Palmer's field study he gave the address of Father Divine's "Heaven": "A portion of West 126th Street between Harlem's Seventh and Lenox Avenues located one branch of Heaven on earth." Palmer, "A Visit to One of Father Divine's Heaven," unpublished. Guy Benton Johnson Papers.

4. Edward Nelson Palmer was on faculty at Fisk University at the time of the study. Born in 1917 in Wilberforce, Ohio, Palmer received his doctoral degree in sociology from the University of Michigan where he wrote a dissertation that examined the impact of unions and mechanization on Black automobile workers and their community organization. See: Edwin Embree *Julius Rosenwald Fund: Review for the Two-Period, 1938–1940* (Chicago, 1940), p. 26. In the Myrdal-Carnegie study, Palmer was a research assistant in the area of Black religion.

5. Palmer, unpublished, "A Visit to One of Father Divine's Heaven," p. 9. Palmer visited the "Heaven" on August 1, 1939.

6. Johnson had a *New York Times* article ("Father Divine Seeks Home Next to President") in his files. Father Divine sought to purchase the Frederick Vanderbilt estate next door to Eleanor and Franklin Roosevelt's Hyde Park home in New York State. The real estate agent gave Father Divine problems when they found out it was him, and not his white secretary, John Lamb, who initially went to purchase the estate. Divine had Lamb write a letter to the Roosevelts to get their approval to purchase the estate. Eleanor Roosevelt initially responded that "there can be no reason against any citizen of our country buying such property as he wishes to acquire." Then, Franklin Roosevelt had his secretary, John Early, send a response to Divine that went over the history of the place and then stated that he thought the "Vanderbilt place should be acquired preferably by some public or government body in order that it might serve the public in perpetuity as a point of interest to visitors from all parts of the nation." This was an interesting response in light of his and Eleanor's earlier response. But Divine responded that "it has been my aim and purpose to lift up a standard of moral betterment for social justice by the act of the cooperative system, to encourage and promote the brotherhood of man and the love of this democracy." He

further noted that the Peace Mission adhered to the Constitution and its amendments, and the Declaration of Independence. The appeals to democracy, even anti-welfare stance/relief rolls, or their businesses that catered to urban residence (such low price of certain goods and services) did not come into the picture in Johnson's analysis. Instead, he only focused on the religious expressions to further exoticize the Peace Mission movement. See: "Father Divine Seeks Home Next to President," *New York Times* (August 17, 1939).

7. Fauset reproduces some of the same arguments about the "cults" as the prewar sociologists, for example how they provide release from psychological tension. But his attention to the different programs and political ideologies paints a more complicated picture of these movements than the accounts of Guy Johnson, Gunnar Myrdal, and others. His functionalist arguments (closeness to the divine, relief from mental or physical illness, race-consciousness, and personality of a charismatic leader) were also informed by actual congregants. He was mainly assessing the "cults" in his criticism of Melville Herskovits and Robert Park. Still, he did recycle the perspective that these were cults. See: Arthur Fauset, *The Black Gods of the Metropolis: Negro Religious Cults of the Urban North* (Philadelphia: University of Pennsylvania Press, 1944). Also, Fauset's career as a folklorist is often ignored. For instance, he traveled with folklorist Elsie Clews Parson to Nova Scotia where they gathered folklore among Black communities.

8. Jackson, *Gunnar Myrdal and America's Conscience* (Chapel Hill: University of North Carolina Press, 1990), p. 116.

9. See: Robert Cherry, "The Culture-of-Poverty Thesis and African Americans: The Work of Gunnar Myrdal and Other Institutionalists," *Journal of Economic Issues*, Vol. 29, No. 4 (December 1995), pp. 1119–1132. Cherry noted that the "The Culture of Poverty Thesis" goes back to the Progressive era.

10. Gunnar Myrdal, *American Dilemma: The Negro Problem and Modern Democracy* (New York: Harper and Brothers, 1944), p. 701.

11. This claim is interesting given his prior claims that folk religion developed out of regional isolation.

12. Guy Johnson, "Notes on Behavior at Religious Service at the Father Divine Peace Mission," 11. Guy B. Johnson Papers.

13. He did mention the "restoration movements" in the Midwest that influenced the Peace Missions movement. William Seymour and Azusa Street were not mentioned in his discussion of the Peace Mission.

14. Myrdal, *American Dilemma*, p. 938.

15. Ibid., p. 645.

16. Ibid., pp. 109–110.

17. Guion Griffis Johnson and Guy B. Johnson (with the Assistance of Edward Nelson Palmer), "The Church and the Race Problem in the United States: A Research Memorandum," Part 2, unpublished, September 1, 1940, p. 300. Guy Benton Johnson Papers, 1830–1882, 1901–1987.

18. For more information on Davis's work with Dollard at Yale, and the American Youth Commission, established by Franklin Roosevelt's administration in 1935, see: David A. Varel, *The Lost Black Scholar: Resurrecting Allision Davis in American Social Thought* (Chicago: University of Chicago, 2018), pp. 108–132.

19. Allison Davis submitted a memorandum, "The Negro Church and Associations in the Lower South," in August 1, 1940. The total amount of the money distributed for Davis's (and Drake's) works was $4,485. This money included monthly rates for the research study, travel, lodging, and missed rent. For submitting a research memorandum, Davis received $1,200 while Drake, as a half-time research assistant, received $800. "Statement of Agreement Reached in Conference between Drs. Myrdal, Johnson, Allison Davis," July 10, 1939. Allison Davis Papers, 1932–1984, Special Collections Research Center, University of Chicago Library.

20. While a graduate student in Harvard University's Anthropology Department, Davis, along with his colleagues, such as the partner, Elizabeth Davis, Mary Gardner, and Burleigh Gardner, did fieldwork in Natchez, Mississippi, for two years, 1933–1935. The field study resulted in *Deep South: A Social Anthropological Study of Caste and Class*, eds. Allison Davis, Burleigh B. Gardner, and Mary R. Gardner (Chicago: University of Chicago Press, 1941).

21. St. Clair Drake was a student at Hampton Institute where he took courses with Allison Davis in the English Department. Drake submitted a memorandum on Black Churches and Lodges in Chicago for the Myrdal study.

22. David Varel, *The Lost Black Scholar: Resurrecting Allison Davis in American Social Thought* (Chicago: University of Chicago Press, 2018), p. 72.

23. Gunnar Myrdal, *An American Dilemma: The Negro Problem and Modern Democracy* (New York: Harper & Brothers Publishers, 1944), p. 75

    This statement highlighted the conundrum of liberalism where folk (lower-class) religion was a reflection of the consequences of their lower social state due to racial segregation. But the preoccupation with right and moral behaviors, at times, framed it as causing the lower social status of the black poor.

24. I'm indebted to late American intellectual historian Walter A. Jackson's erudite book on Gunnar Myrdal for a lot of the background information on
the Myrdal-Carnegie Negro Problem study; see: Jackson, *Gunnar Myrdal
and America's Conscience*.

25. In the "Foreword" to *An American Dilemma*, Frederick Keppel mentioned the Foundation's conventional approach to the Negro problem, set
by Andrew Carnegie. "The wide sweep of Andrew Carnegie's interests included the Negro, he gave generously to Negro institutions, and was closely
identified with both Hampton and Tuskegee Institutions." Gunnar Myrdal,
An American Dilemma: The Negro Problem and Modern Democracy
(New York: Harper & Brothers, 1944), p. vi.

26. Jackson, *Gunnar Myrdal and America's Conscience*, p. 55.

27. Myrdal's original first name was Karl. According to intellectual biographer
Walter A. Jackson, he reportedly dropped Karl out of his rejection of Karl
Marx and Marxism (particularly the Communist Revolution).

28. Trinidadian-American Marxist sociologist Oliver Cox critiqued Myrdal's
homogenizing the "American Creed," and his neglect of interpretative
conflicts of American democracy (constitutional form) in history. Cox
also challenged Myrdal's moralism that ignored the very economic interest that structured the American Creed and race prejudice. See: Oliver
Cox, "An American Dilemma: A Mystical Approach to the Study of Race
Relations," in his *Race: A Study in Social Dynamics* (New York: Monthly
Review Press, reprinted 2000), pp. 206–288.

29. Later, he stood on his optimism by calling attention to the Supreme Court's
decision in *Brown v. Board of Education*, and later the Civil Rights Bills of
1964 and 1965.

30. Jackson, *Gunnar Myrdal*, p. 211.

31. Harvard Sitkoff, *A New Deal for Blacks: The Emergence of Civil Rights
as a National Issue: The Depression Decade*, 30th anniversary edition
(New York: Oxford University Press, 2009), p. 143.

32. Myrdal calls this the "principle of cumulation," "an improvement in the
black standard of living should set in motion a broader cycle of change,
leading to eventual equality and desegregation." See: Jackson, *Gunnar
Myrdal and America's Conscience*, p. 209.

33. Gunnar Myrdal, "Memorandum to Frederick Keppel," January 28, 1940,
The Negro in America: Research Memorandum for Use in the Preparation
of Dr. Gunnar Myrdal's *An American Dilemma*, microfilm.

34. Ibid., p. 3.

35. Ibid., p. 3.

36. Myrdal, *An American Dilemma*, p. 212.

37. I borrowed this quote from Jackson, *Gunnar Myrdal and America's Conscience*, pp. 91. This book was published in 1994 by University of North Carolina Press.

38. Myrdal, *An American Dilemma*, p. 205.

39. Ibid.

40. Myrdal, *American Dilemma*, p. 221.

41. Cornel West referred to Myrdal as a "market liberal" who thought that "African American oppression [could] be alleviated if the state intervenes into racist structures of employment practices and thereby ensures, coercively if necessary, that fair criteria are utilized in hiring and firing black people" (p. 255). Although I think that Myrdal could also very well be a "cultural liberal" who would have supported different governmental programs to prepare people, particularly Blacks, for the market. It is my intention to suggest that Myrdal and other liberals' attention to the market also reinforced certain behavioral and cultural norms. See: Cornel West, "Race and Social Theory," in his *Keeping Faith: Philosophy and Race in America* (New York: Routledge, 1993), p. 255.

42. According to Walter Jackson, Myrdal felt that the agricultural laws were too weak and naïve to make a significant dent in the stagnant southern agricultural economy. He felt that mechanization and surplus population would further displace farmers. In the end, he advocated that the federal government should engineer Black southern migration by placing them in non-agricultural industrial jobs in urban cities. See: Jackson, *Gunnar Myrdal and America's Conscience*, pp. 207–208.

43. My discussion of the NEC Report is inspired by David Carlton and Peter Coclanis's "Introduction," in *Confronting Southern Poverty in the Great Depression: The Report on the Economic Conditions of the South with Related Documents*, eds. David Carlton and Peter A. Coclanis (Boston: Bedford/St. Martin's, 1996), pp. 1–37.

44. "Lowell Mellet to the President," June 25, 1938. Reprinted in Carlton and Coclanis, eds., *Confronting Southern Poverty in the Great Depression*, p. 43.

45. Ibid., p. 77.

46. For work on the radical left in the South, see: Robert D. G. Kelley, *Hammer and Hoe: Alabama Communists during the Great Depression* (Chapel Hill: University of North Carolina Press, 1990). Glenda Gilmore, *Defying Dixie: The Radical Roots of Civil Rights, 1919–1950* (New York: W. W. Norton, 2008).

47. Myrdal overlooked the leftist components of the conference. He simply limited his claims to a discussion on southern liberalism by saying that the conference represented the "lonely Southern liberals" who met in large numbers. He noted that the SCHW conference in Birmingham was the

"nearest approach to an organized political front" in the South. Yet, he felt that the Conference, like his broader critique of southern liberalism, did not have mass appeal beyond the "conference rooms and college lecture halls" (p. 473). For his discussion on the SCHW Conference, see: Myrdal, *American Dilemma*, pp. 466–473.

48. See: Gilmore, *Defying Dixie*, 269. Gilmore shows how the SCHW Conference united liberal politics with "Communist activism." At the helm of the conference were Communist Joseph Gelders and CIO activist Lucy Mason. Both Gelders and Mason connected with the Roosevelts, and organized the conference in light of the release on the *Report on Economic Conditions of the South* (p. 270).

49. Kelley, *Hammer and Hoe: Alabama Communists during the Great Depression*.

50. For information on leftist politics within Black social sciences, see: Jonathan Holloway, *Confronting the Veil: Abram Harris Jr., E. Franklin Frazier, and Ralph Bunche, 1919-1941* (Chapel Hill: University of North Carolina Press, 2002).

51. Benjamin E. Mays, *The Negro's God: As Reflected in His Literature* (Eugene: WIPF & Stock, reprinted 2010), p. 243. This book was originally published in 1938.

52. Negro Congregational Minister, "The Negro Church," Appendix B. The minister attributed the "young people's interest in the social experiment now going forward in Russia" to their distrust in the "static and nonprogressive character of the church" (p. 9), Guy Benton Johnson Papers, 1830–1882, 1901–1987.

53. It is important to note that Myrdal understood, like Charles Johnson, that the Black lower class was not homogeneous.

54. See: Myrdal, *American Dilemma*, pp. 9–12. Myrdal argued that religious freedom was a constitutive part of American Protestantism. Myrdal articulated what Tracy Fessenden calls the "Protestant-secular." In fact, he noted that democracy in America was first religious, before it was political. He acknowledged the myth of religious freedom in the colonies. But he also said that it was a myth was a "social reality with important consequences." He further extended the view that "religion itself in America took on a spirit of fight for liberty" (p. 10). With regard to the Protestant character of private charity that would give rise to the welfare state, he noted: "But I cannot help feeling that the Christian neighborliness of the common American reflects, also, an influence from the churches. . . . It shows up in the American's readiness to make financial sacrifices for charitable purposes. . . . It was not only rugged individualism,

nor a relatively continuous prosperity, that made it possible for America to get along without a publicly organized welfare policy almost up to the Great Depression in the thirties but it was also the world's most generous private charity" (pp. 11–12). To be sure, as other scholars have noted, Myrdal's historical idealization of the American democracy obscured its colonial past.

55. Myrdal, *American Dilemma*, p. 11.
56. Myrdal later regretted his early conclusions about Black religion in light of the Southern Christian Leadership Council and the broader modern civil rights movement. He saw religion as a source for political and democratic change.
57. Myrdal also paid attention to age differentiation in Black life.
58. Lyonel C. Florant's essay, "The Role of Abyssinian Baptist Church in Respect to Migrants," was included in the appendix of Guion and Guy Johnson's "Negro Church and the Race-Relations Problem" for the Myrdal-Carnegie Study. I do not agree with Florant's dichotomy between progressive and traditional. But he still noted the class complexity of the congregation. He basically said the church struck a nice balance between traditional and social gospel politics for the young and old. For instance, he said Adam Clayton Powell, Jr., maintained a "happy median between progressivism and "gestures, carrying-on of proverbial Baptist preacher." Florant, "The Role of Abyssinian Baptist Church," in Guy Benton Johnson Papers, 1830–1882, 1901–1987, pp. 3–4.
59. Myrdal, *American Dilemma*, p. 864.
60. He noted that his take on assimilation into the White mainstream culture was a *practical* argument.
61. Myrdal, *American Dilemma*, p. 863.
62. Johnson and Johnson, "The Church and the Race Problem in the United States," Vol. 2, p. 269.
63. Johnson and Johnson, "The Church and the Race Problem in the United States," Part II, p. 271.
64. Johnson and Johnson, "The Negro Church and the Race Problem in the United States," p. 279.
65. Ibid., pp. 248–269.
66. Ruth Landes, "Ethos of the Negro in the New World," unpublished (Sept. 1, 1940), Guy Benton Johnson Papers. She concentrated on six areas (Jamaica, Haiti, Dutch Guiana, Brazil, United States, West Africa) to demonstrate how the study of Black folkways in the Western world was ultimately a study of acculturated institutions and behaviors (p. 5). She used her research memoranda to show that when studying Blacks in the

Americas and West Africa, one must include a recognition of the contact with several civilizations of Blacks of diverse tribal traditions and physical forms. Also, this recognition must grapple with their contact with diverse peoples of European decent. Yet, she argued that the African forms were "less known than the Europe." She then notes that "intra-cultural phenomena must include a consideration of a) traits Negroes retained universally in the New World, with homologous forms in Africa; b) African traits lost universally in the new world; c) traits retained and/or developed locally."

67. Johnson and Johnson, "The Church and the Race Problem in the United States Part II," Guy Benton Johnson Papers, p. 433.

68. Johnson and Johnson, "The Church and Race Problem in the United States," p. 450.

69. Allison Davis, "Review of Race and Culture by Franz Boas," *Phylon*, Vol. 2, No. 1 (First Quarter, 1941), p. 93.

70. W. Lloyd Warner, "Introduction," in *Deep South: A Social Anthropological Study of Caste and Class*, eds. Allison Davis, Burleigh B. Gardner, and Mary R. Gardner (Chicago: University of Chicago Press, 1941), p. 3.

71. Wright was born a few miles from what was then Natchez, Mississippi. Now, his hometown is considered a part of Natchez, Mississippi.

72. He said that the rental prices ranged from $10.00 for three-room houses to $2.50 for the poorest houses in the alleys. He explained that the average monthly rental for the lower-class Blacks was $4.05 (p. 17).

73. Davis noted that New Orleans, the sixth largest southern city in the Lower South, had a total population of 458,762, with Blacks at 129,632. Half of White men held white-collar positions, while only 6.6% of Blacks held these positions. He said that more than "one-half of all Negro men, and more than three-fourths of all Negro women, who were employed in 1930, had unskilled status" (p. 8). And Black unemployment was "exceeding great" (p. 9). Davis, "The Negro Church and Associations in the Lower South: A Research Memorandum," unpublished, June 1, 1940.

74. Ibid., 2. Yet Davis understood that these sanctions did not apply to sexual unions between white men and Black women. He understood that these sanctions were part and parcel of the legacy of slavery and were brewed in power. These conjugal relationships were norms and rules in the Lower South. He documented how a Black minister protested the unions only to upset white men who were coming to inflict harm and violence on him. They were swayed by the son of a local Black leader who said he would talk to him.

75. Myrdal was clear that he used caste as a concept to "help make [thinking] clear and observation accurate" (p. 667). He further noted that "social relations across caste lines" varied according to region and class in America. But that the caste line is rigid and unblurred. See: Myrdal, *American Dilemma*, pp. 667–676.

76. Davis, "The Negro Church and Associations in the Lower South," p. 3.

77. Ibid., p. 3.

78. Ibid., p. 3.

79. Ibid., p. 29.

80. Ibid., p. 32.

81. In the case of New Orleans, he noted how one of the Mothers of a Spiritualist church was charged in police court for holding programs where Black and whites were congregating together. This was the service in which both Blacks and whites "participated freely." According to the social anthropologist, the white judge directed her, "You go uptown and serve *your* God, and let these white people serve *their* God" (ibid., p. 32).

    On Black mothers ordaining and baptizing white women, Davis gave one example in Mother B's Spiritualist Church. "Mother called on Reverend A (white female): 'Friends, I'm going to ask Rev A. to say a few words. I ordained her and baptized her, and I want to tell you, friends, we are not serving color tonight. We are serving the true living God who says, If I be lifted up, I'll draw all men unto men. He did not speak of color. We are not speaking of color, so I'm going to ask Rev. A to speak to you in her way'" (ibid., p. 33).

82. "Luke Turner" in Hurston's "Hoodoo in America" in the *Journal of American Folklore* (October–December, 1931) was given the name "Samuel Thompson" in *Mules and Men* (New York: HarperCollins, 2008 [1936]).

83. Zora Hurston, "Hoodoo In America," *Journal of American Folklore* (October–December, 1931), p. 319. In fact, we can say that Hurston's claim about the persistence of paganism in Black religion related to her understanding about the role of the state in suppressing Black religiosity. This is seldom attended to in Hurston's work. She mentioned that Blacks had "reverted to paganism" to "revolt against the sterile rituals of the Protestant church," see: "Zora Hurston to Langston Hughes," in *Zora Neale Hurston: A Life in Letters, eds. Carla Kaplan* (New York: Anchor Books, 2002), p. 110.

84. Nick Salvatore, *Singing in a Strange Land: C. L. Franklin, the Black Church, and Transformation of America* (New York: Little, Brown, 2005), p. 6.

85. Davis, "The Negro Church and Associations in the Lower South," p. 46.

86. He observed one minister who told his congregants that a good Christian was an "obedient tenant and faithful worker for his white landlord." He further said that obedient and good work would ensure a "settlement" that would be satisfactory at the end of the year. Davis, "The Negro Church and the Associations in the Lower South," p. 46.

87. It is not certain that Spiritualists used "fortune-telling" to describe their own practices, although whites who visited Black Spiritualists used that term in Davis's memorandum.

88. Davis, "The Negro Church and Associations in the Lower South," p. 52.

89. For information on Davis's upbringing in a middle-class family in Washington, D.C., before his father's job in the Government Printing Office was jeopardized by Woodrow Wilson and his supporters' legislation of segregation in federal and civil services, see: Varel, *The Lost Black Scholar*, pp. 1–42.

90. Davis, "The Negro Church and Associations in the Lower South," p. 137.

91. Myrdal, *American Dilemma*, p. 873.

92. Ibid.

93. "St. Clair Drake to Martin King," March 21, 1956, https://kinginstitute. stanford.edu/king-papers/documents/st-clair-drake.

94. Davis, Gardner, and Gardner, *Deep South*, pp. 414–415.

95. Myrdal, *American Dilemma*.

96. Ibid., p. 877.

97. Gunnar Myrdal, *An American Dilemma*, pp. 877–878.

98. At times Myrdal contradicted himself about the democratic possibilities and impossibilities of the South in the book.

99. Myrdal, *American Dilemma*, p. 463.

100. Ibid., p. 46578.

101. Ibid., p. 465.

102. Gunnar Myrdal, *American Dilemma*, p. 466.

103. For a wonderful book on Owen Whitfield and Claude Williams, see: Erik Gellman and Jarod Roll, *The Gospel of the Working Class: Labor's Southern Prophets in New Deal America* (Urbana: University of Illinois Press, 2011).

104. Johnson and Johnson, "The Church and the Race Problem," Part II, p. 315.

105. Ibid.

106. See: Anthea Butler, *Women in the Church of God in Christ: Making a Sanctified World* (Chapel Hill: University of North Carolina Press, 2007).

Chapter 5

1. Alan Lomax, *The Land Where the Blues Began* (New York: New York Press, 1993), pp. 43–57. The unfinished Coahoma Study resulted in "twenty-five sixteen-inch disc recordings" housed at the Library of Congress. See: *Lost Delta Found: Rediscovering the Fisk University-Library of Congress Coahoma County Study, 1941–1942*, eds. Robert Gordon and Bruce Nemerov (Nashville, TN: Vanderbilt University Press, 2005), pp. 1–26.

2. 1940 US Census.

3. Samuel Adams, "Changing Negro Life in the Delta," reprinted in *Lost Delta Found: Rediscovering the Fisk University-Library of Congress Coahoma County Study, 1941–1942*, (Nashville: Vanderbilt University Press, 2005), pp. 239–240. Adams' "Changing Negro Life in the Delta" was a Master's Thesis that he submitted to the Social Science Department at Fisk University in June of 1947. In his acknowledgments he thanked Jitsuichi Masuoka, Charles Johnson, and Edward Palmer, all faculty members of the department. He gave a special tribute to the late Robert Park due to his "directing [his] initial curiosity in the changing Negro life on a Delta plantation." After leaving the department, he enrolled in the doctoral program at the University of Chicago. He completed the program in 1953. According to Gordon and Nemerov, he was appointed to the federal position as Ambassador to the Republic of Niger, 1968–1969.

4. Ibid.

5. Lomax, *The Land Where the Blues Began.*

6. Ibid., p. 45.

7. There was another exchange with a song seller that was equally as interesting as his interaction with "Rev. Martin" outside the convention. A blind songwriter, Charles Heffner, who marketed himself as a noted "gospel writer and bible lecturer," was selling ballad sheets from his suitcase. Heffner was producing and singing songs that dealt with political turmoil and natural conflict. One of his songs, "These Days Got Everybody Troubled," was classified as a "[p]atriotic [s]ong of the European Conflict," World War II. He replied to Lomax (according to his recollection, of course) that "[a]lthough I am blind, the Lord has blessed me with good understanding and a wife who will read me all the papers" (p. 49). He referred to his songs as "warning songs" that admonished the "uncoverted or unconcerned Christian" or the wicked.

8. Lomax, *The Land Where the Blues Began*, p. 38. "In the Mood" was originally composed by Glenn Miller in 1939. Ellington was among many composers who reformed the arrangement.

9. See: "Introduction to Delta Manuscripts," in *Lost Delta Found: Rediscovering the Fisk University-Library of Congress Coahoma County Study, 1941–1942*, 1-26.

10. Thomas Elsa Jones was Fisk University's fifth president, from 1926 to 1946. Jones, like all the former Fisk presidents, was white (this was the case until Charles Johnson's presidency in 1948). Jones wanted to cozy up with reputable organizations, like philanthropies and governments, to bring prestige and resources to Fisk University.

11. Lomax, *The Land Where the Blues Began*. In a letter to the Division of Music at the Library of Congress, Lomax noted, "I believe that the result will be the establishment of [an] active South-wide folk lore work at Fisk University, and this again will have long-term, deep rooted cultural and scientific results." Alan Lomax to the Division of Music at the Library of Congress, September 18, 1941, *Alan Lomax: Assistant in Charge: The Library of Congress Letters, 1935–1946*, ed. Roland D. Cohen (Jackson: University of Mississippi, 2011), p. 243.

12. Lomax, *The Land Where the Blues Began*, p. xii.

13. Zora Hurston's relationship with Charles Johnson go back to her days as an upcoming writer. She was featured in the edited magazine *Opportunity*.

14. I borrowed "anti-modern modernism" from T. J. Jackson Lears, *No Place of Grace: Antimodernism and the Transformation of American Culture, 1880–1920* (Chicago: University of Chicago Press, 1994).

15. I am thinking of Zora Neale Hurston's distinction between the folk and concert spirituals. Zora Neale Hurston, "Spirituals and Neo-Spirituals," *The Sanctified Church* (New York: Marlowe & Company, 1981), pp. 79–84.

16. John Sr. recalled his state before the 1933 field expedition: "while in 1932 I was barely recovering from an exhausting illness, with a home broken by the death of my wife, my four children scattered, and two of them, Bess Brown and Alan, nine and sixteen [*sic*] years old, respectively, still financially dependent on me." John Lomax, *Adventures of a Ballad-Hunter* (New York: Macmillian, 1947), p. 106.

17. Harvard's English Department played a seminal role in the advance folklore studies. This was first attributed Francis J. Childs and his work in Scottish ballads. Kittredge studied under Childs and replaced his advisor, taking folklore studies to higher heights. What is interesting about the book was that he dedicated it to Theodore Roosevelt.

18. Karl Hagstorm Miller, "That's Right, You're Not from Texas: Exploring Some Outside Influences on Texas Music," pp. 2–3. For more on Roosevelt's masculinist politics, see: Gail Bederman, *Manliness and Civilization: A Cultural History of Gender and Race in the United States, 1880–1917* (Chicago: University of Chicago Press, 1995), pp. 170–216.

19. Lomax, *Adventures of a Ballad Hunter*, p. 112.

20. Alan and John Lomax, *American Ballads and Folk Songs* (New York: Macmillan Books, 1934)

21. Lomax, *Adventures of a Ballad Hunter*, p. 112.

22. I borrowed this quote from John Szwed, *Alan Lomax: The Man Who Recorded the World* (New York: Viking, 2010), p. 36.

23. "Letter to Betty Calhoun," September 17, 1935, *Alan Lomax: Assistant In Charge: Library of Congress Letters, 1935–1945*, p. 13.

24. Swzed, *The Man Who Recorded the World*, p. 37.

25. *The Anti-Slaver Reporter* (Jan.–Feb., 1899), p. 43.

26. For more on the relationship between Black convict labor and modernization, see Alex Lichtenstein, *Twice the Work of Free Labor: The Political Economy of Convict Labor in the New South* (New York: Verso Books, 1996). Lichtenstein rightly contests the notion that the convict labor system underscored the intersections of agriculture and industrial capitalism.

27. *Chicago Daily Tribune*, August 3, 1901.

28. Lomax, *Adventures of a Ballad Hunter*, p. 113.

29. Lomax, *The Land Where the Blues Began*, p. 257.

30. Ibid.

31. Lomax, *Adventures of a Ballad Hunter*, p. 113.

32. In a proposal to the Carnegie Corporation of New York, Alan wrote: "[P]rosperous members of the [Black] community, bolstered by the church and the school sneering at the naivete of the folk songs and unconsciously throwing the weight of their influence in the balance against anything not patterned after white bourgeois culture; the radio with its flood of jazz, created in tearooms for the benefit of city-dwelling whites—these things are killing the best and most genuine Negro folk songs." I borrowed this quote from Szwed, *Alan Lomax: The Man Who Recorded the World*, p. 38.

33. Interestingly, John and Alan told different accounts on what Sin-Killer actually told them about his preaching as it related to the recording machine. Alan recounted the recording of Sin-Killer Griffin's singing sermon in his autobiography. Alan actually said that after hearing his sermon on the recording machine, Griffin responded, "People been tellin' me I was a good preacher for nigh into sixty years, But I never known I was that good." See: *Alan Lomax: Selected Writings, 1934–1997*, ed. Ronald Cohen, (New York: Routledge Books, 2003), p. 52. For John account, see: John Lomax, *Adventures of a Ballad Hunter*, 229

34. John and Alan revisited Lead Belly in the Angola Prison on July 1, 1934. At the time, Lead Belly recorded songs to appeal to Louisiana governor O.

K. Allen to release him from prison. John and Alan let the governor hear it and he released Lead Belly. John and Alan would schedule singing tours with Lead Belly in the mid-1930s. At times, John had Lead Belly perform in prison attire. American writer Richard Wright criticized John Lomax as "one of the most amazing swindles in American history." See: Szwed, *Alan Lomax: The Man Who Recorded the World*, pp. 59–92.

35. Lomax, *The Land Where the Blues Began*, p. ix.

36. Lomax, *Adventures of a Ballad Hunter*, p. 126.

37. Ibid., pp. 1–23.

38. Ibid.

39. Lomax, *Adventures of a Ballad Hunter*, p. 126.

40. Ibid., p. 150. He said Black Samson noted that he learned the songs as a railroad and levee worker.

41. According to Swzed, while a student at Harvard, Alan was head of the student organization that raised money for the miners who were on strike in Harlan, Kentucky, see: Swzed, *Alan Lomax: The Man Who Recorded the World*, pp. 5–58.

42. His father offered his definition of folk in his autobiography. John noted that the folk were "the real people, the plain people, devoid of time and glamour." Lomax, *Adventures of Ballad Hunter*, p. ix.

43. Lomax, "Folk Music in the Roosevelt Era," *Alan Lomax: Selected Writings, 1934–1997*, p. 93.

44. For an excellent book on religion and photography in the New Deal, see: Colleen McDannell, *Picturing Faith* (New Haven, CT: Yale University Press, 2004).

45. "American Songs Are Played and Sung for King and Queen: Sovereigns Hear Our Typical Music," *New York Times*, June 9, 1939, p. 5.

46. Benjamin Feline, *Romancing the Folk: Public Memory and American Roots Music* (Chapel Hill: University of North Carolina, 2000), p. 133.

47. Jerrold Hirsch, *Portrait of America: A Cultural History of the Federal Writers' Project* (Chapel Hill: University of North Carolina Press, 2003).

48. Michael Denning, *Popular Front: Laboring of American Culture in the Twentieth Century* (New York: Verso Books, 1997).

49. Samuel C. Adams, Jr., "Changing Negro Life in the Delta" (Master's thesis: Fisk University, June 1947), reprinted in *Lost Delta Found: Rediscovering the Fisk University–Library of Congress Coahoma County Study, 1941–1942*, p. 226.

50. Phineas Maclean was representative of the, *Land Where the Blues Began*, p. 67.

51. Samuel C. Adams, "Changing Negro Life in the Dealth," reprinted in *Lost Delta Found: Rediscovering the Fisk University-Library of Congress*

Coahoma County Study, 1941–1942, p. 238. Originally Adams submitted the work as his dissertation in June 1947.

52. *America's Folklorist: B. A. Botkins and American Culture* (Norman: University of Oklahoma Press, 2010).

53. Alan Lomax, *The Land Where the Blues Began* (New York: The New Press, 1993), p. 81.

Conclusion

1. Nicholas Lemann, "The Origins of the Underclass," *The Atlantic Monthly* (June 1986). He also wrote the second piece the following month, July.

2. I think Elizabeth Hinton gives a wonderful account of the rise of the Black underclass by tracing it to the John F. Kennedy administration's juvenile delinquency programs, before the War on Poverty policies of his former vice president and successor, Lyndon Johnson.

3. Scholars accredited the coinage "underclass," with journalist Ken Aulette. Others invested in the term, like William Julius Wilson, who felt that scholars have stayed away from charting the pathological and deficient patterns of behaviors of the underclass in fear that they might be perceived as racist or blaming the victim. He attributed this critique to the emergence of the "Black solidarity" movement in the mid-1960s. See: William Julius Wilson, "The Black Underclass," *The Wilson Quarterly*, Vol. 8, No. 2 (Spring 1984), pp. 88–99.

4. Similarly, William Wilson used statistics to described the crime rates in Robert Taylor Holmes housing project. He noted that out of the city's crimes, 11% of all the city's murders, 9% of its rapes, and 10% of its aggravated assaults were committed in the housing project in 1980.

5. Lemann, "The Origins of the Underclass."

6. Lemann actually repeated a lot of William Julius Wilson's arguments.

7. Lemann, "The Origins of the Underclass," *The Atlantic Monthly* (July 1986).

8. After Lemann asked her about her and her family's secret to success, Mildred Nicholas noted that "[i]t might have been that we had a two-parent family." She further said, "father had a fourth-grade education, and my mother had eighth grade—we were middle-class. We lived in town. My father taught us that you have to be a strong person to survive. Willpower! Nothing, nobody is better than you. Nobody. Welfare? No! Jesus No! Because I simply could not be bought." Nicholas was the oldest of five siblings. She had a sister with a master's degree who taught school,

a brother who was an attorney in Jackson [Mississippi], a brother who was a businessman in Canton, a brother who was a graduate of Northwestern Law School, and the youngest sister was a pharmacist.

9. I borrowed this last part of the sentence from the white farm owner.

10. Lemann, "The Origins of the Underclass" (June 1986).

11. Lemann noted, "[a]lthough the problems of the ghettos seem to resist economic solutions, they do seem to respond to the imposition of a different, and more disciplined, culture."

12. Lemann, "The Origins of the Underclass" (July 1986).

13. Lemann asserted, "the programs in the ghetto that work best on a mass scale—most notably Project Head Start, the one poverty program widely acclaimed as a success, which starts giving special instruction to children at a very early age—represent not the ghetto's taking of its own but an intervention by the *mainstream culture*." Allison Davis played a significant role in the Head Start Program. For more on Davis's role on the Head Start Program, see: Varel, *Lost Black Scholar*, chapter 9.

Bibliography

Archival Collections

Clark University, Archives and Special Collections, Robert H. Goddard Library, Worcester, Massachusetts
   G. Stanley Hall Papers
   University Registers

Columbia University, Rare Book & Manuscript Library, New York, New York
   Alumni Federation Cards
   Columbia University Press Records
   Historical Biographical Files

Fisk University, Special Collections and Archives, John Hope and Aurelia E. Franklin Library, Nashville, Tennessee
   Charles S. Johnson Collection
   Julius Rosenwald Fund Archives

Oxford College, Archives and Special Collections Library, Oxford, Georgia
   Davis Papers
   Oxford Local History Collection

University of Chicago, The Hanna Holborn Gray Special Collections Research Center, Chicago, Illinois
   Allison Davis Papers
   Robert E. Park Papers

University of Mississippi, Department of Archives and Special Collections, Libraries, Oxford, Mississippi
   Catalogs and Registration

University of North Carolina–Chapel Hill, Louis Round Wilson Special Collections Library, Southern Historical Collection. Chapel Hill, North Carolina
   Guy Johnson Papers
   St. Helena Papers

Books, Articles, and Dissertations

Anderson, James D. *The Education of Blacks in the South, 1860–1935.* Chapel Hill: University of North Carolina Press, 1988.

Anderson, Mark. *From Boas to Black Power: Racism, Liberalism and American Anthropology.* Berkeley: University of California Press, 2019.

Asad, Talal. *Formation of the Secular: Christianity, Islam, Modernity.* Stanford, CA: Stanford University Press, 2003.

Averbeck, Robin M. *Liberalism Is Not Enough: Race and Poverty in Postwar Political Thought.* Chapel Hill: University of North Carolina Press, 2018.

Ayers, Edward. *Promise of the New South.* New York: Oxford University Press, 1992.

Bacon, Alice M. "The Dixie Work—Is It Worth Continuing," *Southern Workman,* Vol. xxii, No. 12 (1893).

Bacon, Alice M. "Folk-Lore and Ethnology," *Southern Workman,* Vol. xx, No. 12 (December 1893), pp. 180–181.

Bacon, Alice M. "Our Mohammedan," *Southern Workman,* Vol. xxi, No. 2 (February 1892), p. 31.

Bacon, Alice M. "Work and Methods of the Hampton Folk-Lore Society," *Journal of American Folklore Society,* Vol. 11, No. 40 (January–March 1898).

Baer, Hans, and Merrill Singer. *African American Religion in the Twentieth Century: Varieties of Protest and Accommodation.* Knoxville: University of Tennessee Press, 1992.

Baer, Hans, and Merrill Singer. *The Black Spiritual Movement: A Religious Response to Racism,* 2nd edition. Knoxville: University of Tennessee, 2001.

Bailey, Thomas. *Race Orthodox of the South and Other Aspects of the Negro Question.* New York: Neale, 1914.

Baker, Lee D. *Anthropology and the Racial Politics of Culture.* Durham, NC: Duke University Press, 2010.

Baker, Lee D. *From Savage to Negro: Anthropology and the Construction of Race, 1896–1954.* Berkeley: University of California Press, 1998.

Best, Wallace. *Passionately Human, No Less Divine: Religion and Culture in Black Chicago, 1915–1952.* Princeton, NJ: Princeton University Press, 2008.

Blum, Edward. *W.E.B. Du Bois: American Prophet.* Philadelphia: University of Pennsylvania Press, 2007.

Boas, Franz. *The Mind of Primitive Man.* Reprinted. New York: Collier Books, 1963.

Boas, Franz. *Race, Language, and Culture.* New York: The Free Press, 1940.

Brandt, Alan. *No Magic Bullet; A Social History of Venereal Disease in the United States since 1880.* New York: Oxford University Press, 1987.

Brandt, Alan. "Racism and Research: The Case of the Tuskegee Syphilis Study," in *Sickness and Health in America: Readings in the History of Medicine and Public Health,* eds. Judith Walzer Levitt and Ronald Numbers. Madison: University of Wisconsin Press, 1997, pp. 392–404.

Brazil, Wayne D. *Howard W. Odum: The Building Years, 1884–1930*. New York: Garland, 1988.

Bronner, Simon J. *American Folklore Studies: An Intellectual History*. Lawrence: Kansas University Press, 1986.

Bronner, Simon J. *Following Tradition: Folklore in the Discourse of American Culture*. Logan: Utah State University Press, 1998.

Butler, Anthea. *Women in the Church of God in Christ: Making a Sanctified World*. Chapel Hill: University of North Carolina Press, 2007.

Carlton, David, and Peter Coclanis. *Confronting Southern Poverty in the Great Depression: The Report on the Economic Conditions of the South with Related Documents*. Boston: Bedford/St. Martin's, 1996.

Cherry, Robert. "The Culture of Poverty Thesis and African Americans: The Work of Gunnar Myrdal and Other Institutionalists," *Journal of Economic Issues*, Vol. 29, No. 4 (December 1995), pp. 1119–1132.

Chireau, Yvonne P. *Black Magic: Religion and the African American Conjuring Tradition*. Berkeley: University of California Press, 2003.

Cohen, Elizabeth. *Making a New Deal: Industrial Workers in Chicago, 1919–1939*, 2nd edition. Cambridge: Cambridge University Press, 2008.

Cox, Oliver. "An American Dilemma: A Mystical Approach to the Study of Race Relations," reprinted in *Race: A Study of Social Dynamics* (New York: Monthly Review Press).

Crawford, Eric. S. "The Penn School's Educational Curriculum: Its Effects on the St. Helena Songs," *Journal of African American Studies*, Vol. 17, No. 3 (September 2013), pp. 347–369.

Crenner, Christopher. "The Tuskegee Syphilis Study of the Scientific Concept of Racial Nervous Resistance," *Journal of the History of Medicine and Allied Sciences*, Vol. 67, No. 2 (April 2012), pp. 347–369.

Davenport, Frederick M. *Primitive Traits in Religious Revivals: A Study in Mental and Social Evolution*. London: Macmillan, 1905.

Davis, Allison, Burleigh Gardner, and Mary Gardner. *Deep South: A Sociological Anthropological Study of Caste and Class*.

Davis, Allison, Burleigh Gardner, and Mary Gardner. "Review of Race and Culture by Franz Boas," *Phylon*, Vol. 2, No. 1 (First Quarter, 1941), pp. 92–94.

Davis, Michael M. "Wanted: Research in the Economic and Social Aspects of Medicine," *Milbank Memorial Fund Quarterly*, Vol. 13, No. 4 (October 1935), pp. 339–346.

Denning, Michael. *Popular Front: Laboring of American Culture in the Twentieth Century*. New York: Verso Books, 1997.

Dollard, John. *Caste and Class in a Southern Town*. Reprinted. Madison: University of Wisconsin Press, 1988.

Dorr, Gregory M., and Paul Lombardo. "Eugenics, Medical Education, and the Public Health Service: Another Perspective on Tuskegee Syphilis Experiment," *Bulletin of the History of Medicine* (Summer 2006), pp. 291–316.

Du Bois, W. E. B. *Dusk of Dawn: An Essay Toward an Autobiography of a Race Concept*. Reprinted. New Brunswick, NJ: Transaction, 1997.

Du Bois, W. E. B. *The Philadelphia Negro: A Social Study*. Reprinted. New York: Oxford University Press, 2007.

Du Bois, W. E. B. *Souls of Black Folk*. Reprinted. New York: Dover Publications, 1994.

Du Bois, W. E. B. "The Study of the Negro Problems," in *W.E.B. Du Bois: The Problem of the Color Line at the Turn of the Twentieth Century*. Reprinted. New York: Fordham University Press, 2015.

Egerton, John. *Speak Now against the Day: The Generation before the Civil Rights Movement in the South*. New York: Alfred Knopf, 1994.

Ellis, Mark. *Race Harmony and Black Progress: Jack Woofter and the Interracial Cooperation Movement*. Bloomington: Indiana University Press, 2013.

Embree, Edwin R., and Julia Waxman. *Investment in People: The Story of the Julius Rosenwald Fund*. New York: Harper & Brothers, 1988.

Emrich, Duncan. "Folk-Lore: William Johns Thoms," *California Folklore Quarterly*, Vol. 5, No. 4 (October 1946), pp. 355–374.

Epstein, Dena. "The White Origin for the Black Spiritual? An Invalid Theory and How It Grew," *American Music*, Vol. 1, No. 2 (Summer 1983).

Evans, Curtis. *The Burden of Black Religion*. New York: Oxford University Press, 2008.

Fauset, Arthur. *Black Gods of the Metropolis: Negro Religious Cults of the Urban North*. Reprinted. Philadelphia: University of Pennsylvania Press, 2001.

Feline, Benjamin. *Romancing the Folk: Public Memory and American Roots Music*. Chapel Hill: University of North Carolina, 2000.

Frazier, Franklin E. *The Negro Church in America*. Reprinted. New York: Schocken Books, 1974.

Frazier, Franklin E. *The Negro Family in the United States*. Reprinted. Notre Dame: University of Norte Dame Press, 2001.

Fredrickson, George M. *The Black Image in the White Mind: The Debate on Afro-American Character and Destiny, 1817–1914*. Middleton, CT: Wesleyan University Press, 1971.

Geary, Daniel. *Beyond Civil Rights: The Moynihan Report and Its Legacy*. Philadelphia: University of Pennsylvania Press, 2017.

Giggle, John M. *After Redemption: Jim Crow and the Transformation of African American Religion in the Delta, 1875–1915*. New York: Oxford University Press, 2007.

Gilmore, Glenda. *Defying Dixie: The Radical Roots of Civil Rights, 1919–1950*. New York: W. W. Norton, 2008.

Gilpin, Patrick, and Marybeth Gasmen. *Charles S. Johnson: Leadership under the Veil*. Albany: State University of New York Press, 2003.

Gould, Stephen Jay. *The Mismeasure of Man*. New York: W. W. Norton, 1996.

Greene, Alison. *No Depression in Heaven: The Great Depression, the New Deal, and the Transformation of Religion in Delta*. New York: Oxford University Press, 2015.

Grossman, James R. *Land of Hope: Chicago, Black Southerners, and the Great Migration*. Chicago: University of Chicago Press, 1989.

Hahn, Steven. *A Nation under Our Feet: Black Political Struggles in the Rural South from Slavery to the Great Migration*. Cambridge, MA: Harvard University Press, 2005.

Hall, David., ed. *Lived Religion in America*. Princeton, NJ: Princeton University Press, 1997.

Hall, G. Stanley. *Adolescence: Its Psychology, and Its Relations to Physiology, Anthropology, Sociology, Sex, Crime, Religion and Education*, Vol. 2. New York: D. Appleton, 1904.

Hall, G. Stanley. "Proceedings of the Massachusetts Historical Society," February 2, 1905.

Hamilton, Peter. "An American Family's Mission in East Asia, 1838–1936: A Commitment to God, Academia, and Empire," *Journal of the Royal Asiatic Society Hong Kong Branch*, Vol. 49 (2009), pp. 229–265.

Harris, Michael W. *The Rise of Gospel Blues: The Music of Thomas Andrew Dorsey in the Urban Church*. New York: Oxford University Press, 1992.

Hatch, Nathaniel. *Democratization of American Christianity*. New Haven, CT: Yale University Press, 1989.

Hayes, John. *Hard, Hard Religion: Interracial Faith in the Poor South*. University of North Carolina Press, 2017.

Herskovits, Melville. *The Myth of the Negro Past*. Boston: Beacon Press, 1941.

Higginbotham, Evelyn B. *Righteous Discontent: The Women's Movement in the Black Baptist Church, 1880–1920*. Cambridge, MA: Harvard University Press, 2017.

Hinsley, Curtis M., Jr. *Savages and Scientists: The Smithsonian Institute and the Development of American Anthropology, 1846–1910*. Washington, DC: Smithsonian Institute Press, 1981.

Hirsch, Jerrold. *Portrait of America: A Cultural History of the Federal Writers' Project*. Chapel Hill: University of North Carolina Press, 2000.

Holloway, Jonathan S. *Confronting the Veil: Abram Harris Jr., E. Franklin Frazier, and Ralph Bunche, 1919–1941*. Chapel Hill: University of North Carolina Press, 2003.

Hurston, Zora N. "Hoodoo In America," *Journal of American Folklore* (Oct.–Dec., 1931), pp. 317–417.

Hurston, Zora N. *Mules and Men*. Reprinted. New York: Harper & Row, 1990.

Hurston, Zora N. *The Sanctified Church*. Reprinted. New York: Marlowe, 1981.

Hutchinson, William R. *The Modernist Impulse in American Protestantism*. Cambridge: Harvard University Press, 1976.

Jackson, Walter A., *Gunnar Myrdal and America's Conscience: Social Engineering and Racial Liberalism, 1938-1987*. Chapel Hill: University of North Carolina Press, 1990.

Johnson, Charles S. "Present and Future Position of the Negro in the American Social Order," *The Journal of Negro Education* (July 1939), pp. 323-335.

Johnson, Charles S. "Review of Folk Beliefs of the Southern Negro," *Opportunity: Journal of Negro Life* (October 1926).

Johnson, Charles S. "Rise of Liberalism in the South," *World Outlook*, Vol. XXVII, No. 9 (September 1938).

Johnson, Charles S. *The Shadow of the Plantation*. Chicago: University of Chicago Press, 1934.

Johnson, Charles S. "Superstition and Health," *Opportunity: Journal of Negro Life* (July 1926).

Johnson, Guion, and Guy B. Johnson. *Research in Service to Society: The First Fifty Years of the Institute for Research in Social Science at the University of North Carolina*. Chapel Hill: University of North Carolina Press, 1980.

Johnson, Guy. *Folk Culture on St. Helena Island*. Chapel Hill: University of North Carolina Press, 1930.

Johnson, Guy. "The Gullah Dialect Revisited: A Note on Linguistic Acculturation," *Journal of Black Studies*, Vol. 10, No. 4 (January 1980), pp. 417-424.

Johnson, Guy. *John Henry: Tracking Down a Negro Legend*. Chapel Hill: University of North Carolina Press, 1929.

Johnson, Guy. "The Negro Spiritual: A Problem in Anthropology," *American Anthropologist*, Vol. 33, No. 2 (April-June 1931), pp. 157-171.

Johnson, Guy. "Some Factors in the Development of Negro Social Institutions in the United States," *American Journal of Sociology*, Vol. 40, No. 3 (November 1934), pp. 329-337.

Johnson, Guy. *A Study of the Musical Talent of the American Negro*. Dissertation, University of North Carolina, 1924.

Johnson, Sylvester A. *African American Religions, 1500-2000*. Cambridge: Cambridge University Press, 2015.

Jones, Jacqueline. *The Dispossessed: America's Underclasses from the Civil War to the Present*. New York: Basic Books, 1992.

Jones, James. *Bad Blood: The Tuskegee Syphilis Experiment*. Reprinted. New York: Free Press, 1993.

Katz, Michael. *The Underclass Debate: Views from History*. Princeton, NJ: Princeton University Press, 1993.

Katz, Michael. *The Undeserving Poor: From the War on Poverty to the War on Welfare*. New York: Pantheon Books, 1989.

Kelley, Robin D. G. *Hammer and Hoe: Alabama Communists during the Great Depression*. Chapel Hill: University of North Carolina Press, 1990.

Kelley, Robin D. G. "Notes on Deconstructing the Folk," *The American Historical Review*, Vol. 97, No. 5 (December 1992), 1400-1408.

Kirby, Jack T. *Rural Worlds Lost: The American South, 1920–1960*. Baton Rouge: Louisiana State University, 1987.

Klaute, Egbert. *The Mind of the Nation: Volkerpsychologie in Germany, 1851–1955*. New York: Berghahn Books, 2010.

Lamothe, Daphne. *Inventing the New Negro: Narrative, Culture, and Ethnography*. Philadelphia: University of Pennsylvania Press, 2008.

Larson, Edward J. *Sex, Race, and Science: Eugenics in the Deep South*. Baltimore, MD: Johns Hopkins University Press, 1996.

Lears, T. J. *No Place of Grace: Antimodernism and the Transformation of American Culture, 1880–1920*. Chicago: University of Chicago Press, 1981.

Lemann, Nicholas. "The Origins of the Underclass," *Atlantic Monthly* (June 1986), pp. 31–55.

Leonard, Thomas C. *Illiberal Reformers: Race, Eugenics, and the American Economics in the Progressive Era*. Princeton, NJ: Princeton University Press, 2017.

Levine, Lawrence. *Black Culture and Black Consciousness: Afro-American Folk Thought from Slavery to Freedom*. New York: Oxford University Press, 1977.

Lewis, David L. *When Harlem Was in Vogue*. New York: Oxford University Press, 1979.

Lewis, Earl. *In Their Own Interests: Race, Class, and Power in Twentieth-Century Norfolk, Virginia*. Berkeley: University of California Press, 1991.

Lewis, Harriet M. *Southern Workman*, Vol. xxi, No. 6 (June 1892).

Lloyd, Vincent W., and Jonathan Kahn, eds. *Race and Secularism in America*. New York: Columbia University Press, 2016.

Lomax, Alan. *The Land Where the Blues Began*. New York: New York Press, 1993.

Lomax, John. *Adventures of a Ballad Hunter*. New York: Macmillan, 1947.

Martin, Lerone A. *Preaching on Wax: The Phonograph and the Shaping of Modern African American Religion*. New York: New York University Press, 2014.

Mays, Benjamin E., and Joseph Nicholson. Reprinted. *The Negro's Church*. Reprinted. Salem: Ayer, 1988.

Mays, Benjamin E., and Joseph Nicholson. *The Negro's God: As Reflected in His Literature*. Reprinted. Eugene, OR: WIPF & Stock, 2010.

McCrary, Charles, and Jeffrey Wheatly. "The Protestant Secular in the Study of American Religion: Reappraisal and Suggestions," *Religion*, Vol. 47 (2017): 256–276.

McDannell, Colleen. *Picturing Faith: Photography and the Great Depression*. New Haven, CT: Yale University Press, 2004.

Mintz, Sidney, and Richard Price. *The Birth of African American Culture: An Anthropological Perspective*. Boston: Beacon Press, 1976.

Muhammad, Khalil. *Condemnation of Blackness: Race, Crime, and the Making of Modern Urban America*. Cambridge, MA: Harvard University Press, 2010.

Myrdal, Gunnar. *An American Dilemma: The Negro Problem and Modern Democracy*. New York: Harper & Brothers, 1944.

Nemerov, Bruce, and Robert Gordon, eds. *Lost Delta Found: Rediscovering the Fisk University–Library of Congress Coahoma County Study, 1941–1942*. Nashville, TN: Vanderbilt University Press, 2005.

Odum, Howard W. *The Negro and His Songs*. Chapel Hill: University of North Carolina Press, 1925.

Odum, Howard W. *Religious Folk-Songs of the Southern Negroes*. Dissertation, Clark University, 1909.

Odum, Howard W. *The Social and Mental Traits of the Negro: Research into the Conditions of the Negro Race in Southern Towns*. (New York: AMS Press, 1910).

Oghoghomeh-Wells, Alexis S. "She Come like a Nightmare: Hags, Witches and the Gendered Trans-Sense among the Enslaved in the Lower South," *Journal of Africana Religions*, Vol. 5, No. 2 (2017), pp. 239–274.

Orsi, Robert. *Between Heaven and Earth: The Religious Worlds People Made and the Scholars Who Study Them*. Princeton, NJ: Princeton University Press, 2005.

Park, Robert E. "The Problem of Cultural Differences," reprinted in *The Collected Papers of Robert E. Park*. New York: Arno Press, 1974.

Park, Robert E. "Racial Assimilation in Secondary Groups," *The American Sociological Survey*, VIII (1913), pp. 606–623.

Peeler, David. *Hope among Us Yet: Social Criticism and Social Solace in Depression America*. Athens: University of Georgia Press, 1987.

Powdermaker, Hortense. *After Freedom: A Cultural Study of the Deep South*. New York: Viking Press, 1939.

Powdermaker, Hortense. *Stranger and Friend: The Way of an Anthropologist*. New York: W. W. Norton, 1966.

Puckett, Newbell N. *Folk Beliefs of the Southern Negro*. Chapel Hill: University of North Carolina Press, 1926.

Reed, Toure. *Not Alms but Opportunity: The Urban League and the Politics of Racial Uplift, 1910–1950*. Chapel Hill: University of North Carolina Press, 2008.

Reverby, Susan M. *Examining Tuskegee: The Infamous Syphilis Study and Its Legacy*. Chapel Hill: University of North Carolina Press, 2009.

Roll, Jarrod, and Erik S. Gellman. *The Gospel of the Working Class: Labor's Southern Prophets in New Deal America*. Urbana: University of Illinois Press, 2011.

Ross, Dorothy. *G. Stanley Hall: The Psychologist as Prophet*. Chicago: University of Chicago Press, 1972.

Ross, Dorothy. *The Origins of American Social Science*. Cambridge: Cambridge University Press, 1992.

Salvatore, Nick. *Singing in a Strange Land: C. L. Franklin, the Black Church, and the Transformation of America*. New York: Little, Brown, 2005.

Sanders, Lynn M. *Howard W. Odum's Folklore Odyssey: Transformation to Tolerance through African American Folk Studies*. Athens: University of Georgia Press, 2003.

Savage, Barbara. *Your Spirits Walk Beside Us: The Politics of Black Religion*. Cambridge, MA: Harvard University Press, 2008.

Scott, Daryl M. *Contempt and Pity: Social Policy and the Image of the Damaged Black Psyche, 1880–1996*. Chapel Hill: University of North Carolina Press, 2000.

Sernett, Milton. *Bound for the Promised Land: African American Religion and the Great Migration*. Durham, NC: Duke University Press, 1997.

Shaler, Nathaniel S. "The Negro Problem," *Atlantic Monthly* (November 1884).

Shaler, Nathaniel S. "Science and the African Problem," *Atlantic Monthly* (July 1890).

Sharps, Ronald L. *Happy Days and Sorrow Songs: Interpretations of Negro Folk-Lore by Black Intellectuals, 1893–1928*. Dissertation, George Washington University, 1991.

Simpson, Georgiana. *Herder and the Concept of the Volk*. Dissertation, University of Chicago, 1921.

Skaroff, Lauren R. *Black Culture and the New Deal: The Quest for Civil Rights in the Roosevelt Era*. Chapel Hill: University of North Carolina Press, 2009.

Smith, Jonathan Z. *Map Is Not the Territory: Studies in the History of Religions*. Chicago: University of Chicago Press, 1978.

Smith, Jonathan Z. "Religion, Religious, and Religions," in *Critical Terms for Religious Studies*, ed. Mark Taylor. Chicago: University of Chicago Press, 1998, pp. 269–284.

Sorett, Josef. "Secular in Comparison to What?" In *Race and Secularism in America*, eds. Jonathon Kahn and Vincent Lloyd. New York: Columbia University Press, 2016, pp. 43–73.

Sorett, Josef. *Spirit in the Dark: A Religious History of Racial Aesthetics*. New York: Oxford University Press, 2019.

Stephens, Randall J. *Fire Spreads: Holiness and Pentecostalism in the American South*. Cambridge, MA: Harvard University Press, 2008.

Stocking, George W. *Race, Culture, and Evolution: Essays in the History of Anthropology*. Chicago: University of Chicago Press, 1968.

Storm-Josephson, Jason A. *The Myth of Disenchantment: Magic, Modernity, and the Birth of the Human Sciences*. Chicago: University of Chicago Press, 2017.

Storm-Josephson, Jason A. "The Superstition, Secularism, and Religion Trinary: Or, Re-Theorizing Secularism," *Method and Theory in the Study of Religion*, Vol. 30 (2018), pp. 1–20.

Sumner, William G. *Folkways: A Study of the Sociological Importance of Usages, Manners, Customs, Mores, and Morals*. Boston: Ginn, 1906.

Swed, John. *Allan Lomax: The Man Who Recorded the World*. New York: Viking Press, 2010.

Thomas, W. I. "The Scope and Method of Folk-Psychology," *American Journal of Sociology* (January 1896), pp. 434–445.

Thussen, Sarah C. "Taking the Vows of Southern Liberalism: Guion and Guy Johnson and the Evolution of an Intellectual Partnership," *The North Carolina Historical Review*, Vol. LXXIV, No. 3 (July 1993), pp. 284–324.

Tomes, Nancy. *The Gospel of Germs: Men, Women, and the Microbe in American Life*. Cambridge, MA: Harvard University Press, 1998.

Vance, Lee J. "On the Nature and Value of Folk-Lore," *The Chautauquan: A Weekly Newsmagazine* (September 1890), p. 686.

Varel, David. A. *The Lost Black Scholar: Resurrecting Allison Davis in American Social Thought*. Chicago: University of Chicago Press, 2018.

Waters, Donald J. *Strange Ways and Sweet Dreams: Afro-American Folklore from Hampton*. Boston: G. K. Hall, 1983.

Webb, Keane. "Secularism as a Moral Narrative of Modernity," *Transit Europaische Revue*, Vol. 43 (2013), pp. 159–170.

Weisenfeld, Judith. *New Work A-Coming: Black Religion and Racial Identity during the Great Migration*. New York: New York University Press, 2018.

West, Cornel. "Race and Social Theory," in West, *Keeping Faith: Philosophy and Race in America*. New York: Routledge Books, 1993, pp. 251–270.

Wheatly, Jeffrey. "US Colonial Governance of Superstition and Fanaticism in the Philippines," *Method & Theory in the Study of Religion*, Vol. 30, No. 1 (2018), pp. 21–36.

White, Christopher, *Unsettled Minds: Psychology and the American Search for Spiritual Assurance, 1830–1940*. Berkeley: University of California Press, 2008.

White, Sheldon, and Emily Cahan. "Proposal for a Second Psychology," *American Psychologist*, Vol. 47, No. 2 (February 1992), pp. 224–235.

Wilson, William Julius, "The Black Underclass," *The Wilson Quarterly*, Vol. 8, No. 2 (Spring 1984), pp. 88–99.

Woofter, T. J. *Black Yeomanry*. New York: Henry Holt, 1930.

Wright, Gavin. *Old South, New South: Revolutions in the Southern Economy since the Civil War*. Baton Rouge: Louisiana State University Press, 1986.

Zimmerman, Andrew. *Alabama in Africa: Booker T. Washington, the German Empire, and the Globalization of the New South*. Princeton, NJ: Princeton University Press, 2010.

Zumwalt, Rosemary. *American Folklore Scholarship*. Bloomington: Indiana University Press, 1988.

Index